PAUL MORAND

FAUX TITRE

Etudes
de langue et littérature françaises

publiées

sous la direction de Keith Busby,
M.J. Freeman, Sjef Houppermans,
Paul Pelckmans et Co Vet

No. 209

Amsterdam - Atlanta, GA 2001

PAUL MORAND

The Politics and Practice of Writing in Post-War France

Kimberly Philpot van Noort

The paper on which this book is printed meets the requirements of "ISO 9706:1994, Information and documentation - Paper for documents - Requirements for permanence".

Le papier sur lequel le présent ouvrage est imprimé remplit les prescriptions de "ISO 9706:1994, Information et documentation - Papier pour documents - Prescriptions pour la permanence".

ISBN: 90-420-1376-1
©Editions Rodopi B.V., Amsterdam - Atlanta, GA 2001
Printed in The Netherlands

CONTENTS

Acknowledgements	7
Introduction: L'Affaire Morand	9
I. Lacerating Time: History, Penance, and Redemption in *Le Flagellant de Séville*	25
II. Reading the Past: *Parfaite de Saligny* and *La Folle amoureuse*	51
III. Filming the Event: *Fouquet ou le soleil offusqué*	89
IV. Postcards from Venice	121
V. Morand retro	161
Bibliography of Works by Paul Morand	171
Annotated Bibliography of Works Devoted To Paul Morand	177
Works Consulted	182
Index	191

ACKNOWLEDGEMENTS

Many people have contributed in various ways to this book. I would like to thank Jeffrey Mehlman, whose erudition and creativity are a constant inspiration, for his interest in this project and his continued mentorship. Gratitude is also due Roger Shattuck, Jeff Kline, Susan Jackson and Beth Goldsmith for their comments and ideas on earlier versions of the manuscript. A special thanks goes to Joe Breines, for hours of discussion of various aspects of Paul Morand's work, and to Simon Heck for his unflagging, at times long-distance, intellectual and personal support.

Many of my colleagues and friends here at the University of Texas at Arlington and elsewhere have provided important feedback, ideas, wonderful conversations and editorial aid: Chris Conway of Brown University; Toni Sol, Ruth Gross, Aimée Israël-Pelletier and Denis Bettaver, here at UTA; Sonja Kropp-Dams of University of Nebraska-Kearney and Marshall Olds of the University of Nebraska-Lincoln. Many thanks also to Scott Williams, Dennis Tsurkan and Nellainayagam Subramaniam for their technical expertise.

I am also very grateful for the help of Christa Stevens, my editor at Rodopi, for her eagle eye and her always pertinent suggestions.

Grateful acknowledgement is also made to the Humanities Foundation at Boston University for a grant enabling me to attend the Edouard Morot-Sir Institute on Memory and History, and to the Department of Modern Languages, the Dean's Office and the Graduate School at the University of Texas at Arlington for ongoing support of the presentation of portions of this work in various venues.

I can only attempt to thank those people who inspire and sustain me in so many other ways and who have made this book concretely possible: my parents, Howard and Carole Philpot; my brother Scott; Peter, for his endless support; and Hilary and Nathan, for keeping things constantly in perspective.

Finally, I would like to dedicate this book to my mother, for making my dream a reality, and to Etty Horowitz, whose successful fight for life informed the final stages of this book.

L'AFFAIRE MORAND

In 1959, the newly (re)elected President of France Charles de Gaulle blocked the candidature of the writer Paul Morand to the Académie française, warning that he would take the unprecedented step of exercising his right of absolute veto should Morand be elected to that august assembly. The scandal that erupted around the "Affaire Morand," led in the Académie by the writer François Mauriac, was based on Morand's collaboration with the Vichy Government during the Occupation of France. The scandal flooded the national newspapers and laid bare the extent to which the wounds of the Occupation still continued to fester fifteen years after the liberation of France. That de Gaulle himself felt it necessary to intervene points to the urgency of the question, for those on both sides of the situation, of how to deal with the very real fact that French citizens had not only materially but ideologically collaborated with the enemy, thus suggesting a sort of national "flaw," one to be suppressed and denied at any cost. Paul Morand's case is particularly enlightening, not only because of de Gaulle's intervention but because Morand himself had spent the postwar years exploring this very question in his literary works, ceaselessly interrogating the power of the past to impact and reformulate the present. In 1968, de Gaulle withdrew his objections and Morand was elected to the Académie. It is perhaps no coincidence that the post-1968 period, during which the dominant myths of the Occupation came under renewed scrutiny, should coincide with Morand's "re-entry," as it were, into the literary canon.

Morand is perhaps best known for his short stories and travel essays published in the 1920s and 1930s. Prefaced by Marcel Proust, translated by Ezra Pound and hailed as one of the "four M's" of the Grasset publishing empire (Mauriac, Maurois, Montherlant and Morand), he was acknowledged during this early stage of his literary career as one of the great contemporary writers of France. After the war, however, his literary reputation was ruined by his collaboration with the Vichy government. Although he continued writing after the war and, indeed, published some of his most original and noteworthy works during that period, he never regained the acclaim of his early years as a writer. These postwar works are highly unusual for two reasons. First, prior to the war Morand dealt almost exclusively with the contemporary period and garnered fame as a cosmopolitan portraitist of his era. During the Occupation and in all his later works, Morand abruptly shifts his attention to the past in what amounts to an almost total turn toward historical fiction and nonfiction. Secondly, the various historical events and periods Morand chooses as the contexts for these works all reveal uncanny and often inverted links to the period of the Occupation and to acts of collaboration. From Napoleonic Spain to the Boxer Rebellion, the French Revolution, nineteenth-century Russian fur trade in Spanish California and late nineteenth-century Germany, Morand manipulates the past, teasing out certain similarities, in what amounts to an obsessive rewriting of the Occupation in historical guise.

As the title of this book suggests, the postwar oeuvre of Paul Morand provides an excellent illumination of the politicized atmosphere of literature during that period. Beyond the obvious problem that Morand's collaboration posed for his personal and literary reputations, these works presented a further challenge to the dominant myths of the Occupation, myths in large part promulgated and personified by the figure of de Gaulle himself. Morand's debacle before the Académie française may have had less to do with his actions during the war than with the nature of his writing afterward, in the menace that his exploration of the Occupation posed to what Henri Rousso has described as the *"résistancialiste"* ideology of the Gaullist regime. In his magisterial book, *Le Syndrome de Vichy*, Rousso delineates the manner in which France was depicted, after the Liberation, as having presented strong and widespread resistance to its occupiers. The vast majority of the French, according to this portrayal, either actively or passively sought to undermine both the Vichy government and the Nazi occupiers, while only a handful of "traitors" actually collaborated. The history of the development and solidification of this *résistancialisme* between 1944 and 1968 is already well-explored territory, by Rousso, Alan Morris, Richard Golsan and many others, as is the ensuing phase, known as the *"mode rétro,"* beginning after de Gaulle's death and during which the Occupation came under new scrutiny by writers, historians, filmmakers and critics, many of whom belong to the postwar generation, who sought to critique and re-evaluate the prevailing versions of the Occupation by exploring the more ambiguous side of both resistance and collaboration.[1]

Morand's postwar works may be said to participate in both these "movements" – as a dissenting voice during the Gaullist period and as a curiously premonitory voice with regard to the *mode rétro*. By turning his attention to history and to the relation between the past and the present in the writing and "making" of history, both within the fictional and nonfictional contexts of these texts and in

---

[1] Explorations of the *mode rétro* abound. Among the most comprehensive are Rousso and Morris. See also Richard Golsan, Colin Nettelbeck, Pascal Ory, Lynn Higgins.

their extradiegetic links to the period of the Occupation, Morand provides an implicit critique of the contemporary process of historicizing the Occupation. At the same time, Morand's vision of collaboration raises the very questions of concern to many of the revisionist studies of the *rétro* period: the relationship of the past and the present, the various modes of representation of history and their political and literary consequences, the role of individual and collective memory, the psycho-social "working through" of a traumatic historical event, and the vexing question of "tainted aesthetics" and the role of art and literature in collaboration

Alan Morris has argued that the Gaullist, *résistancialiste* process may best be characterized as one of mythification, while the *mode rétro* functions as a demythification of the resulting paradigm. While one might take issue with the terms mythification and demythification, as Morris himself acknowledges, his arguments point to the forces of historicization operating during both periods. Morand's historical prose figures both these movements, presenting historical situations and figures in the course of becoming history, while at the same time, via his exposition of the ambiguities of both the objects of this historicizing thrust and the forces effectuating it, examining the nature of the creation of history itself. In *Le Flagellant de Séville* (1951), to take just one example, the hero Don Luis sets out on a path of collaboration with the Napoleonic Occupation of Spain from 1808 to 1813. The ambiguities and ambivalences of his actions are ironically underscored when he returns to Spain in 1824, after many years of exile in France, to find that he has been proclaimed a hero by the current political establishment. Morand skillfully explores the processes by which the past (here the Napoleonic occupation) is reinscribed and historicized. However, rather than exploiting his new renown, Don Luis renounces his former identity and becomes Don Pablo, the flagellant of Séville, who achieves mythic status as an itinerant penitent.

Many issues are at stake in Morand's late oeuvre, from the genres of historical fiction, biography and autobiography, to the very act of historicization itself in the context of the postwar era. Morand's handling of these issues suggests that literature furnishes perhaps the best space, one of its own creation, within which the complex and highly political question of our ties to the past may be most tellingly examined. Before engaging in such an endeavor, however, a slight detour is called for in the form of a brief return to the past, mirroring Morand's own postwar gesture, in order to recall Morand's early literary success and to better situate the acuteness of his own detour after the war.

12 Paul Morand

In his 1921 preface to Paul Morand's first collection of short stories, *Tendres Stocks*, Marcel Proust hails the young Morand as the prime example of "the new and original" writer in France, and places him at the end of a lineage stretching back to Renan and Stendhal (Proust, 12). Proust goes so far as to extend to Morand a curious invitation to visit the "Hôtel de Balbec," a principal setting in Proust's own novel: "Mais si, avant qu'il devienne ambassadeur et rivalise avec Beyle Consul, il veut visiter l'Hôtel de Balbec, alors je lui prêterai le fil fatal" (Proust, 30). Proust extends the baton, or rather the thread, of literature itself to the soon-to-be twentieth-century rival of Stendhal. But even as Proust plays Ariadne to Morand's Theseus, offering to pass on the secrets of the literary labyrinth, he also affectionately labels Morand "notre minotaure," referring to Morand's taste for casting young girls as the protagonists of his stories. Proust seems to deliberately conflate, in his figure of Morand, the Theseus-like pretender to Stendhal's legacy and the half-human monster of Crete. Another such curious characterization of Morand's literary persona is found in an earlier letter from Proust to Morand's future wife, Hélène Soutzo, in which Proust also evokes Stendhal in reference to Morand. Alluding to Stendhal's novel *La Chartreuse de Parme*, Proust notes that Morand embodies both the youthful naiveté of a Fabrice and the sophisticated refinement of a Mosca, and indeed, of Stendhal himself. How is such a combination possible, he asks, and ends the passage: "Mais j'espère qu'il ne finira pas chartreux, même à Parme" (Proust, Lettre, 148-49). Read in conjunction with Proust's preface, this letter interjects a note of caution into Proust's accolades. Read today, with the advantage of historical hindsight, the letter also appears ironically prophetic. For after his triumphant conquest of literature, Paul Morand was, in fact, destined to end up in seclusion, as something of a monk: "un chartreux," though not, it seems, at Parma.

If I have begun with commentary from so illustrious a reader as Proust, it is because it is little noted today that during the 1920s and 30s, Morand was considered to be one of the best contemporary writers in France. Jean Cocteau, Valéry Larbaud, Jean Giraudoux, Léon Daudet and Bernard Grasset, among others, joined Proust in drawing attention to the author of *Ouvert la nuit* (1921), *Fermé la nuit* (1922), *L'Europe galante* (1925), and *Rien que la terre* (1926). Ezra Pound translated *Tendres Stocks* in 1934, and Céline declared that in the year 2000 only Morand, and of course he, Céline, would still be read (Lacarme, 24). In his 1989 preface to Morand's *New York* (1930), Philippe Sollers seizes upon the Proust-Céline-Morand triangle as a triptych based not on resemblance but rather on stature, representing the three greatest French writers of the twentieth century (Sollers, 7). However, Sollers's rendering of the history of literature is acutely conscious of the vagaries of historicity. Céline and Morand, he suggests, have more in common than artistic talent. Both stood on the "wrong side" during the last World War, an allegiance which, as Sollers points out, had far-reaching effects not only on the individual destiny of each but, perhaps, on the entire course of literature itself as well:

> Que ne sont-ils restés tous les deux de l'autre côté du Channel ou de l'Atlantique au lieu de se mêler à l'explosion du Vieux Continent? Une toute autre histoire de la littérature aurait pu se dérouler alors. (Sollers, 8)

Sollers here suggests that both writers would have been better advised to have remained within the course of their purely literary careers, Céline with *Pont de Londres* and Morand with *New York*, rather than to have taken a political position during the war. Morand did decide to involve himself (prompted, as he himself stated, by his allegiance to Pétain and Laval) by abandoning his post in London and returning to France during the summer of 1940, just days after de Gaulle's "Appel aux Français" (Guitard-Auvuste, 230).[2] After an initially hostile reception in Vichy, Morand was later made director of the bureau of "Censure cinématographique." Between 1940 and 1943, he contributed articles to both *La Gerbe* and *Combats*, pro-collaborationist journals, and to *Voix françaises*, a Catholic, pro-Pétain review.[3] His collection of wartime chronicles, *Chroniques d'un homme maigre* (1941) clearly spells out Morand's support of Pétain and Laval. In Paris, he and his wife Hélène, an ardent fascist supportor, entertained both ranking German officials and known Nazi sympathizers, including Alfred Fabre-Luce, Drieu la Rochelle, Jacques Benoist-Méchin, Abel Bonnard and Marcel Jouhandeau (Guitard-Auviste, 223). In 1943, he was appointed to the post of ambassador of the Vichy government to Romania, an Axis ally, and in 1944, was transferred to a similar post in Switzerland where, after serving only 44 days, he remained in self-imposed exile after the Liberation (Hebey, 395).

Although Morand continued to publish, both his pre- and postwar works remained largely ignored after the war. The effects

---

[2] Morand's allegiance to Laval was not, as Guitard-Auviste suggests, limited to his family's long friendship with the former. Morand established himself early on as a writer of right-wing tendencies. His 1934 novel *France-la-doulce* was an open attack of Jewish dominance of the film industry in France. In a 1933 article, "De l'air, de l'air..." he implored France not to be outdone by Hitler in the "killing of vermin". During the Occupation, he contributed regularly to several collaborationist papers.

[3] The list of Morand's articles appearing in collaborationist reviews and papers may be found in George Place's bibliography of Morand's works.

of his involvement with the Vichy government upon his literary reputation became all too clear during his ill-fated bid for election to the Académie française in 1958. After a bitter polemic within the Académie itself, the new president of the Republic, Charles de Gaulle, threatened to exercise his right of veto, opposing Morand's election: "because of the partisan hatreds the writer would provoke within the Académie" (Rousso, 68). In 1968, de Gaulle withdrew his opposition and Morand was elected. As noted earlier, it was perhaps no coincidence that the post-1968 period, during which the dominant myths of the Occupation came under renewed scrutiny, should coincide with Morand's "re-entry," as it were, into the literary canon. Bordas's *La littérature en France depuis 1968* includes Morand under the rubrique of "Grandes figures du siècle," acknowledging Morand's omission from its earlier anthology, *La littérature en France depuis 1945*, as a mistake which it now sought to rectify (Lecarme, 24). A flurry of interest ensued in France, and in 1992, two volumes of Morand's complete short stories appeared in Gallimard's prestigious series, La Bibliothèque de la Pléiade. Proust, who had offered Morand the "fil fatal," certainly could not have foreseen the labyrinthine path Morand would eventually follow, nor could he have imagined that Morand would indeed "end up chartreux" in a postwar seclusion which had such a profound impact upon his literary career.[4]

Proust's evocation of the Cretan myth is unusually apt, for approaching Morand's work is rather like entering a labyrinth, sure of a destination, but ceaselessly enticed by the complexity of the maze itself. The size of Morand's oeuvre is not only large, over one hundred works, but varied in genre as well: poetry, short stories, travel journals, essays, theatre, chronicles, film adaptations, biography and one extraordinary memoir. Morand tried his hand at practically every generic form, and while it is generally accepted that he excelled in the short story, he was no dilettante in the other domains. Within the work as a whole, the range of subjects is as varied as their forms: six-day cycling races, sexual deviance, hotels in Asia, voodoo, growing potatoes in Paris, Napoleonic Spain, the Habsburg Empire, and Coco Chanel, to name only a few.

Then there is the famous "legend" to get by, a legend which appears everywhere, threatening to engulf the reader in its exotic

---

[4] Ironically, in Morand's 1941 novel, *L'Homme pressé* (Paris: Gallimard, 1941), the hero purchases an ancient "chartreuse" or charterhouse, in the Piedmont, which he dismantles for the antique columns discovered under the chapel. It is as though Morand not only acknowledges the fate lent him by Proust, but also signals his impending turn to the past.

possibilities: the legend of Morand the globetrotter, the modernist and the diplomat, Morand of the "années folles" and their most privileged transcriber. This is the young Morand, the regular at the "Le Boeuf sur le toit," friend of Proust, Cocteau, Milhaud, Coco Chanel, Suzanne Lalique, Satie, Larbaud, Ravel, Auric. Morand the cosmopolitan, the dandy, the eroticist: "cet écrivain réputé, mondain invétéré, voyageur pressé, diplomate à ses heures" (Schneider, Figaro).

It is certainly tempting to linger here amongst the glittering stories of *Ouvert la nuit* and *Fermé la nuit*, to peer through Morand's lens into the bedrooms, the train compartments, the jazz clubs, the private yet ever so public life of his era, an age of political and sexual turmoil through which Morand moves with the ease of a familiar. How seductive his legend of voyager, the last of the great travelers descending through Stendhal and Claudel, relating his long voyages around the world: North America, Asia, Africa, and, of course, Europe. *Hiver-Caraïbe, Paris-Tombouctou, La Route des Indes*: the titles of his travel writings alone evoke the cosmopolitan. And all written in that "style Morand," terse, rapid, electric. Morand's place among the great stylists of the century has been well established. "Le Prince du style," master of the ellipsis and the litote, Morand introduced speed into modern style (Charrière, *Figaro*). His short stories condense into thirty pages what another might barely accomplish in three novels. Philippe Sollers has captured this Morand better than anyone: "Dans ses nouvelles, "l'homme pressé" est sans cesse aux aguets, multipolaire, immergé dans le système nerveux de l'époque" (Sollers, *Le Swing*). Morand at the front lines of his era, this is the Morand most often evoked, perhaps to divert our attention from that other legend, no less notorious, which risks overshadowing the first: the legend of Vichy.

For when dealing with Morand, one is confronted with a problem encountered with so many of his contemporaries, Céline, Montherlant, Drieu la Rochelle, and Anouilh, among others, whose literary greatness is tainted by their political leanings and their activities during the Second World War. Morand was a collaborator under the Vichy regime and his writings, both during and before the war, demonstrate a clear ideological adhesion to many principles associated with National Socialism, including anti-communism, xenophobia and antisemitism.[5] The extent of his activity during the war, beyond the knowledge of the posts he occupied, remains vague. What is clear, however, is the impact of this second "legend" on Morand's place in literature. For many years after the war, his works went unread and unnoticed by the majority

---

[5] For an excellent analysis of these issues see Andrea Loselle, 'The Historical Nullification of Paul Morand's Gendered Eugenics.'

of readers and he virtually dropped from the scene. His ill-fated bid for the Académie in 1958, rather than resuscitating interest in his work, served to demonstrate how powerful an influence his "Vichy connection" exerted upon his literary reputation.

In recent years, as we have noted, interest in Morand has regained momentum, due in large part to the efforts of Jean-Louis Bory, Jean-François Fogel, Philippe Sollers and Ginette Guitard-Auviste, his principal biographer. However, criticial interest has been limited for the most part to his work of the twenties and early thirties, in particular, to the early short stories and travel books. Morand's political leanings are certainly evoked, as is his later involvement with the Vichy government. The end result is not that the early Morand does not emerge in all his facets, but that it is only the early Morand. There exists another Morand, the Morand of 1945 and beyond: the exile, the frustrated Academician and, perhaps most importantly, Morand the historian.

Morand's radical shift away from the contemporary to the historical is often noted but rarely examined in detail. And yet, in the course of Morand's literary career this shift stands as the single most remarkable development in his writing: an almost complete abandonment of that upon which his early works are based and upon which his own reputation rested: the observation of the contemporary world. In place of his voyages through space, recording his era, Morand substitutes voyages into the past, through time, traveling back to Revolutionary France, Napoleonic Spain, the court of Louis XIV, turn-of-the-century Austria and nineteenth-century California in search of material for both his fictional and nonfictional works.

Interesting in and of itself, this shift is even more critical because of its timing. Morand published his first historical work, *Isabeau de Bavière*, a play, in 1938, followed by a biography of Maupassant in 1942; then, immediately after the war, he turned almost exclusively to historical fiction. The aesthetic questions surrounding this shift are compounded by its obvious relationship to Morand's experience of the Second World War and to his collaboration during that period, a relationship confirmed by the works themselves. In all of the immediate postwar works and, to a lesser but no less significant degree, in his works of the late fifties and sixties, the historical contexts and the accompanying fictional and nonfictional narratives reveal a singular obsession with the collision between an individual and an event, most often political: the French Revolution in "Parfaite de Saligny," the Inquisition in "Le Dernier Jour de l'Inquisition," the Spanish Civil War in "La Folle amoureuse," and

Napoleon's occupation of Spain in *Le Flagellant de Séville*. In virtually all of the texts, the choice of the hero or heroine is, perhaps not surprisingly, collaboration, in one form or another, and the result is eventual ostracization. In the texts centering around explicit collaboration, Morand's exploitation of historical situations reveals his use of history as an inverted image of the situation in France in 1940-44. Perhaps the most explicit example occurs in *Le Flagellant de Séville*, published in 1951. The historical situation in Spain furnishes a neat parallel to the situation in France in 1940: Spain is occupied, Napoleon's brother Joseph is placed upon the throne, there is both collaboration with the occupier and organized resistance, England emerges on the side of the resistants; the entire situation demands to be read as a sort of inverted image of the occupation of France.

Most of the full-length studies on Morand recognize the apologetic turn to history in his postwar works. Ginette Guitard-Auviste frequently draws parallels between Morand's situation after the war and that of many of his protagonists. Pascal Louvrier and Eric Canal-Forgues also emphasize the autobiographical character of Morand's later works in a manner which echoes the way in which their biography often tends to amalgamate the man and his fictions:

> Dès 1944, Morand pressent rapidement le fossé qui s'établit entre le pays qu'il a connu et celui qui est en train de naître sous lui: une France qui "déjà avait une autre figure, portait d'autres habits, parlait une langue neuve". (Louvrier, 275)

The citation in this sentence comes from Morand's 1956 novella "Parfaite de Saligny." By failing to note this source, the authors effectively cloak the description with an air of authority implying that Morand's words describe 1944, when in fact, the "new France" in question is, in the context of the novella, that of 1793. Louvrier and Canal-Forgues slyly, perhaps unwittingly, suggest the relationship between the historical and fictional context and Morand's present, but offer no insight on how Morand uses history or of the implications of such an enterprise.

Stéphane Sarkany, in his highly biographical study of cosmopolitanism in Morand's oeuvre, suggests that the works written after 1945 constitute an effort of "moral elucidation," aimed less at an apology of his past actions, than at a blueprinting of future conduct (Sarkany, 169-73). Sarkany's observations are provocative and deserve more attention than the four-page chapter he devotes to them.

Likewise, Jean-François Fogel's ideas on the importance of the concept of time in Morand merit more than the passing commentary they receive. In his view, the notion of speed in Morand's early works has less to do with space, that is, with the amount of ground covered, than with a race against time. Fogel perceptively notes that time is indeed the central question in all of Morand's works, and hints that the post-1945 move to history may be only a subtle shift of gears (Fogel, 44-48).

It is my intention to carry these observations one step further and to examine several of Morand's postwar works and the ways in which the past is made to comment upon the present. Arguing that these texts constitute an obsessional rewriting, in historical guise, of the experience of the Occupation and its aftermath, I shall attempt to elucidate the mechanisms: stylistic, thematic, and structural, which make such an endeavor successful. In addition, I will explore the implications of Morand's uses (and misuses) of history with regard not only to the works themselves, but to the larger question of the role of the past in the present as well.

The decision to remove this project of rewriting from the more immediate context of the Occupation of France and to place it into historical contexts offered several specific advantages to Morand. Most obviously, for a writer who as a former collaborator found himself in a quite precarious situation after the war, history no doubt provided a tool for establishing a certain distance between himself and the recent debacle in France. History emerges as a sort of safe haven, certainly not without resemblance to the relative safety of Switzerland where Morand remained after the war. History itself, as we have seen, also provided previous instances of collaboration, models against which Morand could, in a sense, superimpose collaboration "Vichy style." Morand's manipulation of these models is such that a link is created between the past (the historical context) and the present, through a refashioning of their connections of similarity and difference which repeatedly refers the historical situation beyond the work. The experience of the Occupation comes to be seen in a new, redemptive light when read against Morand's fictional pasts.

One technique of detaching the contextual event from its historical position consists of the periodic "lifting out" of the protagonist from his historical context by inserting the character into an order transcending history. The many references to mythological and biblical figures serve to establish a network of "mythic" recurrence operating outside of the historically specific. This network functions to minimize the link between the narrative and the particular historical moment in which it is located. A similar effect is produced by the presence of extended parallels, either explicit or implicit, with other texts. *Le Flagellant de Séville* reveals strong ties to the art of Goya, most particularly to the series *The*

Caprices and *The Disasters of War.* Each chapter carries as epigraph the title of one of Goya's works and many descriptions of particular scenes are directly inspired by Goya's paintings and sketches. At the same time in this novel, another parallel is drawn, less obviously, to Stendhal's *La Chartreuse de Parme.* Don Luis emerges as a Spanish Fabrice in his love for the Emperor and as a Count Mosca in his political dealings. "Parfaite de Saligny" contains many parallels with Flaubert's *Education sentimentale,* and "La Folle amoureuse" is loosely based upon a nineteenth-century Russian legend, itself gleaned from the history of Russian trade in California. The intertextual systems in these works, I shall argue, operate as a sort of subtext which periodically erupts through the fabric of the narrative, calling attention to the fictionality of the narrative by means of its ties to other texts. This has the effect of dislocating the story, in a sense, from itself. We shall see, in the final chapter, this technique carried to the extreme in *Venises,* in which a complex system of references to other literary representations of Venice subtends the entire work and in which the city itself functions as an intertext.

Another striking feature of these works is the recurrence of the figure of a pariah. Each of Morand's protagonists emerges as an example of an historical loser. In the fictional texts, don Luis is shunned after the ouster of Joseph Bonaparte, Loup de Tincé is executed for counter-revolutionary activities, and the mad Escholastica waits in vain for the return of her Russian lover. The actual historical figures cast as main characters also reflect this destiny: Nicolas Fouquet, Ferdinand Lassalle, and others from works not considered extensively in this study: Sophie Dorothée de Celle, wife of George of Hanover, and the entire Habsburg dynasty. Morand admits to his taste for great failures and to his repetition of stories of historical condemnation:

> J'ai toujours aimé les causes perdues: Fouquet, Caillaux, Berthelot, Laval. Quand ils furent envoyés en forteresse, traînés en Haute Cour, mis ignominieusement à la retraite, attachés au poteau, mon affection pour eux a crû d'autant.... L'échec après le succès, ce devait être encore le thème de mes livres entre 1950 et les années soixante; après *Fouquet, Le Flagellant de Séville, Les Clés du souterrain, Le Dernier Jour de l'Inquisition, Hécate....*
> (Morand, *Venises,* 84)

Invariably, however, in Morand's reworking of history, his protagonists' failures and persecutions are ultimately redeemed by the very history which served to condemn them.

This subversion of history is reflected in the manner in which the historical event serving as context is consistently absorbed into "another" story, a technique which furthers the process of detachment noted above. Don Luis's story is also one of blind jealousy,

Loup de Tincé's real objective is love and not political involvement, the fascist dona Escholastica forgets her politics when in love with a communist, Fouquet is caught up accidently in Louis XIV's unresolved oedipal complex. The effect is that of a weakening of the ties which bind the protagonists to their particular historical positions, thus enabling Morand to project their experiences onto his own.

This is not to imply that these techniques somehow negate or strip the historical event of signification. On the contrary, I shall argue that history fulfills several important functions within the narratives. At its most general level, history as a referent works to ensure the vital sense of verisimilitude surrounding the narratives. Morand crams the works full with historical information: names, dates, descriptions of social and political milieux, battles, etc, all of which are scrupulously accurate. Or almost all, for the use of history, far from being an autonomous, objective tool, reveals itself to be as subject to the demands of Morand's ideological supersystem as the components of the fictional narrative. We shall examine in detail the rare historical "errors" which, although they appear slight: a date miscalculated by several months, the wrong person in the right place, are thrown into sharp relief by the accompanying abundance of accurate information. Now it is true that these errors have come to my attention perhaps only because I was in the process of tediously verifying Morand's accuracy, and one might argue that to a reader who is reading from a less pointed perspective, these errors would most probably remain imperceptible. But this is exactly the point. Morand appears to go to great extremes in order to render these errors practically invisible and upon closer examination it is revealed that these are no mere lapses but in fact examples of a careful manipulation of history directed toward a specific end, or rather to a specific effect, namely the reader's attitude toward the central figure. The most striking example of this manipulation occurs in *Le Flagellant de Séville* where the reader's response to the protagonist, don Luis, depends a great deal upon a subtle historical sleight-of-hand on the part of the author. Because this novel offers a clear example of this particular use of history and also contains many of the other structures with which we are concerned, Chapter One will be devoted to its extended examination. As the longest work of the four historical fictions in question, it can be expected to contain more structures and more uses of these structures than the other three fictions I shall consider, which are short stories.

Another function of the historical situation operates on yet another level, between the event itself and the larger notion of History. In each of the texts in question it is repeatedly emphasized that the historical event around which it revolves is most significant not in and of itself, as an isolated event, but because of its position as both the end of one era and the beginning of another: the French Revolution as the watershed between the Ancien Regime and the Republic; the Napoleonic Wars in Spain as the end (for all practical purposes) of an autonomous monarchy and the beginning of the cortès; the death of Mazarin as the advent of Louis XIV. It is indisputable that these events marked great changes, some more radical or more enduring than others, and Morand is certainly not alone in marking these points in history as crucial. But what is significant is that these events are not represented as mere turning points but as points of definitive rupture with the past.

Morand will in turn exploit this notion of rupture as a metaphor for his act of superimposing, as it were, two distinct historical "events": the event constituting the context of the work and the "event" of the Occupation of France. In Chapter One I will suggest that Morand perversely reproduces, unwittingly, the model proposed by Walter Benjamin in his *Theses on the Philosophy of History* of a constellation, formed of fragments of the past and the present, in the wake of what Benjamin terms an "blasting out of the continuum of history" (Benjamin, 263). Specific models of Morand's use of history and of points of historical rupture will be examined in Chapter Two in relation to two of Morand's postwar novellas "Parfaite de Saligny" and "La Folle amoureuse." In this chapter I will again evoke Benjamin in relation to Morand's work and will briefly examine a 1959 play, *Le Lion écarlate,* as a possible means of dealing with the paradoxical similarities between Morand's and Benjamin's ideas on history.

In Chapter Three, I will examine a nonfictional work, *Fouquet ou le soleil offusqué* (1959), Morand's biography of Nicholas Fouquet. By extending the study of Morand's historical techniques to a nonfictional text, certain literary traits emerge more clearly, in particular, Morand's use of a highly figural language. In addition, Morand's exploitation of the figure of a pariah, or historical loser, clearly parallels similar models in his fictions. I will pursue the discussion of such a figure in reference to other contemporary texts which bear upon Morand's interpretation of Fouquet's situation.

The last chapter is devoted to another "nonfictional" work, Morand's memoir, *Venises* (1971). This text is important in many ways. Firstly, it is, quite simply, an extraordinary memoir. Secondly, this text is as much a city portrait, in the vein of his portraits of New York, Budapest, and London, as it is a memoir of his own life, and yet the two are inseparable. Venice serves as a sort of "sign" for Morand's life, which is recollected as a series of encounters with the city, hence, perhaps, the plural of the title: Venice as many Venices seen at different points during the course of the author's life.

Venises is also plural in that it is not only Morand's Venice but also the city, or rather, cities of Byron, Chateaubriand, Goethe, Stendhal, Ruskin, Proust, Barrès, Lawrence, Corvo, and many others. Morand repeatedly alludes to Venice's place in literary history, either by direct evocation or quotation of the great literary figures whose ghosts seem to inhabit the great city, or by slipping in a phrase or image, here and there, which immediately recalls the Venice of these writers. Thus Morand would situate himself not only in relation to the city, but also in the long literary tradition of those who "dipped their pens in the canals of Venice" (Morand, *Venises*, 33).

I will also examine Morand's "use" of Venice and the ways in which the strategies revealed resemble those of the previous works, notably his manipulation of temporal and spatial relations and his use of history. I will suggest that the latter functions, as does the city of Venice, as a surrogate and as an instrument which permits Morand to represent his own experience through its dislocation onto an "other," whether a character, a structure, a text, a city, or history itself.

It is this continual displacement of the self onto an "other" which permits Morand's later works to be situated within the larger context of the politicization of literature during the decades following the Second World War. By obsessively inscribing and rewriting his own struggle to deal with the aftermath of the war onto and through his various historical protagonists, Morand reflects a similar if not identical gesture carried out individually and institutionally in France after the war. Although it may be argued that Morand mimics what might be termed a "universal response" to traumatic events, a topic which shall be raised throughout this book, more interesting is the manner in which this at once highly personal and universalizing reflection rehearses, as it were, the particularities of the same phenomenon operating on a larger scale during the contemporary period. Writers, historians, journalists and politicians alike scrambled to "represent" the Occupation by imposing upon its terms models of meaning, translating it through the various grids that constitute the making of history and literature. Michel de Certeau has argued that all history, like literature, is displacement, the removal of an event from itself and its reconstruction from a present perspective: "Le réel représenté ne correspond pas au réel qui détermine sa production. Il cache, derrière la figuration d'un passé le présent qui l'organise" (de Certeau, *Histoire*, 70). De Certeau's use of the verb "cacher" may be especially significant as regards Morand's endeavors, for Morand's practice of displacement is just this movement of hiding one identity or operation behind another. As for de Certeau, this displacement or concealment operates in the space articulated between the past and the present, in the web of relations created by Morand in this space. Alan Morris has admirably traced this same operation in the discourse of the Gaullist period as it came to bear on the interpretation/(re)creation of the Occupation. There were significant voices of dissent, as Morris acknowledges, seeking to "correct" the official history by pointing out dissonances between the Gaullist version and the far more ambiguous experiences of others. Morand certainly falls into this category of dissenters, but his work is unique in that it also self-consciously enacts the process of historicization at work, critiquing the system from within. As such his postwar oeuvre also belongs, if not chronologically then ideologically, to the *mode rétro* in its focus on the problematic nature of the representations of the past that constitute history. Of course, Morand works within a highly literary conception of history, but this only helps him to underscore the blurred boundaries between fiction and history as distinct discourses and to explore the political implications of this blurring in the highly particularized arena of literature in France.

I
LACERATING TIME

History, Penance and Redemption in *Le Flagellant de Séville*

In 1946, Paul Morand broke the two-year isolation of his self-imposed exile in Switzerland to travel to Spain where he joined his long-time friend Alfred Fabre-Luce.[1] Between 1946 and 1951, Morand returned repeatedly to Spain, most often to the Andalusian city of Seville and it was during one of these sojourns that Morand claims to have been inspired to write his first major postwar novel, *Le Flagellant de Séville*:

> J'habitais Séville. Un jour je suis allé à l'académie San Fernando et je me suis trouvé en face de la palette de Goya, avec toutes les couleurs qui étaient restées dessus depuis sa mort. J'ai pensé qu'il faudrait remployer ces couleurs. (Guitard Auviste, 249)

At the Academy San Fernando in Madrid, Morand also probably saw one of Goya's *Five Paintings on Panel*, "Procession of Flagellants," to which he later refers in the novel and which may have furnished Morand with a more concrete model for his novel.

The choice of Goya reaches far beyond mere aesthetic considerations and, as we shall see, reveals a great deal about not only Morand's novel but about the author himself. Goya, best known perhaps for his darkly humorous caricatures, *Los Caprichos*, and his stunning portraits which reveal the artist's uncanny psychological insight, was also significantly the painter of his own particular era. Few historians have succeeded in grasping so vividly the passions and horrors of early nineteenth century Spain and few were, like Goya, so intimately involved in the great upheavals of the time. The artist was painter to three Spanish kings, one imposed French king and a celebrated British general, all of whom at one time controlled the country. His most famous "historical" works, those contained in the *Disasters of War*, a series of etchings brutal in their depiction of the horrors of war, center around the bitter struggles under the Napoleonic occupation of Spain. A later work, *The Second of May* (*El dos de mayo*) records the ruthless massacre of Spanish patriots by French troops. Goya, however, also included

---

[1] Fabre-Luce, at that time living in exile in Madrid, had been one of the leading literary figures in Paris during the Occupation and one of the most out-spoken collaborators. He contributed numerous articles to the NRF under the direction of Drieu la Rochelle, as had Paul Morand, and, in his *Anthologie de la Nouvelle Europe*, cited Hitler as one of the spiritual origins of the "New Europe."

harsh images of the Spanish partisans, known as guerrillas, often shown in acts of mutilation and savage murder. Indeed Goya achieves a certain balance in which neither side bears the greater part of the responsibility for the tragedy and from which the figure of war itself emerges as the ultimate enemy.

Goya's own activities during this period are just as ambiguous as his art. He found favor with the Spanish monarch, Charles IV, and painted several portraits of the favorite, Manuel Godoy. In 1808 he traveled to his home province to witness and record the valliance of the citizens of Saragossa during the siege of that city by French troops. And yet he swore an oath of allegiance to Joseph Bonaparte, the king imposed by his brother, Napoleon, and accepted the Order of Spain, an honor established by Joseph. During the occupation many French officers sat for Goya as well as a great number of their Spanish sympathizers, who had come to be known as "afrancesados." Then, after Joseph and his government left Madrid, Goya painted General Wellington just before the Englishman set out to drive the French out of Vitoria and subsequently from Spain itself.

Goya's loyalties are difficult to ascertain from his artistic production during and after the war and he emerges as a rather slippery figure, intent upon adapting himself to the present situation without wholly committing himself to any side. Many attempts have been made to paint Goya as a dedicated patriot. For instance, it has been noted that although Goya supervised the removal of a large number of Spanish paintings and other objects of art to France, he selected only works of lesser quality and importance, a feeble justification at best for his agreement to engage in the pillage at all (Williams, 113).[2] And when, in 1824, Goya found himself in a rather awkward situation with Ferdinand VII after the latter's violent repression of the attempted constitutional revolution in 1823, the painter sought exile in France. He remained in Bordeaux until his death in 1828, living out his last years among old friends, most of whom were former afrancesados who had been living there in exile since 1813.

In light of this rather more compromising side of Goya's activities, Morand's claim to inspiration takes on new meaning. Was it the chance encounter with the relic at San Fernando that planted the seed for *Le Flagellant* or did Morand's experience of his own war, not unlike that of the artist, compel him to seek out Goya as a vehicle for recasting his own disaster, that of 1944? Morand wrote, in a letter to Louis Kornprobst dated July 17, 1972, that: "J'ai écrit

---

[2] On Goya's role see also Anthony Hull, *Goya, Man Among Kings* (New York: Hamilton Press, 1987).

Le Flagellant pour mettre en repos un coeur ulcéré" (Guitard-Auviste, 247). Is the novel then a case of art imitating art, as suggested by the first citation, or an attempt by Morand to repair his own life, broken after his period of collaboration, a subject upon which he is completely silent? It is almost as if Morand, refusing to flagellate himself publicly, found the perfect instrument with which to accomplish it artistically: the palette of his fellow artist.

Which, then, of Goya's palettes does Morand employ in his novel? That of the artist or that of his life? Perhaps this question cannot nor need not be answered, first of all because in Goya's case the two are only difficultly distinguished, and secondly, because Morand, in fact, utilizes both. He appropriates not only Goya's art and era but the very person of the painter himself who appears in the novel near the end. Before moving on to a more thorough discussion of the novel itself, let us pause for a moment to consider this "use" of Goya, the ramifications of which weigh heavily upon the rest of the novel.

The most obvious reference to Goya comes in the form of chapter headings: each chapter takes its title from a particular work of art, the title itself being the French translation with the original title in Spanish serving as epigraph. Morand's attention to detail, which will be explored further on in this chapter, is already apparent in these headings. Each title is followed by a precise notation of the particular collection to which it belongs or by a description of the medium followed by its date. The titles borrowed from Goya aptly indicate the content of Morand's chapters. For example, the chapter entitled "Rare pénitence" ("Rara penitencia"), deals with the ceremony of self-flagellation performed by a group of illustrious Sevillians on Good Friday and from which the book takes its title. "Voici le Croquemitaine" recounts the arrival of Napoleon in Spain. Perhaps more important is the function of these titles as a sort of metaphorical link which by sheer force of association serves not only to lend a veracious historical aura to the narrative but also enables Morand to set himself up as Goya's surrogate, whose palette is now his own. As earlier noted, Morand's reputation prior to the war rested upon his obsession with and depiction of the contemporary world. In contrast, *Le Flagellant de Séville* marks a radical turn to the past which will characterize all of his postwar fiction. By linking himself to Goya and his art, achieved by the relation created by the use of Goya's titles, Morand rather craftily asserts his authority as an observer of the historical world as well.

Goya himself appears as a character in the third part of the novel where he occupies a central position at the gatherings of the Spaniards in exile in Bordeaux after Napoleon's defeat. His character fulfills an important function: to bring don Luis, the hero of the novel, back into contact with society and eventually back to Spain itself. Don Luis sits for Goya, and during these portrait sessions views the paintings of the *Disasters of War* collection. Goya, in painting don Luis, lends authority to the protagonist who is thus guaranteed entry into posterity. By allowing the hero to see his as yet unfinished *Disasters*, he also permits don Luis access to his vision of the war, a vision which inspires the very novel in which don Luis exists. One day, in the painter's atelier, Goya shows don Luis his painting of a Sevillian scene: a procession of flagellants. Don Luis reaction is striking, the sight of the painting touches off a series of reminiscences of his childhood and don Luis begins to think of returning to his native Seville. Thus, as Goya's "presence" in the form of chapter headings serves to orient the novel's exterior structure, his interior role in the narrative is indispensable to the reorientation of the protagonist towards Spain and ultimately towards don Luis' own scene of flagellation. Just as each of the chapters responds to the work designated by its heading, the entire novel tends toward the scene announced by the title, painted by Goya and reenacted in the novel.

There is, however, a problem concerning Goya's appearance in this meticulously documented historical novel. In 1823, Goya was not in Bordeaux. He did not leave Spain until 1824 and then stopped only three days in Bordeaux en route to Paris. It was not until 1825 that Goya established his permanent residence in Bordeaux. However, as we shall see, his presence in that city in late 1823 is vital for the denouement of the novel. This is but a first example of Morand's carefully concealed manipulations of history, the examination of which will ultimately aid in revealing the underlying intentions of the author's historical techniques.

In 1808, the political situation in Spain teetered on the brink of civil war. The monarchy, led by the ineffectual Charles IV, was plagued by scandal after scandal and the support of the populace was at its lowest point. Not the least of the king's problems was the Treaty of Fontainebleau signed with Napoleon and intended to "safeguard" Spain against England's imperialistic ambitions. Napoleon, with one eye on England and the other on the Italian states, clearly viewed Spain as the shortest available route to Portugal, considered both a buffer-zone and a stepping-stone to England. The securing of Spain as an Imperial satellite would spare Napoleon, the bulk of whose army was engaged in the east, from diverting precious troops and capital to his western frontier.

In the meantime, the monarchy in Spain was crumbling. Public protest of the corruption of the favorite, Manuel Godoy, joined with the growing ambitions of the Prince, Ferdinand, came to a head at Aranjuez in April, 1808. Fearing that the royal court verged on fleeing the country ahead of Napoleon's forces, the mob was easily incited to action by Ferdinand's confidants who disguised as commoners urged the people to the home of Godoy. Godoy escaped certain death by hiding in the attic of his residence and the crowd continued on to the royal lodgings. Terrified by the riot and fearful for the safety of their favorite, the king and queen agreed to abdicate on condition that Godoy's life be spared.

Napoleon, recognizing his moment of opportunity, refused to recognize Ferdinand's claim to the throne and proposed a meeting near the frontier to discuss the matter with the new king himself. Against the advice of many of his councilors, Ferdinand traveled to Bayonne, where Napoleon acquainted him with his intention to remove the Bourbon monarchy in favor of his brother, Joseph Bonaparte.

Before any action was taken, however, the events of the second of May, the infamous "dos de mayo," precipitated matters. This uprising of the citizens of Madrid against the French troops garrisoned in the capitol was followed by the severe repression and execution of many of the participants on the following day. Clearly the situation was out of control in the eyes of both Napoleon and the weary, terrified Charles. Ferdinand, a cowardly and impressionable man, was easily persuaded to relinquish the throne to Joseph, the emperor's brother and then King of Naples. French troops poured across the frontier and Joseph entered Madrid on July 20, 1808, beginning a period of occupation that was to continue until 1813 and which would plunge the country into a bitter civil war.

This specific historical period, with all its fascinating political intrigues, spanning three regimes and engulfing all levels of society, is rich in material ripe for novelistic inquiry. Paul Morand recognized not only this but also a situation well-suited to his own purpose. And the nature of this purpose? Morand meticulously refrains from stating it explicitly, but the most cursory glance at the manner in which he exploits the historical material suffices to suggest his intent. This, coupled with the extra-textual knowledge of Morand's own political background and the date of the publication of the novel, 1951, affirms our suspicions. For the protagonist of the novel, don Luis Almovar y Saiz, is an "afrancesado," one of the many Spaniards who collaborated with the French during their occupation of Spain.

Without reiterating all of the various aspects of the situation in Spain during the Napoleonic incursion, the analogies to the occupation of France during the first half of the 1940's are easily perceived. Spain replaces France as the occupied country while France assumes the role of occupier; the afrancesados find their counterparts in those who collaborated with the Vichy government and the guerrillas or freedom fighters in the members of the Resistance; England emerges as a force supporting the guerilla movement as it will later provide a base of operation for the Resistance. In 1808, England sunk the Spanish fleet, a move not unlike the events at Mers-el-Kébir in 1940. Morand manipulates these implicit analogies in such a way that there is little doubt as to his intent to provide an indirect commentary on the events in France.

Le Flagellant de Séville presents a view of collaboration that is sympathetic and yet not unambiguous. At its most basic level it is the story of one man's struggle to reconcile his love for his country and an equally compelling love for France. This latter force appears in two distinct yet related forms. Don Luis, educated in France, displays a ravenous hunger for knowledge and in particular the knowledge of the Enlightenment. In the opening pages of the first part of the novel, don Luis exults over the arrival of the latest edition of the Encyclopédie. Ridiculed by his family members who represent the ignorant, backward character of Spain, don Luis caresses the volumes lovingly: "la divine manne de la pensée française." Set against this adulation of the France of the eighteenth century, don Luis' admiration of Napoleon is rooted in his belief that the emperor alone holds the key to the future. Morand's tour de force in this novel is to lead the reader, who has been inured with the view of collaboration as constituting a betrayal, into the mind of a collaborator who acts out of love and fidelity to France.

Fueled by this francophilia, don Luis is compelled to action upon hearing of the ascension of Joseph Bonaparte to the Spanish throne. His first collaborative effort comes in the role of intermediary when he offers his services to the mayor of Seville, hoping to facilitate the entry of the French. The meeting with the Sevillian alcade, however, proves more than a simple act of political mediation when don Luis encounters there a former school-mate and present French hussard, Poupard. The presence of the French official, seen as an act of provocation by the growing partisan movement in the city, results in the execution of the mayor and the flight of don Luis and his wife to Madrid.

Once in Madrid, don Luis, still struggling with his divided loyalties, witnesses the coronation of Joseph, but his attempts to join the government of Napoleon's brother are thwarted by the August uprising in Madrid which forces the French and don Luis back to Vitoria where they wait for the arrival of the Emperor himself. Napoleon personally leads the recapture of the capitol and don Luis returns to his uneasy position of afrancesado-without-a-post.

In the meantime, Maria Soledad (Marisol), the wife of don Luis, returns to Seville which is then under English occupation. The family there continues to support the resistance movement and Blas, a cousin, is an important guerrilla leader. Marisol, alarmed by her husband's continued collaboration and the growing anti-francisard sentiments, agrees to spy for Blas and his guerrillas in exchange for a guarantee of don Luis' safety. The opposing ideologies of don Luis and his wife offer a potential vehicle for examining the function of such a conflict within an intimate relationship. But Morand carefully subverts such a possibility by portraying Marisol's resistance as motivated by personal rather than political fidelity, a devaluating technique applied to the other fictional resistance figures as well. The women of the family embrace the movement as a means of satisfying their romantic desire to rebel. Blas, the cousin, is depicted as the underprivileged younger male, whose zeal arises in part from his rivalry with don Luis, a conflict rich in references to the fraternal struggle of Cain and Abel. By situating Blas in the position of Cain, Morand effectively undermines the credibility of Blas' position and synedochically that of the entire movement as well.

The discovery of Marisol's dealing with Blas, incorrectly interpreted by don Luis as proof of a love affair, marks a turning point in don Luis' collaboration. In exchange for police surveillance of his wife, don Luis agrees to aid the French police in their search for the guerrillas and those who aid them. Soon after, Marisol disappears; she is last seen in the company of two guerrillas who have presumably abducted and later murdered her.

The loss of his wife, corresponding in the text to the loss of all ties to his country, transforms don Luis into a ruthless denunciator. He joins the French investigative forces and begins to take a perverse pleasure in ordering the executions of scores of suspected resistance fighters, justifying his crimes as acts of vengeance for the murder of Marisol. Don Luis pursues his role as the "butcher of Seville" until the English force the French out of Andalusia and finally from Spain itself following Wellington's victory at Vitoria in 1813. Don Luis follows the flood of afrancesados to Bordeaux where he remains in exile until 1823.

Following the constitutional revolution of 1820 and with a return to order effectuated by French troops in 1823, this time under the flag of the restored French monarch, don Luis returns to Seville. Once there, he presents himself to the chief of police, expecting to be tried and punished for his collaborationist activities. He is stunned when the chief greets him almost as a hero and brushes aside his attempts to confess his crimes, choosing instead to focus on the criminality of the liberals, many of them former resistance fighters themselves. In fact, the prison houses the most celebrated among them, Blas. Don Luis obtains an audience with his cousin and confronts his old enemy. As don Luis apologizes for his actions and questions Blas about his relationship to Marisol, the prisoner reveals to him Marisol's resistance efforts and the circumstances surrounding her death. It was not the guerrillas who were responsible for her death but the French, and don Luis realizes that it was he himself who had ordered the ambush that resulted in the horrific death of his wife.

What happens next, in the final pages of the novel, is not the end of the story, for the very last scene of the story is actually the scene upon which the prologue ends. In the prologue, the three chapters forming a unit before the First Part, the activities of Good Friday in Seville are described. The narration focuses on a particular group and their ceremony: the "Confrérie de la Grande Discipline," a group of men who, after flagellating themselves, ritualistically whip the leader of the group, don Pablo. The prologue ends with the departure of a bloodied and weak don Pablo leaving the city on foot to wander about until the following year. It is not until the end of the novel that the identity of don Pablo is revealed: he is don Luis who, having renounced his worldly identity, has become the Flagellant of Seville.[3]

This brief overview of the plot of the novel allows me to outline several generalizations which when considered more systematically provide important clues to Morand's treatment of the question of collaboration so central to this work. Firstly, the novel, rooted so firmly in a particular historical context, not only employs history as a device for orienting and shaping the narrative but also as a political tool. Collaboration emerges as an ultimately repeatable phenomenon arising in response to a particular situation, thus suggesting a sort of cyclical perspective in Morand's own view of history. The manner in which Morand appropriates and then manipulates history reveals his project for the recuperation of the collaborationist figure.

---

[3] While in Séville, Morand became friends with the Sevillian writer Joaquin Romero Murube. In Murube's circle, Morand became known as "Don Pablo", a revelation which provides yet another link in the autobiographical aspects of this novel. Pascal Louvrier and Eric Canal-Forgues, *Paul Morand: Le sourire du harakiri* (Paris: Perrin, 1994) 306. In addition, a letter written to Murube explicitly signals the value Morand attached to this novel:

> Et quand ils (les Français) disent qu'une armée régulière n'avait pas le droit de fusiller une population civile qui tirait sur les soldats... ils seront obligés d'admettre que Napoléon a toujours donné des ordres contraires, exécutant des villages entiers qui n'avaient pris aucune part active à la lutte; en peu de mots, que les représailles sont aussi vieilles que les guerres." (Louvrier and Canal-Forgues, 309)

Secondly, the question of political engagement and of the vagaries of public opinion is used to bolster the reader's perception of the protagonist, don Luis, as a well-intentioned if misguided collaborator. As is the case in many of Morand's postwar works, the hero emerges as the one steadfast character in the midst of often wildly vacillating political loyalties. Don Luis remains true to his initial principles throughout the novel, unlike the majority of the others, notably the Spanish elite and even Poupard, the French hussard.

Finally, the impact of the denouement, don Luis' discovery that he carries the responsibility for his wife's murder, provides yet another means of desensitizing the collaborationist figure. Don Luis is unwittingly guilty; his blindness to the truth of his own crime, referred to upon numerous occasions prior to the final peripeteia, suggests a form of Oedipal innocence, one of mistaken identity. The problem of identity, as we shall see, occupies a central position in all of Morand's mature works, where the answers to the questions of "Who am I? What have I done?" produce disastrous results not only for the fictional characters but for the very possibility of narration as well. The impossibility of fixing an individual's identity, that is, of narrating that identity, increasingly seems to obsess Morand's work, culminating in the 1965 novel, *Tais-toi* which takes as its central subject the futility of any attempt to discover let alone recount the ontological status of an individual.

As we previously noted, when, at the end of the novel, don Luis returns to Séville, he is astonished to discover that he is no longer considered an enemy of the state. When he persists in confessing his collaboration with the French under Napoleon, the official laughs:

> "Napoléon! Mais c'est de l'histoire ancienne! que nous contez-vous là? Pourquoi pas Nabuchodonosor?" - le corregidor riait, charmé de sa plaisanterie." (426)

Don Luis finds himself acquitted not by trial but by history itself, or rather the latest version of history in which the events of the Napoleonic occupation have been recast in relation to the more recent liberal uprising, suppressed once again through the intervention of French troops in 1823, this time to secure the Spanish monarchy. This, of course, is not an unusual phenomenon, but neither does it present an adequate means of dealing with his situation, as don Luis discovers soon after.

Strangely enough, Morand, in acquitting don Luis on the basis of "ancient history" echoes an indictment of the hypocrisy of that practice in his own time. In his article, "De la paille et du grain," Jean Paulhan chides the members of the CENE (Comité nationale des écrivains) for having forgotten that they too once acquitted by forgetting:

> Il [l'amour de la patrie] oublie volontiers. On dirait même qu'il a plaisir à oublier (il a peut être tort). Romain Rolland, lui aussi, a bel et bien trahi la cause de la France en quatorze..., Pourtant, dès l'année vingt, nous lui avions tous pardonné et qui de nous eût refusé d'écrire à ses côtés? [...] A qui nous eût dit: "Mais il a trahi la cause," nous aurions volontiers répondu (comme l'enfant qu'on gronde parce qu'il a cassé une potiche): C'était il y a cinq ans. (329)

If we leave aside for a moment the rather questionable nature of Paulhan's polemic and concentrate on the notion of selective loss of memory, it would appear that both Morand and Paulhan point to the generally, if only recently accepted notion of the subjective nature of historiography and to its potential as a political instrument by which the most recent "official" version of historical events can be used to shape policy and public opinion. Indeed, the most pertinent example of this politicization of history can be seen in the propagation and acceptance of the "deGaullian" version of the occupation of France which held that collaboration with Nazi Germany was limited to a few individuals and that the vast majority of the French people resisted the Occupation from the outset, an account which has only recently been called into question.[4]

At this point is may be useful to point out what appears to be a discrepancy between Morand's exploitation of a subjective historiography as evidenced in don Luis' acquittal via historical pardon and the global project of the novel itself which, as historical fiction, purports to pose as historiography. Is it not odd that even as the novel proposes to tell the story of don Luis in a highly accurate and detailed historical context, it then, at the end, suggests that history can only be rendered subjectively or, in a sense, fictionally? Thus this historical novel would subvert its own claim to authority by calling attention to its own fictionality. Odd perhaps, but certainly not uncharacteristic of what one critic labels the "metahistorical novel" of the twentieth century which, by thematizing historiography itself, is characterized by "the assertion of the very indeterminancy of factual verification." The same critic continues:

> Whether the artist-hero of modernist fictional auto-biography encounters the horror of contemporary history by evasion, denial or self-flagellation, the effect is similar: the referent may be an object of cognition, but the knowledge that it yields is either trans-historical or ahistorical. (Foley, 194)

---

[4] See Colin Nettelbeck, "Getting the Story Right: Narratives of the Second World War in Post-1968 France." On the persistence of this myth and others and their effect upon policy and opinion, see also Henry Rousso, *The Vichy Syndrome*.

Foley's observations seem directly to address *Le Flagellant de Séville*, not only in her reference to self-flagellation, but also in the qualification of the knowledge produced by this type of fiction as transhistorical or ahistorical, terms which are relevant to this novel in two important ways.

It is not difficult to perceive the transhistorical quality of the novel when one considers exactly how Morand is using history. We earlier noted that the period of the Spanish civil war of 1808 bears many resemblances to that of the occupation of France from 1940 to 1944. Morand is certainly not alone in drawing this analogy. Among others, Céline, interestingly enough, points to it in a passage from *D'un château l'autre*:

> ...nous étions peut-être?... peut-être?... aussi ordures à l'Europe aussi à jeter à la première voirie venue, crocher à n'importe quelle fourche, que les amis de Napoléon?... une fois Sainte-Hélène!... peut-être?... Surtout les amis espagnols!... collaborateurs hidalgos!... les joséfins! un nom à toujours se souvenir!... ce que nous étions aussi nous!... adolfins! (106)

"Joséfins" and "adolfins," the same roles, the same collaboration and, dare we say, the same story? If it has become apparent that in the novel the France of 1940-44 is seen as a repetition of the Spain of 1808-14, then it is also apparent that on one level, Morand views history as eminently repeatable, implying a sort of cyclical view of human behavior. Thus by positing the transhistorical quality of the collaborationist experience, Morand also points to certain common factors which spark or motivate collaborationist behavior. Since collaboration occurs in diverse historical periods, the motivations or determinants must be similar if not identical. Indeed, *Le Flagellant* emerges as an attempt to describe or illustrate these determinants. Don Luis does not become the butcher of Séville overnight and it is the process of coming to collaboration which occupies the bulk of the text. In this sense, the novel can be read as a case-study in which the forces propelling don Luis, and thus anyone like him, to collaboration are revealed throughout the observation of his activities and the way in which don Luis justifies to himself his position.

The collaborationist "logic" emerges most clearly in two types of moments in the text: the contemplative moment of self-examination and doubt, upon which we will comment shortly; and those instances where don Luis is called upon to defend the Napoleonic project. The recurring theme of the latter polemic is don Luis' vision of Napoléon as a savior figure, as evidenced in the following passage from an exchange between don Luis and the other members of his family, who are firmly opposed to the occupation. Don Luis admits the suffering which will result, but while the others remain rooted in the perception of the present situation, don Luis projects his argument into the future:

> Je préfère essayer de vous faire comprendre que Napoléon est le chef moderne [...] d'un pays moderne [...] qui a engendré une ère [...] barbare si tu veux, dont nous voyons le début et dont plusieurs siècles ne verront pas la fin. Des formes nouvelles sont nées: elles portent encore haut d'antiques drapeaux nationaux, mais c'est pour soûler les patries qu'elles vont anéantir. Bientôt les querelles entre nations paraîtront aussi puériles que les tournois entre mon secrétaire et mon intendant mettant flamberge au vent pour ou contre la tauromachie de Ronda ou de Séville. De même que Ronda et Séville, Paris et Madrid seront de simples chefs-lieux et les frontières sauteront comme ont déjà sauté les octrois. Sortons du Moyen Age, je vous en supplie, et entrons dans notre siècle. N'est-il pas suranné notre raidissement devant les événements qui ne nous demandent pas notre avis pour se dérouler selon la logique des choses? L'arrogance est toujours risible, mais l'arrogance du pauvre est d'une risible témérité." (65-66)

Several of the large issues surrounding collaboration are embedded in this defense of Napoléon's imperial project, a defense which, as presented by don Luis, is based upon the notion that progress is not perceptible from the limited vantage point of the present. According to this scenario, the sacrifices of today can only be judged from the future. This "historical" perspective of events is similar to that explained by Sartre in his essay "Qu'est-ce qu'un collaborateur?" in which he claims that collaboration can be explained only by individual pathology rather than by societal pressures (43-61). One "error" latent to the psyche of the collaborator is just this tendency to validate events by viewing them as necessary links in a process mistakenly seen as progress. In projecting his argument into the future, the collaborator sets up a scenario in which current events are judged from an historical perspective. This process absolves the collaborator from facing the moral decisions that such a situation provokes and, in addition, serves as a sort of alibi against future judgment. For the collaborator also suffers from what Sartre calls an "intellectual malady," namely historicism, which, in Sartre's own terms teaches that: "ceux qui résistent aux grands soulèvements, bien qu'ils apparaissent comme de belles âmes, seront considérés plus tard comme inefficaces, égarés et attardés" (52). That don Luis suffers from a variation of this illness is evident in his ridicule of the "risible témérité" associated with the arrogance of the poor, an obvious reference to the militarily weak Spanish, or later to the French in 1940.

Also characteristic of don Luis' polemic is what Sartre calls "realism," the tendency to submit to any outcome simply because it has been accomplished (51). Don Luis again refutes the utility of a resistance that fails to recognize the fatalistic quality of events which "ne nous demandent pas notre avis pour se dérouler selon la logique des choses." His solution is to submit to this overpowering logic simply because it is already in motion.

If Sartre's analysis of some of the characteristic ways that a collaborator fashions a version of current events seems to be pertinent in the study of this novel, the underlying premise of his argument is even more so. Without proposing either that Sartre's argument provides a convincing rationale of collaboration or that Morand was in some way influenced by his article, it is striking that Morand's polemic should resemble that of Sartre in many ways save the implicit goal of each. Whereas Sartre proposes a sort of "expert testimony" of collaborationist behavior, made available to the prosecution of collaboration, Morand uses many of the same arguments to construct a means of acquittal. Sartre proposes that collaboration is an individual pathology explicable by existential psychoanalysis and, as stated before, this novel is, at a very basic level, the study or the exteriorisation of don Luis' mental journey into collaboration. Faced with the possibility of a choice between Spain and France, don Luis agonizes and wavers in "un de ces voyages minutieux où l'on visite tous les lieux avant de se fixer définitivement" (60). This "voyage" is to form the basis of don Luis' collaboration, for don Luis proves incapable of fixing himself firmly on the side of France, haunted by his inability to convince himself of the role he should assume and by a persistent perception of his solitude vis-à-vis his fellow Spaniards, an obsession bordering on paranoia:

> Il éprouvait le sentiment pénible d'être seul, physiquement et moralement, seul, égaré dans un autre élément, comme un insecte chez des poissons, comme un ours au milieux d'un vol de mouettes. (68)

This self-marginalization echoes that of don Esteban, the hero of an earlier short story, 'Le Dernier jour de l'Inquisition," who likewise is obsessed with his solitude, seen as the result of his failure to reconcile the contradictory temptations of good and evil despite the faith which promised to free him of this burden. And like don Esteban, who sees in the Inquisition a ready-made situation which seems to offer him a community in which his own responsibility for decision making is rendered unnecessary by the clear rules set forth, the decisive factors which influence don Luis in his moments of self-doubt are the ease of the path of collaboration and the self-assurance of those involved. Don Luis' journey is marked by recurring cycles of self-doubt resolved by the all too fortuitous appearances of Poupard, the French officer, and Juan Bautista d'Alcaraz, a young Spaniard fanatically devoted to Napoleon.

Poupard invariably arrives on the scene just as don Luis becomes mired in his inability to direct his own action and offers a concrete solution. Likewise, when don Luis begins to doubt his own courage and the prudence of Napoleon's campaign, his path crosses that of Juan Bautista whose fervor and unwavering adoration of the Emperor restores to the Sevillian his own doubtful zeal.

Neither Poupard nor Juan Bautista represent actual historical figures; there is, however, a strong symbolic value attached to each. The first time that don Luis meets (or rather re-acquaints himself with) Poupard, the Sevillian's reaction to their handshake is striking:

> Pour dissimuler une gêne qui est presque de la peur, il fait un calembour: "Ce n'est pas la main du commandant, c'est la main du Commandeur." Il songe qu'il est à Séville, comme don Juan. (80)

This image recurs later in the novel as well when he again meets the Frenchman, this time in Madrid after don Luis' flight from Séville:

> "La poigne du Commandeur" se dit à nouveau don Luis. "Je suis don Juan, vainqueur de mille et trois idées, entraîné aux enfers par la main de pierre." (139)

Poupard, via his association to the commander of the myth, symbolizes destiny, a destiny to which don Luis, as don Juan, is condemned to suffer. Once again don Luis inserts himself into a ready-made order, one might say a text, this time mythological and literary. Morand had already employed the Don Juan myth in his first collaborationist text, "Le Festin de pierre" (1941); but whereas it is Hitler who plays the role of the Commander in the earlier version, exacting vengeance on decadent France, here it is Poupard, a relatively low-ranking French officer. However, given the degree of verisimilitude for which Morand aims in this novel, Poupard provides a convenient surrogate for the hand of Napoleon himself. This position of representative extends to the other figure, Juan Bautista, who likewise functions to shape don Luis' decisions.

Juan Bautista, by virtue of his name alone, signals recourse to yet another level of intertextuality, this time biblical. The young soldier displays a zeal which approaches religious fervor, echoed in his choice of words used to describe his adoration of the Emperor:

> Tu penses, n'est-ce pas, comme moi, que hors Napoléon, il n'y a pas de salut? (239)

> Leur cause est sainte, disent-ils? La nôtre est plus sainte encore car c'est la cause de l'Empereur! (306)

This vision of Napoleon as savior expresses directly the tendency of don Luis to attribute to him this role. Juan Bautista has the effect of a disciple/soldier, serving as go-between and promoter of his god. As we noted before, Juan Bautista's appearances in the novel coincide directly with don Luis' most anguished moments of self-doubt, and the Sevillian invariably emerges from these encounters rejuvenated and reaffirmed:

> Le Sévillan sentait son cœur s'alléger. (306)

> Cette rencontre avait été salutaire pour don Luis: c'était la tête dans un seau d'eau froide au réveil. (240)

Just as he cast himself in the role of don Juan, he is here depicted as the recipient of divine inspiration and salvation, granted baptism in the image of the bucket of cold water. These ready-made roles relieve don Luis of the burden of assuming responsibility. As don Juan he is merely obeying the fatalistic principle of the myth, and as the wayward sinner he has only to pronounce his belief in order to be absorbed into grace. The paradox here, however, is that the road to hell (Commander/Napoleon) is also the road to heaven (John the Baptist/Napoleon). Certainly, in the text, the morality of the day-to-day aspects of Napoleon's project remains in the eyes of don Luis ambiguous at best. But here, as before, Morand's earlier text, "Le Festin de pierre" provides a clue to another possibility. In the 1941 text the Commander (Hitler), in congruence with the myth, emerges not as an evil entity but as the exactor of "divine" justice. The Commander would then be in the service of a severe but just god. Set against this punitary justice of the Old Testament is the pardoning god figure of the New Testament, in the figure of John the Baptist, harbinger of Christ. Napoleon would thus simultaneously represent the threat of a just damnation and the opportunity of redemption.

We also earlier noted an allusion to the fraticidal struggle of Cain and Abel, which again situates don Luis in relation to a biblical model, this time as the gentle, credulous counterpart of the evil brother:

> De son côté, Blas voyait en son cousin le contraire de ce qu'il était lui-même. Toujours il avait supporté malaisément cet esprit innocent et affranchi, qui avait fait son miel très tôt, au hasard de beaucoup de fleurs; il avait haï cette générosité inflammable alternant avec l'indifférence oublieuse des gens comblés que le voisinage d'un être difficile ne gêne pas parce qu'ils ne pèsent jamais à son vrai poids (si même ils le sentent) le ressentiment de l'infirme moral, la bosse du frère défavorisé, le cœur louche du proche qui ne pardonne pas. (92)

The qualities hated by Blas are exactly those developed by Morand in order to render his collaborator more appealing and more human. Moreover, although don Luis's transformation into a ruthless avenger reverses this characterization somewhat, his position as Abel is recuperated at the end of the novel when Blas symbolically "kills" don Luis by revealing to him his crime, the expiation of which leads don Luis to renounce his earthly identity and assume the persona of don Pablo.

Thus even as don Luis projects into the future to defend his ideology, he reaches into the past in order to describe and to model his present self. This sense of re-enactment and déjà-vu echoes the position of the novel itself as a re-enactment of a fixed past which allows it to situate itself in the present. The choice of myth reinforces what we have termed the "transhistorical" quality of the novel's strategy by developing the idea of repetition within the narrative itself. Don Luis repeats just as the novel repeats. By a process of a continued "lifting-out" of history at crucial points in don Luis' story, the actual historical situation is abstracted and in a sense severed from contemporary judgement as such. Nowhere is this process so apparent as in the transformation of don Luis into the Flagellant of Seville, don Pablo.

In speaking of the assumption or re-enactment of myth, we deal with phenomena which are essentially mutable across time. The meaning of the myth changes according to the circumstances surrounding its re-enactment, as pointed out by a theorist of memory, John Connerton, who gives as example the various results of the treatment of Greek myth by classical dramatists:

> The symbolic material of such myths does not have the invariance and inertia of something already pre-signified and formalised. On the contrary, it constitutes something more like a reservoir of meanings which is available for possible use again in other structures [...]. As is the case with much of the material in the Old Testament, for instance, although there more in the form of narrative reprise and commentary, a network of mythic events enjoys a significant historicity, a long interpretative process of renewal and variation. The re-use of Greek myths, both within the culture of ancient Greece and beyond that cultural domain, depends upon what may be called a surplus of meaning - a surplus which can be realised in variable interpretive arrangements when the mythic material is restructured in other dramatic forms. (56-57)

The situation is entirely different in the re-enactment of what Connerton terms ritual or commemorative ceremony. The two main distinctions are firstly, that ritual specifies the relationship between the performance of the ritual and the ritual itself, and secondly, that the commemorative ceremony explicitly refers to prototypical persons or events which are formally re-enacted (57-61). Thus while minor modifications may occur, the central meaning of ritual remains fixed and the emphasis is placed upon the pure re-enactment. The meaning as such would emerge as ahistorical, for although the re-enacted scene takes as its object a particular person or event, historical, mythological or both, the ritual itself is (ideally) untouched by history. The act of flagellation is just this type of commemorative ceremony whose motives are described by the New Catholic Encyclopedia as: "expiation of personal sin and the sins of others, self-conquest, the impenetration of divine graces and favors, and especially *conformity with Christ* in his passion" (954) (my emphasis). The practice of penitential processions of flagellants originated in Italy in the twelfth century and was sanctioned by the Church as part of the liturgical observation of the events of Holy Week (New Catholic, 955). Thus the flagellant would re-enact or represent the figure of Christ in his passion, transcending history and situating himself in an ahistorical position established by the sheer repetition of a prescribed ritual.

Such is the depiction of the procession of flagellants and their leader, don Pablo, in the prologue to *Le Flagellant de Séville*. The rituals of Good Friday are described in an essentially ahistorical setting. We do learn that the ceremony is taking place in Seville sometime in the fourth decade of the nineteenth century, but the only reference to an actual date is the rather vague notation: "Ce Vendredi saint de l'année 183...." Of the leader, don Pablo, we know very little at this point, except that he has been a flagellant for twenty years and that he has suffered something in the past for which he seeks expiation. There is no mention of the situation of the outside world, of anything which might situate the prologue in a specific and significant historical context. All that emerges is the eternal sense of the ritual itself, revolving around the anonymous don Pablo, a suffering and almost sacred figure.

When at the end of the novel the identity of don Pablo is revealed, the reaction of the reader is at first one of surprise and then of sympathy, something akin to "Don Luis is a moral man; after all, he recognizes his crime and punishes himself, even as the institution of justice has acquitted him." But while it is true that don Luis punishes himself, the sin for which he seeks expiation must be examined more closely.

When don Luis presents himself to the "frère majeur," the administrator of the confraternity of flagellants, he confesses his crime:

> [...] maintenant que vous connaissez mon nom, señor, vous savez que c'est celui d'un grand pêcheur qui se repent. J'ai erré dangereusement, mais non dans mes opinions que je ne songe pas à renier; je sais que la cause embrassée par moi était la meilleure; l'état où se débat l'Europe a fait une certitude de ce qui, jadis, a pu par moments être un doute. Ce dont je m'accuse ce sont des excès où

m'a poussé une abominable passion, une jalousie qui m'a jeté dans le crime. (436)

Don Luis has no intention of repenting for his crimes of collaboration but rather for his crimes of passion, that is, those he committed as vengeance for Marisol whose true actions he ignored, blinded as he was by jealousy. Thus his actions take on meaning worthy of the punishment he now proposes *only* as a result of his discovery. This is even clearer in the statement of his intent which comes immediately after his "confession":

> Je suis perdu d'honneur; j'ai été policier, délateur; en revenant à Séville j'avais décidé de faire don de tous mes biens à une communauté religieuse, pour retrouver cet honneur que nous mettons au-dessus de tout. Mais depuis mon retour j'ai appris... (Il s'arrêta, la gorge nouée.). Je sais aujourd'hui que je me suis couvert du sang de l'être que j'aimais plus que ma vie [...]. L'avoir perdu est un épouvantable châtiment [...]. Mais il ne me suffit pas. (437)

It would seem that of all the blood with which don Luis is covered, only that of his wife is of sufficient value to exact payment in kind. And while don Luis does propose to pay for Marisol's blood with his own, he chooses to shed it not by giving up his life, but by allowing it to flow in a ritualistic whipping which besides serving as penance must, by the nature of the re-enactment of the passion of Christ, symbolically raise don Luis to the status of martyr.

If one re-examines don Luis' words, it is not difficult to perceive exactly of what don Luis is the martyr: "je sais que la cause embrassée par moi était la meilleure." Don Luis acquits himself of the crimes of collaboration this time by appealing to the present situation: "l'état où se débat l'Europe a fait une certitude de ce qui, jadis, a pu par moments être un doute," far different from his previous appeals to the future and to the past. In other words, had Napoleon triumphed, had my ideology triumphed, we would not be in the mess we are in now.

Two remarks are called for at this point. First of all, if one has accepted my argument that this novel is intended as a veiled analogy of and commentary upon the situation of France in the 1940s, this observation, written in 1951, would seem to refer to the crisis in Europe surrounding the escalation of the Cold War, a situation which, according the this logic, would have been averted or simply rendered non-existent had Hitler (as counterpart to Napoleon) triumphed.

Secondly, with regard to the text itself, don Luis acquits himself of ideological crimes by pointing out the state of affairs at a very specific time, late 1823 or early 1824 according to the text. At that time in Spain, Ferdinand VII was cementing his hold on the country, re-established by the intervention of French troops in

April, 1823. The king achieved his goal through a series of repressive measures aimed at snuffing out the constitutional revolutionaries (the liberals), thus inaugurating a period many historians refer to as "white terror." Now, at the end of the novel, as we have remarked, the revelation of don Luis' transformation into don Pablo greatly affects our sentiments towards don Luis. Morand cleverly uses the structure of the novel to recuperate his collaborator by referring the reader back to the pitiful and yet admirable flagellant. In this process the ultimately historical don Luis becomes the ahistorical, anonymous don Pablo, but at a very particular point in time. Our final vision of don Luis remains fixed in the context of 1823-24, a time when history provides the means for his acquittal. Yet, in the prologue there is absolutely no mention of the contemporary situation either in Spain or in Europe as a whole, thus inducing the reader to ignore or downplay the possibility that perhaps don Luis could be proved wrong in his convictions by the very "history" called upon to prove him right.

The conspicuous absence of history in the prologue, when contrasted with the copious and scrupulous historical detail of the rest of the novel, should give pause. Morand uses history as a narrative and ultimately political strategy in creating his hero. And yet in the prologue it is the absence of this context which proves to be the most powerful tool wielded by the author. It is as if the author "doth protest too much," as if Morand crammed the bulk of his novel with facts in order to conceal his true intent, in order to divert attention from the way in which he manipulates the reader's sympathy for don Luis by a subtle sleight-of-hand. And yet, in the instant in which don Luis pronounces the name he has chosen, don Pablo, the narrative space separating the prologue and the final chapter collapses. Don Luis becomes don Pablo in an act of transformation which symbolically and literally obliterates his former identity. To reread the prologue is an acutely uncomfortable experience, uncanny in the fullest sense of the word; where one expects to find reassurance of a certain continuity is found only its lack. A sort of short-circuit has been effectuated, one which throws the two poles of the novel into contact and volatizes the intervening circuitry.

But is this not characteristic as well of many of the other structural techniques employed in the novel? Don Luis' reunion with Blas throws the reader backwards to the moment of Marisol's disappearance. Don Luis' physical reaction to Blas' revelation repeats the image of the blind beggar seen at the time of Marisol's death. And in his declaration to the frère-majeur the emphasis placed upon his adherence to his original ideologies operates a curious reversal of the traditional Bildungsroman, a model which this novel at first glance seems to emulate. Despite his many experiences, his perpetual self-examination and his crimes, don Luis seems strangely untouched, rather like a Frédéric Moreau whose final pronouncement upon his life consists in a reference to a long-ago episode, one lived before his "education" began. The importance of don Luis' development, the narration of which comprises the bulk of the novel, is devaluated. To understand him requires only that one be informed of his initial characterization. This is, of course, a gross simplification, but one which illustrates the persistence of a technique which essentially represses what might be termed the "middle." The many extra-textual references in the novel achieve roughly the same effect: lifting the story out of the narrative and placing it in direct relation to its referent. In likening Poupard to the Commander, Morand, in constructing the metaphor, at the same time momentarily severs Poupard from his historical (and narrative) context in a manner which unites for an instant, the hussard and the statue of stone.

These techniques of abolishing a certain textual space respond to what we have postulated as the primary force behind Morand's choice of Napoleonic Spain as the context of *Le Flagellant de Séville*: the curious and inverted parallels between this historical situation and the events of 1940 in France. Just as the intervening textual space melts away at the end of the novel, there is a simultaneous dropping away of the temporal space separating 1808 and 1940, a temporal short-circuit which functions to suppress the one hundred and fifty-odd years between them. The past becomes the present and, at one and the same time, the present becomes the past. There is simultaneously a resuscitation of the past and an historicization of the present, a dual movement which has as its effect to desensitize both. In the prologue, don Pablo pauses before his ancestral home and marvels that he can look at it with indifference:

> Il ne souffrait plus. Quelque chose était brisé entre le présent et le passé; c'était une rupture sans brusquerie, un vide à l'intérieur de quoi il repensait ses aventures sans plus les sentir. Ce dédoublement était l'œuvre de milliers et de milliers de nuits, d'abord sans sommeil, ensuite plus calmes, de matins de moins en moins torturants, de soirs où la plus atroce amertume s'était muée à la fin en une démangeaison sourde, puis en une sorte de sécheresse qui avait trempé jusqu'à la plus inflexible résistance ce qui lui restait de cœur; juste ce qu'il faut pour faire marcher un corps. (25)

This passage directly addresses the relationship of the past and the present in a manner which invests this link with a very particular character. To the notion of a break between the past and present is added that of a breaking (down) of what is between (entre) the two poles. The latter, the rupture itself, provides don Pablo with a "vide," a null space emptied of content within which he may contemplate the past without pain, but which also renders the present tolerable. That the rupture or break is more the creation of a certain neutral zone between the past and the present than their definite separation is further evidenced by its qualification as a "dédoublement." The verb from which "dédoublement" takes its derivation, "dédoubler," in addition to being the act of division, has as its primary definition the undoing of a duality: "défaire le double" (Littré) and "défaire ce qui est double en le ramenant à l'unité" (Robert). Thus a certain unification would be achieved by the fracture of the intervening space. It is as though the content of this interval has been sucked away, joining the two temporal extremes.

This is not to say that the "middle" has been actually abolished, but rather, as in the case of the novel, devaluated. This "something" between the past and the present has been broken, "brisé": rendered useless, without value, suppressed (from "supprimer," Robert). The process of this suppression itself consumes time: "de milliers et de milliers de nuits." But duration here functions not to fill but rather to empty don Pablo's days and nights. Strangely, if anyone undergoes an evolution in this novel it is don Pablo prior to the prologue, that is, in a space outside the novel itself, between its end and its beginning. But this development tends not toward a fullness of being but rather to an evaporation, culminating in a dryness (sécheresse) which hardens what remains of his heart. The "middle" emerges as suppressed, broken up, dried up. If change there has been, it is less a transformation of don Pablo's "self" than a modification of the manner in which the present and the past co-exist. In the following passage, coming immediately after the above, Morand provides a concrete image of the movement(s) between the past and the present:

> La flûte d'un marchand de lait de brebis se fit entendre et pénétra très loin dans son passé. Les hommes changeront, quitteront le sol d'un coup de talon pour s'élever dans les airs, n'auront qu'un oeil ou s'en grefferont un troisième, mais ce seront toujours les mêmes chats, les mêmes femmes, les mêmes chèvres, les mêmes enfants; cette flûte d'un marchand de lait sévillan surgissait du fond de sa huitième année. (26)

The structure of this passage is quite striking. It begins and ends with the sound of the milk vendor's flute, a sound which evokes the past, in the manner of Proust's madeleine, for example. But the two phrases of the flute differ from each other in that they indicate two temporal movements in opposite directions. In the first, the flute penetrates the past (pénétra très loin dans son passé), moving from the present to the past. The second moves from the past toward the present, it surges (surgissait) from a fixed point in the past. The sound thus provokes a dual movement: spiraling first into the past and then resurging back toward the present. This ricochet effect, that of an echo, is made possible by the image of time which is compressed, as it were, between the two flutes. In this middle, one again finds two movements, this time both moving in the same direction but presenting radically different perceptions of their flow. From one such perspective, things happen, progress or change occurs: men will learn to fly, will lose or acquire an eye. But, from the other, nothing changes: there will always be the same cats, the same women, etc. This dual image effectively rejects any notion of causality in history - either future history, in this instance, or past, as with the notes of the flute - by emphasizing the homogenous quality of the time that links great events. What is emphasized is the recurrence, or rather the perception of a link between the present and the past, on the one hand, and the present and the future on the other, a link repeated in the movement of the flute: first penetrating the past and then moving from the past, at that moment itself a present moment, towards a future which, in this instance, is don Pablo's present.

This is exactly the movement of the novel itself: beginning with don Pablo's "present" in the prologue, jumping backwards to a point in his (don Luis) past (1808), moving forward to the final scene (1823) and then leaping into the "future" as the narrative wraps around, returning to the prologue, to don Pablo's present. Of course, in the case of the narrative the "return" to the present spans some two hundred pages, while the sound of the flute rebounds almost instantaneously. However, as noted above, the transformation of don Luis into don Pablo at the end of the novel, coupled with the stark contrast between the prologue and the rest of the novel, suppresses the bulk of the story of his return by creating the loop which throws the reader forward, that is, back to the beginning.

This structure of an *aller-retour* or round-trip between a present moment and a past moment characterizes many of Morand's postwar fictional and non-fictional works and it is perhaps here that we may begin to delineate Morand's conception of history as it relates to the problem of collaboration in these texts. To this end I propose a rather strange detour through Walter Benjamin's "Theses on the Philosophy of History." Odd, perhaps, to cite the ideas of a man who committed suicide while fleeing the Nazis in 1940 as a model which would further our examination of the works of a collaborator, but, as I shall ultimately argue, it is precisely this tension which renders such a comparison fruitful. There is no evidence that Morand read or was indirectly influenced by Benjamin's last work, published posthumously in 1947, nor shall this study attempt to argue to the contrary. Rather, Benjamin's work shall be seen as putting forth a particular view of history which resembles that of Morand and which might be usefully compared with it so as to further illuminate the latter.

Commenting upon Benjamin's "Theses," Timothy Bahti remarks that Benjamin, in the second thesis, advocates a historical presentation which rather than looking forward from the present to the future (prolepsis), would instead redeem the past in the present (metalepsis or the retrospective assignation of a relationship between past and present). However, as Bahti points out, this metalepsis cannot occur without an accompanying prolepsis, that is, you cannot go back without returning forward:

> The movement connecting the present to the past - metalepsis strictly speaking - as, for example in having the present be an effect of a past cause or an answer to a past claim or need, necessarily involves a correlative prolepsis - with which one moves from a past back to the present: the past anticipated its effect, response or fulfillment in a present that was "future" for it but is present now. This two-way street is actually a single, unitary tropological structure: the metalepsis that gets one from the present to the related past presupposes a corresponding "return" prolepsis, and this prolepsis is predicated upon the metalepsis and as such is a "metaleptic prolepsis." (189-90)

This, Bahti argues, is the structure of what Benjamin calls the "secret agreement" between the past and the present (190). In Bahti's configuration of the structure of metalepsis/metaleptic prolepsis, Morand's "round-trip" finds an apt formulation. The dual movements evoked by the sound of the milk vendor's flute and by the structure of the novel itself respond to this view of the "secret agreement." The notion of agreement chez Benjamin, however, does not so much imply resemblance or complementarity as it does a pact or promise. It is not a question of the present looking to the past for precedence or antecedence; indeed, Benjamin rejects the notion of causality in history as the "additive" method of historicism. The past, rather, should be, can only be, truly grasped by a historical materialism which understands that the past becomes historical only as it is (ful)filled or redeemed in and by the present:

> History is the subject of a structure whose site is not homogeneous, empty time, but time filled by the presence of the now (Jetztzeit). Thus, to Robespierre, ancient Rome was a past charged with the time of the now which he blasted out of the continuum of history. The French Revolution viewed itself as Rome reincarnate. (263)

Many of Morand's war-time writings center around a persistent sensation of just this type of reincarnation. Past and present coincide at every turn and Occupied Paris appears to Morand as a series of set pieces reincarnated from the past. Just as the present is scattered with images of the past, here the reverse is also true: the present "appears" in the past. In Thesis A Benjamin gives this structure an image:

> [...] he (the materialist historian) grasps the constellation which his own era has formed with a definite earlier one. Thus he establishes a conception of the present as the "time of the now" which is shot through with chips of Messianic time. (265)

This constellation is formed by the "blasting open of the continuum of history," a figure used repeatedly in the theses, an explosion clearing away the debris of historicism's chain of causality and allowing the perception of the "secret agreement" which the historian must grasp in order to situate himself in the present - a present revealed as "now-time" (Jetztzeit) in the constellation. Now, is this not the effect of the ricochet of the notes of Morand's flute? Don Pablo's present enters into a constellation with a specific past, his eighth year, via the eruption of the continuum of time effected by the juxtaposition of progress/non-progress situated in the middle. It is also recalled that the "flute" passage immediately follows the passage concerning the "vide," the break (down) of "something" between the past and the present which allows the two temporal poles to co-exist in a vacuum, like a constellation in the great empty space of the heavens. And would it not also be possible to insert into this series the act of flagellation as it explodes open the past, bringing don Pablo into relation with Christ in this prologue bereft of historical content other than that of the ritual itself? The lashes of the whip open wounds in don Pablo's flesh but they also ulcerate time.

It must not be forgotten, however, that these lacerations paradoxically serve to heal: flagellation as an act of penitence seeking redemption. Now, Benjamin's "secret agreement" is predicated upon the redemption of the past, upon an implicit pact between past generations and our own. We in the present are endowed with a "weak Messianic power," an incomplete power of redemption.[5] As we saw, don Luis' crimes of collaboration are redeemed by the political situation in 1823-24. Don Pablo seeks redemption by conforming to the figure of an ever-present Christ. But what of the novel as a whole as it relates to Paul Morand's present? The constellation created between Napoleonic Spain and

---

[5] The study of Benjamin's messianic structures is complex and as such is beyond the bounds of this study. See Irving Wolfarth and the various articles contained in *Materialien zu Benjamins Thesen "Uber den Begriff der Geschichte": Beiträge und Interpretationen.*

Occupied France, between the afrancesado, lover of France in 1808, and the collaborator, the "super-patriot" of 1940, does it not, on the contrary, signal an effort to redeem the present in and by the past?

I shall, for the moment, leave open the question of Morand's use of this structure as it related to his own experience of the "present." In the following chapter, I will extend the discussion of history and redemption to two novellas: "Parfaite de Saligny" (1946) and "La Folle amoureuse" (1956); and a historical drama, *Le Lion écarlate*. These works, in addition to further clarifying the structure perceived in *Le Flagellant de Séville*, provide explicit images of the spatialization of history as Morand continues to construct or add to his constellation of collaboration.

II

READING THE PAST

"Parfaite de Saligny" and "La Folle amoureuse"

In 1947, Paul Morand published *Montociel: le rajah aux grandes Indes*, a novel reminiscent of his 1922 work, *Bouddha vivant* in which a disenchanted Frenchman travels to the Orient and discovers there what he believes to be "paradise on earth." *Montociel*, likewise, is the account of a Frenchman's accidental discovery of the exotic realm of Oudore and how he becomes the sovereign of this mythical land by marrying the Begum. But the novel tells another story, that of the deciphering of the first story which in its initial form exists only as a coded document: the personal journal of the European Rajah, now considered a relic by the present ruler, the son of "Montociel," who carries it with him to France where he seeks therapeutic treatment. The story of the document's decipherment centers around the eccentric Ferdinand Le Galeux, a master cryptanalyst whose services the Rajah reluctantly engages.

Le Galeux becomes obsessed with the emerging tale of the European-become-rajah and of his ultimate repudiation of his throne and ascension in a hot air balloon, an escape which earned him the status of legendary hero in the kingdom and the name "Montociel" - "monte au ciel." As Le Galeux deciphers the final page, he makes an astounding discovery: the Rajah was none other than his own father who ultimately returned to France to marry the young girl Célina, Le Galeux's mother. He, the lonely puzzle solver, is the half-brother of the present Rajah.

What particularly interests me in this novel is the central image of the decipherment of Montociel's journal. The Rajah's story is decoded by Le Galeux, that is, it is read by him. And, naturally, it was previously encoded by Montociel. The terms "encoding" and "decoding" are certainly not unfamiliar to readers of modern literary criticism, but without provoking a discussion of the use to which these terms are often put, we may discern here a generally accepted metaphor: writing, particularly of fiction, is akin to coding to ciphering in that it condenses a particular vision into a form which is then to be deciphered by the reader. Le Galeux's activity in this novel is that of "reading"; more specifically, he reads not just a document but the past as well, a past which constitutes his own history. The ultimate import of the coded document proves to be that it furnishes a link to the past, one which gives meaning to the present.

52 Paul Morand

Le Galeux's endeavor resembles greatly the operation which we, as readers of Morand's postwar fiction, are called upon to perform. In *Le Flagellant de Séville*, for example, we are invited to read or decode the parallels drawn between the Napoleonic occupation of Spain and a specific present: namely that of the Nazi occupation of France. In this chapter I propose to examine similar figurations of the "reading" of the past and how such a reading functions to illustrate not only the mechanisms of Morand's use of history but also the particular political ends to which these techniques are put.

It is to two historical novellas, the first published immediately after the war in 1946 and the second ten years later, that I now turn. "Parfaite de Saligny" (1946) is the story of Loup de Tincé, an impoverished noble who desperately in love with the daughter of the usurper of his ancestral lands, engages in the forces in the Vendée opposing the tide of the Revolution in 1793 in order to locate his beloved, Parfaite de Saligny. Tincé joins the counter-revolutionary leader Charette and takes part in the attack on Nantes. He is arrested and at the moment of his execution, death by drowning while bound hand and foot to another condemned, finally finds Parfaite as she is tied to him, his eternal partner in death.

"La Folle amoureuse" (1956) revolves around the experiences of two women, both named Escolastica. The first Escolastica, daughter of a Spanish commandante in nineteenth-century California, is a madwoman. Her sanity is restored only by the arrival at the nearby Russian settlement of a young Russian prince whose embrace returns the girl to reality. He falls in love with Escolastica and promises to return for her after settling his affairs in St. Petersburg. In the second part of the story, the second Escolastica recounts her experience of the Spanish Civil War. Taken prisoner at Guadalajara, she was turned over to the Russian commander of the anarchist forces for his personal "use." The fascist Escolastica falls in love with her captor who asks her to wait for him when he is called away to quell a fascist raid. Despite her desire to flee to Russia she does not remain, citing the memory of a great-aunt, also named Escolastica, who did wait for her Russian lover - all her life.

These two stories, despite differences in subject, share certain characteristics which invite comparison. The historical context of each furnishes a situation which, not unlike that encountered in *Le Flagellant de Séville*, presents both a choice concerning political alignment and interesting parallels to the situation in France during and immediately after the Second World War. Of the latter, "Parfaite de Saligny" offers perhaps the most explicit example, set in the Vendée, the site of the bloodiest resistance to the Revolution.

In what amounted to a provincial civil war in western France, this conflict was divided into two main factions: the Revolutionaries, known as the "Bleus"; and the Counter-Revolutionaries, often identified by their regional divisions, known as the "Blancs." The Blancs, who were in essence resisting the Revolution, emanated from the emerging political right - the monarchists (Roberts 113-14). Loup de Tincé, a Blanc, would therefore be a resistant but, in contrast to the Resistance of 1940-44, would be situated on the right of the political spectrum, while collaboration with the Revolution would be situated on the political left. England, besides accepting many Royalists emigrants, provided intermittent and reluctant support to the Counter-Revolution. Morand's exploitation of this situation, as I shall argue, is consonant with his use of history as observed in *Le Flagellant de Séville*, with two important differences. First, adding to the confusion of the chiasmic relationship between the political situation in the Vendée and that of the Occupation of France is the ambiguity of the former. A long tradition of resistance to centralized authority, coupled with a relatively harmonious arrangement with local seigneurs, complicates any attempt to describe the Vendéen Counter-Revolution along the lines of a political spectrum. Their uprising sprang more from economic, religious and societal concerns than from a wholesale political rejection of the principles of the Revolution. The vast majority of the insurgeants, it must be stressed, were poor peasants who rather than seeing the Revolution as an opportunity for economic betterment, remained firmly opposed to the centralization which would disrupt their feudal society (Roberts 30-43). The Vendéens were "neither right nor left," to borrow the title of Sternhell's study of fascism in France between the two World Wars, but rather a complex mixture of the two. Secondly, Tincé himself acts not out of an explicit, declared love of his country but out of love for a woman, a subtle departure which rather than weakening the argument of collaboration as an act of patriotism, serves to further displace attention from the political situation to the personal concerns of the hero.

Similarly, in "La Folle amoureurse" the accent falls upon the amorous adventures of the two Escolasticas rather than upon the specific political situation of each. This story is peculiar, however, in that in addition to presenting historical contexts offering parallels to the Occupation of France in 1940, the two contexts within the novella themselves provide parallel historical structures. Both parts of the story relate an encounter between Spain and Russia: the first in California in roughly 1812 and the second in Spain in 1937. The spatial and temporal compressions observed in connection with Morand's use of history are here effectuated in and by the repetitive nature of the novella itself.

Morand's exploitation of the historical contexts used in "La Folle amoureuse" is rather puzzling. The second part of the novel, set during the Spanish Civil War, a conflict often described as a dress rehearsal for the Second World War, might be expected to be the more fully developped of the two sections. However, it is by far the shorter and more skeletal of the two. The first part, in contrast, takes as context a little-known episode from the history of Russian fur-trading in California, one marked more by its romantic aspects than by political consequences.

It is within this tension created by the radically different styles of the two parts and their equally dissimilar contexts that I shall further examine Morand's techniques for suppressing spatial and temporal distance. This compression, strangely set into motion by figures of difference and expansion which first appear in the earlier story, "Parfaite de Saligny," enables Morand, I shall argue, not only to draw political conclusions regarding the present but to postulate a particular method for reading the past in relation to that present as well.

"Parfaite de Saligny" opens neither with Parfaite nor with Loup de Tincé, but with the "grand tour" of Harold Janeway, a young English aristocrat who, in 1783, sets out to see France. After an unfortunate fall from his horse, Janeway seeks aid for his injury at a nearby chateau but is discouraged by the sight of a huge party on the lawn. He continues on and discovers a humble abode inhabited by the rustic Loup de Tincé who promptly resets Janeway's dislocated shoulder. Upon hearing of the Englishman's futile visit to the neighboring chateau, Tincé informs him that the garden party was taking place on his ancestral lands, forfeited by his mother for taxes. When Janeway mentions having seen a particularly lovely girl, Tincé pales. Since childhood he has been in love with Parfaite, the daughter of the slave trader Babud who has erected the magnificent Huchière seen by Janeway. His obsession with Parfaite is compounded by the distance which separates him, an impoverished noble, from the daughter of this wealthy man. Janeway, with typical English pragmatism, urges Tincé to take control of the situation by going to the West Indies where he can quickly amass the fortune needed to win Parfaite.

Tincé returns from America in 1793, landing first in London, which he finds teeming with Royalist emigrés. Intent upon finding Parfaite, he joins Royalist volunteers returning to France. Tincé's political convictions here remain quite unclear. In explaining to Janeway his reasons for returning to France, he states simply: "Vous savez pourquoi je suis parti, Janeway, vous devinez pourquoi je reviens, et vous me posez cette question (Vous nous resterez?)?" (154). As for the Royalists, Tincé explains: "Ils ne m'emmèneraient pas [...] si je ne leur avais donné de gages" (155).

Even when he tells Janeway: "je fais mon devoir," it is not clear whether this duty is to France or merely to Parfaite. Indeed, all of Tincé's subsequent adventures in France reflect this ambiguity of motive. His participation in the Counter-Revolution seems at times accidental and secondary to his search for Parfaite. As with many of Morand's historical characters, Loup de Tincé is likened to a comedian, accidentally thrust into the unfolding drama of history: "L'entrée de Loup de Tincé dans le drame vendéen débuta par une scène de comédie" (156). Before the gates of Nantes, Tincé is struck by a "balle perdue," one destined for another. After fleeing the Blues by donning a dead Revolutionary's uniform, he enters Nantes, climbs a tree to avoid detection, and falls through a window into a house he later discovers to be none other than the Hôtel de Saligny. This "comedy" of errors culminates in his arrest for having unwittingly paid for a meal with Royalist currency. In prison, Tincé observes the calling of names of those to be tried and executed and the eerie immobility which reigns in the prison after their departure:

> A Tincé, l'Entrepôt apparaissait alors comme une de ces boîtes pleines de marionnettes, que le montreur cache dans l'ombre, sous le rideau de son théâtre, et d'où il tire au moment voulu les personnages du drame. (203)

And, awaiting his execution, when Tincé prepares to escape he recognizes Parfaite and abandons his attempt. Throughout the story Tincé reacts rather than acts, as if he were one of the marionnettes pulled at random from the box onto stage. He is a royalist despite himself, a sort of molièresque "résistant malgré lui." The ambivalence of Tincé's political position echos that of the Vendéen uprising itself which, as we earlier noted, arose from a complex reaction not readily politically defined. In addition to the enigma "left or right" posed by this particular conflict, Tincé's actions raise the question "Parfaite or France?" that is, personal motive or political conviction? Although the former constantly threatens to overshadow the latter, the two emerge as mutually dependent to a degree which leads us to question Morand's own motives behind the creation of such an opposition.

We have yet to look at the object of his obsession, Parfaite de Saligny. It is clear from her role in the story that the beautiful Parfaite functions as little more than a symbol. She "appears" only four times in the course of the story: first, when Tincé recounts his obsession with her to Janeway; next as the object of the speculations of two gentlemen who attend one of her "meetings"; third, again as the object of conversation between two emigrants in London; and finally, as she is tied to Tincé just before their dual execution. On only two of these occasions is she actually present: at her salon and at the river, and it is only at the former that she speaks. However, even in this instance her speech emerges as a sort of choral response to the running commentary by the Chevalier d'Oncet and M. de Vieille Aure. She remains very much an object which, although providing the motor of the plot, has no autonomous existence. Even at the end of the story, when reunited with Loup de Tincé, Parfaite gives no sign that she actually recognizes him or that his love is in any way reciprocated: "Elle ne l'avait pas reconnu. Mais sans doute le son de cette voix remonta-t-il alors du fond de sa mémoire?" (210). This recognition comes in the form of a question, revealing its speculative nature. And when Tincé again calls her name, she trembles, but "Etait-ce lui, ou la mort qui la faisait défaillir?" (210). Finally, after his third try: "Le visage de Mlle de Saligny, qui n'avait eu jusque-là aucune expression, parut s'éveiller à un sentiment lointain comme un écho et plus fort que l'angoisse" (211). But her face appears only to react and then only to an ambiguous faraway emotion which may only be related to the repeated pronouncement of her name. It is clear that Morand has deliberately inserted an element of uncertainty which undermines what otherwise would be a supremely pathetic moment. It is as though she is denied, to the very end, her own role and remains an object to be characterized by others.

If Parfaite functions as a purely symbolic figure, of what is she the symbol? Since we are uninformed of her feelings for Tincé, the notion of eternal love does not provide an adequate response. This would, indeed, be a purely speculative question were it not for one brief allusion to a statement by Parfaite herself as it is, of course, reported and interpreted by another. While in prison, Loup de Tincé encounters a Monsieur Beautiran who responds to his queries about Parfaite's safety by saying:

> Je l'avais conjurée d'émigrer, avait dit à Tincé un M. Beautiran, arrêté pour fédéralisme, mais elle m'a répondu: "La France est belle, comme à elle il ne m'arrivera rien." C'est justement parce que la France est belle qu'il lui arrive toujours quelque chose; plaise à Dieu qu'il n'en soit pas de même pour Mlle de Saligny; mais elle a toujours été ainsi: de la raison dans le sentiment, de la déraison dans le raisonnement. (198)

Even more telling than Parfaite's own comparison of herself to France is M. Beautiran's description of Parfaite: "elle a toujours été ainsi." The "ainsi" or "thus" obviously refers to the chiasmic description of her mental faculties which follows. But could it not also refer back to the "de même" of the preceding clause: as for France, thus for Mlle de Saligny? Thus the description following the colon would not only describe Parfaite but also France? Before answering this question, we must first examine the character of

Parfaite as she is interpreted in the text and then look to Loup de Tincé's own interpretation of the situation in France.

Parfaite de Saligny walks a tightrope between her ties to the Ancien Régime and the revolutionary tides sweeping over Nantes. Described as rather frivolous, she maintains her position as social innovator by presiding over a salon frequented by both the nobility and the latest proponents of reform. The obvious motive of self-preservation is secondary to Parfaite's naive obsession with the "latest" fashion, whether it be in matters of scientific discovery or political ideology: "Elle ne pouvait voir un mouvement sans y participer" (130). This enthusiasm results in an almost comic description of Parfaite's "adaptability":

> "Sous le ministère de M. de Calome, on l'avait vue sensible, anglaise, constitutionnelle; peu après elle devenait agricole, helvétique, humanitaire; aujourd'hui, elle était romaine, enflammée d'amour pour la liberté, et prête à aller défendre la République aux frontières." (133)

If Parfaite is guilty of complicity with the party in power, however, it is not due to any moral or intellectual conviction, but rather because of her desire to be included in the changes sweeping over the country. Her intent is not criminal but fashionable:

> Distinguée, comme tous ceux que rien ne distingue, et tout à fait convenable, elle était la convention de cette Convention qui n'avait pas encore un mois d'âge. Remplaçant l'amour par l'amour du prochain, Mlle de Saligny restait une demoiselle respectueuse des usages; ce n'était pas sa faute si les usages changeaient. (133)

As her name suggests, Parfaite is "perfect" in that she immediately senses change and adroitly manoevers herself into position. As a derivative of the verb "parfaire," her name also implies her status as product, an "ouvrage" carried to its extreme degree of completion. In the case of Mlle de Saligny, this extreme, as we have noted, borders on the comic, to the point that her very "perfection" functions as parody. As a woman "respectueuse des usages," she can be seen on one level as the incarnation of a certain eighteenth-century ideal of conventionality. Parfaite's physical appearance responds to this sur-perfection, she is more a classical statue than a woman: "son cou semblait un fût de colonne posé sur le socle des épaules; son front, un fronton; on eût dit que ses oreilles avaient été moulées et ses cheveux sculptés" (129). To the conventionality "à la Ancien Régime" is added a physical appeal to Antiquity; Parfaite embodies the past.

One might also cite, at this point, a similar female figure drawn from Antiquity: Jean Giraudoux's Hélène of *La Guerre de Troie n'aura pas lieu*. Hélène's nature emerges as capricious and self-interested; I would also recall her ability to "see" the future and to adapt her behaviour accordingly. The novella's final scene, the "embrace" of Tincé and Parfaite, echos that of the play, as a twist on the couple of Hélène and Troilus kissing outside the walls of the city. From Menelaus to Paris to Troilus, Hélène seems to have no more difficulty than Parfaite in transferring her alliances. Like Hélène, Parfaite's role seems to serve to blur the lines between love and politics. And if, as some have argued, Hélène ultimately represents the destiny of the Trojans, might one not equally venture that Parfaite likewise emerges as the figure of destiny, not only the destiny of Loup de Tincé but of France as well?

For even as she appears as a symbolic embodiment of the past, Parfaite is the convention of "la Convention," the ideal reflection of the Republic created by that assembly which was subsequently to undergo such frequent and violent change. In her obsession with the latest "fashion," Parfaite is in perfect alignment with what Trimoutiers labels the fundamental change in society after the 1789 revolution:

> Autrefois, on cédait aux mœurs, c'est-à-dire aux lois invisibles qu'une minorité longue et continue avait fixés - généralement pour son bien-être ou pour sa défense - à travers les siècles; aujourd'hui, c'est aux modes qu'on cède, simple expression d'une majorité momentanée, sorte de convulsion sentimentale affichée partout, de grande vague mesmérique de goûts et de dégoûts, moins communs à un pays ou à une classe qu'à une génération, et qui vous submerge le monde tous les deux ou trois ans. (146-47)

Parfaite is the "perfect" example of this tyranny of fashion, of the taste for the present moment, just as she is the "perfect" product of the past. Her salon, the "Amis des lumières et de la Révolution" reflects this intersection; it is a moderate group only in that it includes members of both extremes: a M. de Vieille Aure and a Demophile Grapin.

This, perhaps, accounts for Parfaite's eventual downfall, a fall from grace neither described nor explained in the story, but concerning which sporadic allusions allow us to piece together possible scenarios. Her wealth presents one problem: "N'oubliez pas que les Babud de Saligny sont des gens riches, très riches; si l'on permettait aux gens riches d'appartenir en outre aux partis avancés qui dépouillerait-on?" (147). Even more convincing, however, is the perception of Parfaite's enthusiasm itself:

> [...] si Mlle de Saligny veut des Jacobins, qui nous dit que les Jacobins veuillent d'elle? Aux modérés qui l'affaiblissent, la Convention préfère les émigrés, dont elle vit... Danton n'a que faire des louanges d'une Mlle de Saligny; elles le compromettraient... il ne se passera pas longtemps que notre Parfaite ne soit pas parfaitement dévorée, elle et ses enthousiasmes. (141)

Hence, as we suspected, her very perfection may well be the cause of her condemnation. Inextricably linked to the past by virtue of her social position and her conventionality, she must be rejected as compromising to a Revolution eminently in revolt against that past, indeed against History itself. Parfaite incarnates the arbitrary nature of conventionality as she passes from one convention to another, eventually arriving at the Convention itself. For this alone she represents a danger to a body whose founding principal rests upon the expurgation of the arbitrary: "'Mlle de Saligny, c'est la Révolution,' avait dit un jour M. de Trimoutiers; 'Si vous dites vrai, alors la Révolution est finie,' avait répondu le Président" (131). Parfaite's conventionality threatens; if she succeeds in attaining the status of symbol of the Revolution, that Revolution would be compromised from within. She would stand as an only too visible indicator of that which the Convention must repress: its own arbitariness.

Interestingly enough, this is the exact situation, emanating from the opposite angle, in which Loup de Tincé finds himself. After his imprisonment in the Entrepôt de Nantes, Tincé, for the first time, takes to reflecting upon the situation of his country:

> Tincé regardait ces hommes couchés comme des morts surpris dans leur sommeil, au fond d'un immense fossé, ce fossé qui déjà séparait la France du passé et celle de l'avenir; tous victimes d'un monstrueux accident géologique pareil à ceux qui font s'écrouler les montagnes dans les plaines et les océans submerger les civilisations [...]. Une France nouvelle naissait au dehors, sans lui, sans eux, après les avoir enfermés moins pour les punir que pour ne plus les voir, pour n'avoir plus à penser à eux, pour fuir leurs reproches muets de fantômes. Une France qui déjà avait une autre figure, portait d'autres habits, parlait une langue neuve. (199)

Again we have the notion of Tincé's involvement as an accident, here compared to an immense geological disaster. The description of this catastrophe coincides with Trimoutiers' comments on the vicissitudes of contemporary society which periodically submerge the world ("qui vous submerge le monde tous les deux ou trois ans"). The victims of this disaster are stretched before Tincé as if in an immense "fossé" or ditch, which Tincé then likens to the metaphorical "fossé" separating the France of the past from the France of the future. We would do well to pause briefly to reflect upon this image and the word describing it, fossé, as it both figures the commentary which follows and swings around to rejoin Parfaite.

In geological terms, a rift valley, a "fossé" marks the location of a "faille" or fault, the intersection of crustal plates. A rift is the result of one plate being dropped or subsided as it pulls away from its bordering plate, creating a valley. In architectural terms, a fossé is a "moat," a ditch dug for purposes of fortification. Now, those in the Entrepôt are interred there not as a punitive measure but so as to render them invisible and mute, so that the France of the future, the "new" France might ignore their existence: not to be obliged to see them, to think of them and, above all, to hear them in their mute reproach. The latter represents, indeed, their most powerful threat: that of a persistent criticism, of a phantom voice which is eminently the voice of the past. They would then be subsumed by the pulling apart of the past and the future, but also shut away at the bottom of a moat designed to protect the Revolution.

Moving backwards to the second definition of "fossé": a ditch or conduit of water, we approach Parfaite. For where does this "fossé" symbolically lead but to the Loire, the site of the watery execution of Tincé and Parfaite? Indeed, "fossé" phonetically and etymologically recalls "fosse" or grave, a relation signalled by Tincé himself: "couchés comme des morts." How then does Parfaite arrive at the same destination? On the deck of the galiote hollandaise, speculations abound as to Parfaite's identity: a nun, a counter-revolutionary, a dévote; no one seems quite certain of why she is there. But in this scene, as we noted, the focus falls not upon Parfaite's crimes but on her failure to recognize Tincé. It is precisely in this lack of recognition that Parfaite may be inserted into Tincé's vision of the new France: a France which already wears new clothes, has a new face and speaks a new language. Would it not be possible that this new France should fail to recognize its ancestor? That Parfaite should not acknowledge Tincé because he represents all that she has labored to forget, all that she has attempted to cast off just as she discarded the familiar in search of the new?

But is this separation so complete? As they are bound together, their bodies mold to one another, creating a single form: "Dans le brouillard plombé, il allait devenir difficile de distinguer un supplicié de l'autre; les contours de leur masse devenaient incertains" (209). Tincé and Parfaite, the past and the present, are bound one to the other, in and by an eternal and deadly bond. There is, in the text, a certain pessimistic premonition of this destiny. Contemplating his escape, Tincé decides that he will flee Europe:

> L'Europe, pour lui, ce n'était plus l'Ancien Monde, c'était déjà l'autre monde, la Révolution, une première attaque d'apoplexie. On changerait les régimes, les médecins, mais on ne changerait pas l'âme du malade; les régals, privilèges, fermes, tailles, bénéfices s'appelleraient désormais taxes, droits, perceptions, contributions ou reprises du Trésor, mais ce serait la même évolution du même cancer, dont mourrait l'homme européen. "L'Europe a trop

Reading the Past 61

vécu, trop blasphémé, trop expliqué, trop profané," se disait-il; "un cœur ferme doit prendre ses sûretés ailleurs." (201)

Names, systems, figures may change, but all essentially remains the same. Europe is dying, attacked by a cancer within, one that the Revolution can only exacerbate, and change reveals itself to be superficial and volatile. The past and the present coexist in a permanent bond, one which, without radical change, will lead to their mutual death. Similarly, despite her efforts to the contrary, Parfaite can never surmount who or what she is; she can never become "new," not only because the "new" changes just as she touches it, but also because there can never be, in the current situation, a "new." And nor does Tincé truly evolve; at the end of the story he is the same love-sick adolescent whom Harold Janeway met in 1783. His recognition of the ailments of Europe, his experiences first in America and then with Charette result not in a prise de conscience but in what is essentially a suicide.

This immobility finds its image in the spectacle of their bound bodies, an image which also reflects the more general position of each with regard to their historical situation. Both Parfaite and Tincé are engulfed in a whirlwind from which neither can escape. Parfaite is doomed to fail in her efforts to remain "comme-il-faut." Tincé finds himself in a similar dilemma: escape and lose Parfaite or stay with her and die. They are both trapped in a no-win situation, literally and figuratively in a "double-bind."

After the Liberation of France in 1944, a great deal of concerned speculation arose as to the immediate future of the country. Would 1945 prove to be a new 1789, a founding of a democratic republic, or a 1793, terror in the form of épuration, the purging of Nazi sympathizers?[1] Morand, in writing the story of 1793 onto that of 1945, signals in "Parfaite de Saligny" the latter. But his careful manipulation of the historical situation nuances this "terror" in such a way as to call into question the very principles behind such a purge. By creating an atmosphere of indeterminacy, Morand seeks to demonstrate the difficulties associated with a clear determination of guilt. Are the Vendéens counter revolutionaries or politically illiterate peasants seeking self-determination? Is Tincé a Royalist or a determined lover? Is Parfaite's conventionality criminal or capricious? Morand leaves all of these questions open, perhaps too much so, for the result is that of a constant movement back and forth from one side to the other, effectively deflecting attention from any attempt at resolution. In much the same way, the personal stories of Tincé and Parfaite intersect at angles seemingly designed

---

[1] On this period see Pierre Assouline, *L'Epuration des intellectuels en France, 1944-45*.

to relegate the latter to mere functions of the former. We observed exactly the same situation in *Le Flagellant de Séville* where Don Luis' jealousy provided the impetus and justification of his deadly collaboration which ironically resulted in the murder of the very woman for whom he sought vengeance. In "Parfaite de Saligny" Tincé's pursuit of Parfaite not only leads to his involvement in the conflict but remains his primary motive throughout and eventually impels him to reject his plan of escape and to accept death as a strange attainment of his goal.

This is nowhere more evident than in the strange scene which ends the novella. One is tempted to dismiss this episode as a regretful lapse into a romantic pathos at once contrived and unoriginal. While the image of their bound bodies provides a fitting metaphor for their individual situations, it fails utterly as the representation of a supremely dramatic moment. This failure stems from several obvious considerations, too glaring to have been unintended, which undermine the impact of what might otherwise be read as the dramatic uniting of lovers in death. For one, the entire story reads more like a comedy than a drama. Tincé is an almost farcical figure, falling through windows, hiding in haystacks, falling victim to a "lost" bullet. Parfaite herself is no less comical in her flitting from one fad to another, listening rapturously to Revolutionary discourses even as her thoughts are on her table service. Indeed, Parfaite herself represents the locus of the problem in the final scene. Her presence on the galiote remains entirely inexplicable, we know nothing of her actions since her last "appearance" some two years and seventy pages earlier. Her sudden appearance is devoid of meaning except insofar as it provides the necessary link closing Tincé's quest. Perhaps most importantly, Parfaite's feelings toward Tincé, as we earlier noted, never once receive mention, nor is her recognition of Tincé on the deck of the ship certain, but merely suggested as an admittedly dubious possibility. The ultimate tragedy, if one is to be found in this scene, lies in the possibility that Tincé agrees to die for a woman who neither loves nor even recognizes him. Tincé involvement in the Counter-Revolution would thus be rendered superfluous, just as don Luis' discovery of the true assassins of his wife (the French acting on a tip from don Luis himself) reveals his collaboration to have been pointless. I would, however, not carry the comparison of don Luis to Tincé too far. While the former resembles a Stendhalian hero in his zeal for Napoleon and in his sincere political convictions, Tincé emerges more as a Frédéric Moreau whose involvement, if it may be characterized as such, in the political events of his time emerges as incidental to his quest for

Mme Arnoux.[2] The main point of convergence between the Sevillian and Tincé is that they are both political losers, not because of the criminality of their acts, but because of the personal drama of each which slices across any political considerations, essentially severing them from the conflict.

"Parfaite de Saligny" ends with what is, literally and figuratively, a "geological fatality." Tincé and Parfaite are thrown into the Loire, and thus into the ditch or fault (fossé) separating the past and the present, subsumed by the immense accident that is the Revolution. "La Folle amoureuse," written ten years later, opens on a similar accident, one of fortuitous destiny, this time geographical:

> La partie s'engageait entre les deux vieux joueurs; ils en avaient perdu ou gagné plusieurs milliers, depuis vingt années qu'il vivaient face à face; par une fatalité géographique. L'un Espagnol; l'autre Russe. (11)

Spain and Russia are thrown together, here in the beginning of the story, over a chessboard, just as they will again confront one another, one hundred years later and on a different continent, in the second half of the novella. While "La Folle amoureuse" is essentially the story of two women, at the same time it is the story of temporal and spatial encounters both outside of and within the text itself.

As I argued in the previous chapter, Morand's 1951 novel, *Le Flagellant de Séville* contains an abundance of historical parallels and inversions of the events in France during the Second World War. Likewise, the Counter-Revolution in the Vendée also parallels, again at times inversely, the Occupation of 1940. "La Folle amoureuse" revolves around similar patterns of repetition and difference, structures related not only to the events of 1940-44 but also to the internal make-up of the novella itself. Divided into two sections, as mentioned earlier, "La Folle amoureuse" recounts stories separated by both time and space. The basic plot of these encounters is identical: a Spanish woman meets a Russian man, and the repetition of details is such that in many ways they form a single story. But the subtle differences and the injection of a particular political context into the second narrative, reveal much about Morand's development of his historical techniques. Indeed, if the choice of historical contexts here reveals ties to his earlier postwar works in that they all create resonances with Morand's own historical context, "La Folle amoureuse" reproduces the mechanism of Morand's endeavor within the confines of the story itself.

---

[2] I would also note that Loup de Tincé is inadvertently caught in the Hotel Babud during the auction of its contents - an echo of Frederic witnessing the liquidation of the possessions of Mme Arnoux.

The first part of the "La Folle amoureuse" was no doubt modelled after a curious episode in the history of Russian fur trade in America. In 1805, Nikolai Petrovich Rezanov, chamberlain of the Czar, was sent to inspect the Russian colonies in the North Pacific. Arriving at Sitka in southern Alaska, he found a starving settlement plagued by scurvy, and in the spring of 1806 Rezanov set sail for California in seach of supplies, accompanied by a German surgeon and naturalist, Dr. Georg von Langsdorff. Relations between Spanish California and the Russian traders were strained. Following the establishment of the Russian-American Fur Company in Alaska in 1799, the Russians had slowly extended their influence southward. The lack of foodstuffs in Alaska prompted Alexander Baranov, head of the Russian Company, to send parties south as early as 1803 in hopes of establishing trade. The venture proved initially profitable, but as Russian hunters began to exploit agreements made with the Aleut Indians and to penetrate ever farther south, Spain became increasingly alarmed. Rezanov was by no means certain of a hospitable reception when he reached San Francisco later in the summer where he was, however, courteously received although Governor Arrillaga was initially unwilling to furnish him with supplies. Then, a new development arose which influenced the negotiations: Rezanov fell in love with the beautiful Concepcíon Argüello, the fifteen year-old daughter of the commander of the port. His suit was at first opposed by the girl's family and the Franciscan friars who objected to the marriage of the Catholic girl to the Orthodox Russian. Rezanov proposed that he return to St. Petersburg to obtain dispensation and to propose new agreements governing the commerce between the two powers in California. Argüello consented and the couple was betrothed. Rezanov set off for Russia, but never returned to California. Concepcíon, after waiting for years, took the vows of the Dominican order in Monterey, and only later learned of the death of Rezanov in Siberia, en route to St. Petersburg. Rezanov's expedition did, however, serve as a catalyst for Russian expansion to the south and in 1812, Ivan Ruskov established Fort Ross, north of Bodega Bay in California (Chevigny 105-124).

In his 1956 novella, Morand retains only the barest outline of this curious story and takes great liberty with its chronology. Rezanov is transformed into the dashing Prince Tobolsky, a fugitive from the Grand-Duke whose mistress he had unwisely seduced. The locale moves from San Francisco to the fictional San Esteban, located near a Russian outpost probably modelled after Fort Ross. The Russian commander in the novella, Igor Menckendorf, is the chess partner of his Spanish neighbor, don Nemesio, counterpart to Argüello whose daughter had caught the eye of Rezanov. And, in Morand's most striking addition, the young Spanish girl, Escolastica, is mad.

Reading the Past 65

Only the end of the story remains intact: after promising to return, Tobolsky sets off, like Rezanov, for St. Petersburg and is never heard of again.

Strangely, this tragic conclusion to the love story of Tobolsky and Escolastica is not immediately revealed at the end of the first part but rather deferred until the end of the novella, that is, after the story of the second Escolastica. Odd, but not unmotivated, for the end of the latter half of the novella repeats the end of the first. Indeed, in many ways, the story of the second Escolastica appears as a repetition of the first, to the degree that the distinction between the two women is blurred. And yet, significant differences ensure that even as the reader equates the two stories, he or she must also simultaneously separate them. This dual procedure of assimilation and distinction is crucial to an understanding of the way in which the two stories convey a particular message.

The most explicit repetition, of course, occurs in the basic premise of each story, which I have already outlined. Like the first Escolastica, the second also falls in love with a Russian who promises to take her to Russia with him, but under entirely different circumstances: taken prisoner by the anarchists at Guadalajara in 1937, she is "raffled off" to the captain of the Russian forces; they fall in love and he promises to return to her. The Russian captain may have been modeled after the commander of the anarchist forces at Guadalajara, Enrique Lister, a Spanish communist trained in Moscow.[3] The political situation complicates the second story in that Escolastica comes from a family rallied to Franco, and it is here that the issue of political alliance comes into play.

Supporting the identical nature of the two stories are several important details. First, the descriptions of Tobolsky and the Russian captain coincide exactly:

[...] yeux d'aiguë marine, un nez desinvolte, relevé, racé. (24)

---

[3] The Russian captain may have been modeled after Enrique Lister, a Kremlin-trained anarchist who led the assault on Guadalajara and who also may have served as a model for Manuel in Andre Malraux's novel *L'Espoir*. It may not be implausible to suggest that Morand gleaned this character, as well as certain images, from Malraux's novel. Indeed, there may be some basis for a comparison of Morand's and Malraux's respective uses of history; they were, of course, acquainted, and in addition to a certain parallel between their careers as diplomats and writers, on opposite sides of the political spectrum, both were published at Grasset in the thirties. On the character of Manuel and his historical counterpart, see James W. Greenlee, *Malraux's Heroes and History* (Dekalb: Northern Illinois University Press, 1975) 126.

[...] yeux magnifiques, transparence d'aiguë marine; d'une nez comme chez un garçon de vieille race. (47)

Both have the habit of clicking their heels "militarily" and, both, significantly, are devoted chess players, frequenting clubs in Russia (possibly the same?) where they regularly play.

In both instances the relationship of the lovers occurs on an "other-worldly" plane, one removed from reality. The first Escolastica is not only mad, and thus in Tobolsky's eyes raised to that order of the demented cherished by Russians, but, as we shall see, she is also endowed with all the qualities of a vampire, a creature not of this world. The second Escolastica describes the Russian captain as bewitching: "cet être tombé d'une planète scélérate [...] m'ensorcelait" (48), and their affair as occurring in an supernatural realm: "Nous entrions ensemble au fond du miroir magique, dans un crépuscule enchanté, couleur de perle" (48).

One significant effect of the repetition of both plot and detail is the enticement of the reader to "read" the first Escolastica into or onto the second, to naturally superimpose the two. That this, in fact, is Morand's intention is revealed in the stylistic differences between the two stories. The first part, thirty-two pages in length, contains extensive descriptions of the landscape, characters and events. In contrast, the second employs a mere seven pages to tell the "same" story. Description in the second part is minimal and very little is provided in terms of background description. The result is that the reader fleshes-out the spare framework of the second story with information from the recently acquired resevoir of facts from the first story, an operation reinforced by the coincidence of detail between the two. In the same way, the first story functions to interpret the second. Doña Escolastica herself exemplifies this operation when she explains why she decided not to wait for the captain's return:

> Parce que dans le vide de ma cervelle un souvenir était tout à coup revenu: celui d'une fille de notre maison, une arrière-grand-tante. Elle s'appelait Escolastica, comme moi; elle est morte il y a cent ans. Elle aussi, un Russe lui avait commandé de l'attendre, et elle l'avait attendu... toute sa vie. (49)

Doña Escolastica interprets her own situation by utilizing information from the first Escolastica's story. She derives meaning for her own story by discerning the parallels between the two.

And yet we would recall that only at this point, at the end of the second story, does the conclusion of the first story reveal itself. The story of the first Escolastica, at the same time that it is called upon to "complete" the story of doña Escolastica, is itself completed by the second. The two stories co-exist in a mutual relationship of narrative dependence: one cannot be "understood" without the other, each alone is insignificant in that it lacks a specific meaning which can only be provided by its juxtaposition with the other.

Now, to return to our initial premise, this is exactly the structure observed in two of Morand's other historical works, *Le Flagellant de Séville* and "Parfaite de Saligny." In those works, emphasis is placed upon particular aspects of the historical context: the Napoleonic occupation of Spain in the former and the Counter-Revolution in the Vendée in the latter, which resemble those of another context, the Occupation of France in 1940. Morand creates a network of parallels between the two, the one historical and the other "present" in such a way that they coexist in a relationship of signification. These parallels work to unite the events via a system of repetition which creates the impression that one is "reading" the same story. Yet at the same time, Morand plays upon significant differences which ensure that the story is always "another" in order to achieve his own ends. In *Le Flagellant de Séville*, for example, one major difference between the Spain of 1808 and the France of 1940 is that in the former France is the occupier rather than the occupied. This inversion permits Morand to oppose the figure of don Luis, who collaborates out of love for France, to the received figure of a collaborator "1940's style," who is a traitor to France. In this sense, following Morand's rhetoric, 1940 cannot be fully completed or interpreted without 1808.

In "La Folle amoureuse" Morand similarly manipulates difference, again to a political end, but in a very subtle way, one operating between the text and the exterior context (here again Occupied France) but orchestrated within the text itself. The second Escolastica is embroiled in a very particular political context, that of the battle of Guadalajara during the Spanish Civil War. The fight for control of this city and the surrounding area centered around the Italian push to break through to Madrid. The anarchists held the region, but only through persistent resistance to fascist raids (Thomas 383-88). Doña Escolastica, from a fascist family, thus collaborates with the enemy out of love. Collaboration is again a love affair, like don Luis' love affair with France and Tincé's devotion to Parfaite. But the meaning attached to this relationship arises, we argue, not from its own isolated occurrence but from its superimposition with the love of the first Escolastica and Tobolsky. The major difference between the stories, the most glaring, is that the first Escolastica is a madwoman, whereas the second lives up to their shared name when, in making her decision not to wait for the Russian, she displays her learnedness, her "scholaticism," her reason. It is just this path from the first Escolastica to the second, from madness to reason that we must examine in order to perceive Morand's play(ing) of difference within this text.

One morning, over their daily game of chess, Tobolsky hears don Nemesio ordering a servant to seal well the doors and windows that evening in order to shut out the noises of the "Fête des songes." Responding to Tobolsky's curiosity, don Nemesio explains the native rite: "Une fois l'an, les indigènes se réunissent dans la forêt autour de grands feux et se chuchotent l'un à l'autre les rêves qu'ils viennent de faire; et ce rêve doit se réaliser aussitôt" (30). Fascinated, Tobolsky resolves to observe the ritual and that night hides behind a tree from which he may watch the ceremony, unnoticed by its participants.

Lost in thoughts of his own desires, Tobolsky watches, mesmerized by the spectacle of the Indians releasing their desires in a wild dance of sexual gratification. The spell is broken when Tobolsky suddenly sees a white woman, half naked, who jumps from a tree into the midst of the natives. They greet her with cries of "Escolastica! Escolastica!" She alone seems able to see him, and advances towards him, close enough for Tobolsky to see her eyes and their horrifying fixity. Terrified he flees back to the fort and falls asleep, dreaming of Escolastica. His dream is very "real" and Escolastica, on top of him, speaks and responds. Tobolsky realizes his error only when he extends his hand which comes into contact with the warm flesh of the girl: Escolastica is there, real and present. The Fête des Songes has worked its miracle on him, fulfilling his wish in the form of the living Escolastica.

But the true miracle is that she is lucid; she speaks, understands and recognizes him, a transformation that is the direct result of their passion:

> Dans ce corps égaré, dont le frisson s'amplifiait en ondes frémissantes, l'intelligence revenait; c'était là le miracle. Effet renversé et bouleversant de la volupté qui fait délirer les êtres de raison et ici, au contraire, chassait la démence. L'extase charnelle qui désorbite les femmes ramenait celle-ci dans le cycle des échanges sains. (35)

In the midst of their erotic frenzy a strange reversal has taken place: just as Escolastica differs from others in her madness, her reaction to sex opposes the "normal." The orgasm which disorients and "makes crazy" other woman, has the contrary effect upon Escolastica. Sex with Tobolsky makes her sane.

At the same time, sexuality is at the very origin of her madness itself. The mother-superior reveals to don Nemesio that Escolastica's affliction first manifested itself at puberty: "C'est quand la fillette est devenue adulte que le mal a commencé, que la tête lui a tourné. Aujourd'hui on dirait qu'elle a ses périodes comme la mer, comme la lune" (13). Her malady reveals itself to be particularly female in nature: its inception coincides with the beginning of menstruation, recurring in monthly cycles like that of the moon. In fact, Escolastica's condition, normally benign, worsens at the full moon when she suffers what Mother Dolores terms a "bouleversement des humeurs"; and the girl is repeatedly described as "lunatique," that is, crazy about the moon.

But if her mental state alienates her from other people (notably the Spaniards), at the same time she appears in harmony with nature and "natural" phenomena. At night she escapes the fort with her Indian maid and wanders the fields and forests, perching in the trees: "Entre le jus vertical qui monte des racines et la sève horizontale épandue dans les feuilles, Escolastica s'interposait; elle en captait l'essence" (20). Escolastica is full of this fecundity, her breasts are "poussées à bout par la jeune sève, jusqu'à faire craquer l'étoffe" (20). Lunar and pubescent, Escolastica herself is ripe for bursting. Her madness, which recedes when she lies with Tobolsky, may thus result from a lack of release of this sexual potential. Sex with the prince alleviates the problem by allowing Escolastica the expression of this repressed sexuality, a sort of Freudian sex cure. Tobolsky wonders, in the midst of their coupling: "si ce qu'elle cherchait ce n'était pas, mieux encore que de le posséder, de se posséder elle-même?" (35). But Escolastica's sexuality reaches beyond a young girl's natural desire. Witness the description of their coupling:

> Escolastica était là... et lui prenait sa vie pour s'en nourrir. (34)
> Dévoré vivant, il se demandait [...]. (35)
> [...] ce qu'il donnait, vain verseur de liqueur, c'était du sang [...]. (40)
> Abîmé comme une effigie [...] il défaillit. (40)

Escolastica sucks life from him, devours him alive, leaves him half dead - certainly these are fairly conventional images of intense sexual activity. But when coupled with other scattered allusions, our hypothesis is confirmed: Escolastica is a vampire. She behaves like a bat: "Escolastica vivait perchée..." (20); she is active only at night and at dawn her entire being reverts to a state of non-life: "épuisée, détachée de tout [...] elle restait, pieds écartés, sur le lit, petrifiée, pareille à un mort" (21); and, when describing herself to Tobolsky, she says: "Je suis presque morte [...] dans un cerceuil" (34). Escolastica fulfills all the stereotypes of the "un-dead."

But why a vampire? Several responses immediately present themselves. For one, Escolastica's madness originated with and mirrors the occurence of her menstrual cycles, with the loss of blood. Her affliction worsens, again in rhythm with her cycles, at the approach of the full moon, a time when vampires reputedly emerge in search of victims. But Escolastica receives from Tobolsky not blood but semen. Her return to sanity and, by extension, to life depends on her reception of a masculine emission. One pertinent reading of her vampirism would be that of a quest for the masculine which as a traditional symbol of reason would restore that which Escolastica lacks. Such a reading is supported by two images used to describe their strange relationship:

> [...] il était le socle et elle la statue, magnifique, mais sans lui, creuse. (35)

> Le prince était le pôle magnétique nécessaire à l'autre pôle, au rétablissement d'un circuit humain. (36)

Tobolsky is not only a remedy for her madness, but vital to her very existence as well. Without him, she is "creuse," hollow, and not even human. The connection of the circuit rendering her human - and it will be noted that at first, her moments of lucidity only occur during the sex act - is operated by his maleness, here translated as his "pole" or "pedestal."

The many aspects of the complex relationship between Escolastica and Tobolsky all point to one common factor: the transformative quality of their love. Morand reinforces and repeats the movement from insanity to sanity by inserting both the element of vampirism, by which insanity is linked to "death" and reason to life (double comparaisons which certainly are not in themselves unique), and the notion of the completion of the female by the male which equates the non-human (outside the "circuit humain") with the original state of Escolastica. This web of analogies and the insistence on the all-encompassing quality of Escolastica's "cure" serve to signal the importance of the role this transformation plays in the narrative. The Russian's embrace brings Escolastica simultaneously to sanity, to life and to humanity.

When at the beginning of the second story, doña Escolastica declares: "Moi, les échecs m'ont sauvé la vie," it is by no means apparent that we have before our eyes any other than the first Escolastica, brought back from death (insanity) by the chess player Tobolsky. The life of the second Escolastica was also saved, brought back from death, via a Russian chess player. But what was this certain death faced by doña Escolastica? Certainly it is one threatened by the anarchists who had captured her, by the very captain with whom she would later fall in love. But it is also a death coming from her own hand. When brought to the captain's room, she spies a musket on the table. The captain and his partner are so absorbed in their chess game that she is able to silently inch her way toward the gun, with which she intends to kill not them but herself. As she extends her hand to touch the weapon, the captain raises his eyes. Instantaneously she sees the move to be made and reaches instead for the chessboard, pushing his opponent's pawn and checkmating the captain. Chess doubly saves her life, not only by diverting the attention of the players from her real intention (to seize the gun) but also by "intervening" to prevent her own suicide.

This, of course, is the most obvious intention of the expression "chess saved my life." At the same time, it would be fruitful to approach the notion from a slightly different angle. As we argued, the story of the first Escolastica is called upon to complete and to give meaning to the second. By commencing the second story with a phrase recalling one of the aspects of the first Escolastica's transformation (death to life), Morand invites the reading of the first transformation, in all its facets, onto the second. Indeed the second Escolastica undergoes a process of change: from hatred of the Russian to love for him. The Russian tongue, which she first describes as a "glouglou" becomes to her ears: "la plus belle des musiques russes; ces notes basses qui montent en arpèges, au plus haut" (48). Escolastica has learned to distinguish, from this garbled mess, the tonal and rhythmic subtleties of the language. True to her name, Escolastica learns, she is a scholar, she comes to reason. And yet doña Escolastica does not wait for her Russian captain, choosing instead to rejoin the fascist forces outside the city. The lesson she has learned is not that love conquers all; nor, however, is the lesson one of purely political fidelity. Escolastica's return, in the text, has less to do with her commitment to fascism than with her commitment to her heritage and to the example of her great-aunt, the mad Escolastica. The personal again slices across the political, as in "Parfaite de Saligny," valuing individual decisions over a blind following of any collective movement. Morand suggests that political actions and, by extension, his actions are highly personal and based upon considerations not easily discerned by others if one does not know the rest of the story, as exemplified by the dual stories of this novella.

In the two works previously treated in this study, *Le Flagellant de Séville* and "Parfaite de Saligny," I argued that each contains a specific figure of Morand's historical method. In the 1951 novel, it will be recalled, the notes of the milk vendor's flute, as they instantaneously travel from the present to a moment in don Pablo's past and then back again, effectuate a sudden juxtaposition of the past and the present so immediate that both moments are separated from their place in the chronology of history and are placed in their own "chronological" order. This is the image of Morand's use of the series of repetitions and differences which create a short-circuit between two specific historical moments: 1808 in Spain and 1940 in France, a circuit which likewise blasts both moments out of the continuum and places them in immediate relation. In "Parfaite" de Saligny" the image of the "fossé" functions in much the same manner. The subsuming of the "middle," in the text, of the space separating the "old" France from the "new" mirrors the dropping away of the historical space between the Vendeen uprising and the Occupation of France in 1940.

I would propose that in "La Folle amoureuse" it is chess which functions as the figure of Morand's use of history. The game infiltrates the entire novella, involving every character, providing the initial motor of both plots, and serving as the ultimate site of all action. No matter what activity engages the characters, they are always, at the same time, playing chess: don Nemesio and Menckendorf have a game going at all times, even from a distance; and while Tobolsky lies with Escolastica at night, he continues his regular chess games with don Nemesio during the day. Significantly, the only major character who does not play is the mad Escolastica.

In addition to this omnipresence, Morand, in the opening pages of the novella, signals that chess is to function as a metaphorical figure:

> L'un Espagnol; l'autre Russe. Posés sur l'échiquier du monde, à la frontière de deux empires: l'empire russe, qui s'arrêtait là, vaincu par l'espace; l'empire espagnol, qui s'abolissait dans le temps, en cette zone où les terres des tsars et celles du roi d'Espagne s'affrontaient, sur le continent nord-américain. (11)

The world is likened to a chessboard with the "zones" of the two empires as "cases." And what do don Nemesio and Menckendorf do but themselves play out the moves of this larger game? The two are in a constant state of political flux, one day they are allies, the next they are at war. Nemesio detains or "captures" Menckendorf when Spain, allied to France, goes to war with Russia. Menckendorf returns the "move" when Napoleon, and with him Spain under Joseph Bonaparte, invades Russia. Don Nemesio and Menckendorf essentially play out History itself.

Chess as a metaphor for the state of conflict of the world certainly, of course, does not originate with Morand. Early Persian literature refers to chess as the symbolic re-enactment of battle. When the game was introduced into southern Europe the nomenclature of the chess pieces evolved to mirror feudal society: the Persian elephant was replaced by the knight, for example. Medieval moralists saw in the game of chess a microcosm of the European state (Finkenzeller 10-27). Don Nemesio and Menckendorf, by playing chess, mirror the larger game in which they themselves are pawns. When they are unable to play face to face their game does not cease. Moves are relayed via signal flags placed upon their ships: a red flag for the king, a green for the "fou," et cetera. Likewise, messengers bear the "moves" to be made on the larger board on the part of the global opponents, Spain and Russia. Nemesio and Menckendorf are playing out history within History itself.

Chess is thus perceived as re-enactment, which leads us to speculate as to the nature of the game itself. On one level, chess may be described as the confrontation of two intellects, with each move pitting the wit of one against the other. But, when one player moves his Kin, or, for that matter, any of the pieces, he or she symbolically enters into the order upon which that nomenclature is based. This order would vary, of course, depending upon the "language" in which the game is played: a francophone moves his "fou" whereas an anglophone moving the same piece, moves the bishop. But linguistic differences aside, when one plays chess (in the West) one re-enacts not only the world but also a particular historical phase of that world: feudal society.

It may be argued that the nomenclature of the pieces is merely incidental or, more to the point, that it is archaic. But this is precisely the point. Chess is a game which, while reproducing a particular historical order, may be played outside of that order, that is, outside of the historical continuum. Now, while Nemesio and Menckendorf play, in a sense, within the feudal order, that is, in their proper place in history, one image in the text demonstrates just this break from that position. While detained at San Esteban following the outbreak of war between Russia and Spain in 1799, Menckendorf assumes a peculiar attitude:

> [...] il resta au fort San Esteban, cajolé et festoyé jusqu'à la paix d'Amiens, qu'il attendit, assis à la turque, fumant de longues pipes de tabac levantin, tirant sur un tuyau en cerisier de Perse. (11)

Even as Menckendorf plays out his role in one order, he dons the costume of another, that of the Orient, sucking on a cherry-wood hookah from Persia - the site of chess' origins.

Chess permits a displacement in yet another way, again thematised in the text. Nemesio and Menckendorf continue to play chess, whether they be "at peace" or "at war." The game of chess, or any competitive game for that matter, obliges the participants to enter into a pact for the duration of the game. They must agree to a specified set of conditions which govern the game and which require them to act as if they were enemies. Thus, even when allied on the board of global politics, the Russian and Spaniard play at being enemies. And when in a state of hostility, they agree to the terms of the pact. Chess permits its players to be detached from their individual historical contexts and to enter a context created by the game.

Now, as I argued, chess may be characterized as a re-enactment of a particular order, one which for any player, save the first, is necessarily other than his or her own. It may be then be described as an essentially mimetic game. And, because it requires those players to enter into a competitive pact which may not be consonant with their individual situations, it thus displaces them doubly from their position in history.

But if chess removes its participants from the continuum of history, it cannot be said to be an achronological game. Indeed, it belongs to a particular chronological order but one which is confined to the limits of the game itself. More precisely, chess creates its own chronology, both spatial and temporal, as the players move the pieces in a particular sequence over a period of time, a sequence which varies with each new game.

Based upon the observations made thus far, chess may be described as mimetic, in that it imitates an original context; representational, in that it constitutes a metaphor for the universe; ahistorical, as it displaces its players from their own particular historical contexts; and generative as it creates its own chronology, both temporal and spatial. Chess may be provisionally described as fictional in that it contains all the traits proper to fiction.

In the second half of the novella, another game of chess is played, between doña Escolastica and the Russian captain, a game which further reveals Morand's use of chess as a figure. In pitting a Spaniard against a Russian, the "second" game emerges as a re-playing of the first. Not only is there a coincidence of nationality, but of the global situation as well. In revolutionary Spain, Russia, as supporter of the Revolutionaries, is at war with the Fascists led by Franco. Doña Escolastica and the captain function as pawns on the chessboard of global politics, just as did don Nemesio and Menckendorf one hundred years earlier. But the twentieth-century players are not only playing within the same world/chess metaphor, but they are re-enacting the same "order" as well. In playing chess, the second Escolastica and the captain re-enact the first story: that of a Spanish woman brought into contact, via chess, with a Russian man with whom she falls in love. At the same time that doña Escolastica and the Russian (re)play out their roles in history, they also reproduce the "original" story. It is the tension between these two "games" that cuts the stories loose from the temporal and spatial chronology which holds them a century apart and thousands of miles away from each other. Chess is the lever with which Morand pries the two stories out of their fixed historical positions and places them together in a mutual relationship of signification.

But while the second Escolastica is a player of chess, the first is not. Or is she? Soon after Tobolsky discovers that Escolastica regains sanity under his touch, he has an intimation of the power he possesses: "Maintenant il connaissait le secret, savait manier la clef de l'automate. La touchait-il, elle s'animait" (36). The description of Escolastica as an automaton brought to "life" fits in neatly with the series of characterizations brought to bear on the girl: madwoman brought to sanity; "un-dead" brought to life; incomplete (female) being brought to completeness. But the image of an automaton, in this story so insistently centered around the game of chess, evokes another reference as well. In 1770, the Baron Wolfgang von Kempelen introduced his latest invention, a mechanized player of chess that became known as the Automaton Chess-player (Poe 132). A figure in Turkish attire sitting at a table, the automaton appeared able to respond to its opponents' moves. Hidden under the table, in an ingenious series of compartments and trick mirrors, was a master chess player who controlled the movements of the automaton (Poe 142-45). Lest there be any doubt as to Morand's intention to bring to mind this particular automaton, it would be recalled that Menckendorf, while awaiting the peace of Amiens, assumed a Turkish attitude, sucking on a long Persian pipe.

The figure of the automaton necessarily presents a dual image, that of the "mechanized" chess player and that of the person under the table, who controls the action even as he or she remains hidden to the audience. In the first story, Tobolsky is explicitly cast in the latter role. In addition, he is twice portrayed in a hidden position: once in a reminiscence of a childhood game and then at the "Fête des songes." Escolastica herself is depicted as an invisible presence, but one which lends her a seductive rather than a controlling power. Who then is the hidden hand in the second story? Upon initial consideration, it would appear to be the Russian captain whose powers of enchantment are readily acknowledged by doña Escolastica. And yet it is doña Escolastica who emerges as the ultimate locus of control: not only is it her story, but she tells it. Whereas in the first story the narrator is omniscient and anonymous, the second is related from a specific point of view by an identifiable narrator. Doña Escolastica pulls the strings if not of her relationship with the captain, then certainly of its story.

Now, while acknowledging the dangers of identifying an author-figure in a text with the actual author, it may be neither implausible nor fruitless to suggest that doña Escolastica is representative of Paul Morand, if one places such an analogy within the global perspective of his postwar works. To support the notion of such a scenario, one might for instance cite the retrospective character of both events: doña Escolastica tells her story twenty years after its occurence; Morand tells and retells his some fifteen years after the fact. Both use the game of chess as a central point upon which to construct their narratives: doña Escolastica uses the game as both a point of departure and as the central metaphor upon which "her" narrative is based. But while doña Escolastica's employment of chess as a narrative figure is occasional, the entire story having been provoked simply by her presence at a chess tournament, we would argue that Morand's use of chess is highly motivated. As I pointed out earlier, chess may not only be seen simultaneously as a metaphor of the world and of a specific historical order, but also of literature itself in that chess displays the mimetic, representative and generative traits of literature. At the same time, chess, as it appears in the text, was conceived of as mirroring Morand's own techniques of using history: the tension between the playing of chess simultaneously within and outside history enables Morand to displace the two stories from their fixed positions in time and space. To further examine this dual role of chess: as a metaphor for both literature and Morand's historical "method," we must return to our chess-playing automaton and to another figure, also familiar, but no less puzzling in his relationship to Morand.

To this end we would cite the first thesis of Walter Benjamin's "Theses on the Philosophy of History," whose central metaphor is striking to a reader of "La Folle amoureuse":

> The story is told of automaton constructed in such a way that it could play a winning game of chess, answering each move of an opponent with a countermove. A puppet in Turkish attire and with a hookah in its mouth sat before a chessboard played on a large table. A system of mirrors created the illusion that this table was transparent from all sides. Actually a little hunchback who was an expert chess player sat inside and guided the puppet's hand by means of strings. One can imagine a philosophical counterpart to this device. The puppet called "historical materialism" is to win all the time. It can easily be a match for anyone if it enlists the services of theology, which today, as we know, is wizened and has to keep out of sight. (255)

Benjamin's counterpart to the automaton, the historical method he terms "historical materialism," or simply Marxism, wins every time because it functions with the aid of a hidden partner, here theology itself. The theological nature of Benjamin's brand of historical inquiry may, for our purposes, be described as centering around the notion of messianic time: history, or more generally the past, is to be redeemed or understood only in the present, and even then only "incompletely" in anticipation of an eventual messianic revelation. For Benjamin, this implies not only that the past receives its full value in the present and vice versa, but also that this relation is not to be construed as a mere chain of events (Benjamin strikingly uses the metaphor of a rosary) but rather as a split-second configuration composed between a past moment and a present moment, dislodging them or "blasting" them out of the "homogenous course of history" (265). The latter, Benjamin explains, is the domain of historicism which "gives the eternal image of the past," whereas historical materialism "supplies a unique experience with the past" (264). Hence the puppet called historical materialism wins every time by providing the most authentic, most constructive perception of history.

Morand might be said to use the figure of the chess-playing automaton in a similar if ultimately perverse manner. In order to pursue such an argument, I would now return briefly to Ferdinand Le Galeux, the protagonist of *Montociel, rajah aux grandes Indes*. Le Galeux's profession of cryptanalyst in that novel, we recall, casts him in the role of a "reader" in that he decodes texts. But as the "reader" of the particular text in question, the journal of Montociel, for all practical purposes a historical document, one might equally envision him as occupying the position of historian or, more precisely, of Morand's figure of an historical materialist. Cryptanalysis might be described as the seizing of the moment in which the ciphered language encounters "real" language at the point where they reveal their secret relationship of signification, thus making possible the "reading" of the encoded document. This would be analogous to the seizing of the constellation formed between the past and the present which enables the past to be redeemed or "read" in and by the present.

And like the puppet called historical materialism, Le Galeux employs a special tool: a "passe-partout" or skeleton key, which allows him to unlock any document, to "win" every time:

> Ce passe-partout est en fait un mot, continua Le Galeux, le mot ESARINTULO. Les dix lettres de ce mot-là expriment l'ordre de fréquence où elles se présentent dans la langue française. C'est avec cette notion de fréquence qu'un déchiffreur arrive peu à peu à faire sauter toutes les serrures d'un texte. (30-31)

Le Galeux's "dwarf" is not theological but linguistic. The key lies in the discovery of the disposition of letters as words and, consequently, of words as units of meaning.

Le Galeux leaves no doubt as the the result of this operation: "Arrivé au mot, le décrypteur est sur la terre ferme: le voilà sauvé" (31). The passe-partout (or more generally cryptography) saves not only figuratively but, as Le Galeux explains, literally as well. In fact, the art of "decoding" saved his own life, just as chess saved the life of doña Escolastica. Pressed to describe how he came to be a cryptanalyst, Le Galeux describes his childhood discovery of some of his father's papers written in cipher. Later, penniless and starving after the death of his mother, he set about deciphering the papers, convinced that they contained a hidden message: some clue about a treasure-hoard or some secret that would produce a fortune. He does find "gold," not in the content of the documents which themselves were devoid of meaning, but in his abilities as cryptanalyst:

> Comme la cassette de la fable de La Fontaine qui ne contenait rien, mais enrichit sa propriétaire en la forçant de travailler, ainsi ces papiers qui étaient vides de tout sens utiles, simples procès-verbaux de séances d'une junte française de carbonari, que mon père avait chiffrés pour dépister la police de la Restauration. (33-34)

There is perhaps an analogy to be drawn between *Ferdinand* Le Galeux and Paul Emile Charles *Ferdinand* Morand, one which surpasses a mere coincidence of name. As Le Galeux learns to decipher the past (his father's documents) and thereby "saves" himself, so Morand, by learning to decode or to "read" history similarly stumbled upon an equally salutary solution. Le Galeux, it will be noted, translates for Napoleon III in Vichy, the site that Morand would symbolically flee in 1944 by remaining in Switzerland - by his own description a penniless and hermitlike figure. Morand's art of reading history must have appeared, at least to him, as lucrative as Le Galeux's passe-partout, if not financially, then as a means for re-establishing his reputation. Much as for doña Escolastica who declares "les échecs m'ont sauvé la vie," Morand himself may be said to have been "saved" by both chess (les échecs), as metaphor for his historical method, and by his stories of failures (les échecs).

But if Morand emerges as a "decoder" of history he must also be situated as author, for his "reading" produces a written text. One might postulate the movement from decoder to encoder as follows: after Morand himself deciphers the past, he then puts it into his own cipher, in the form of a novel or story which is then presented to "us" that we might in turn decode Morand's constellation.

The scenario of the automaton thus takes on a new twist. Morand's puppet would be labelled "historical materialism," in that Morand employs virtually the same techniques described by Benjamin in the construction of the historical works discussed thus far. And, in a particularly perverse manner, Morand's dwarf is also that of a certain redemptive theology. One has only to consider the figures of don Luis and Loup de Tincé, not to mention doña Escolastica and, to a degree, Le Galeux, to observe this redemption at work, for what do they represent but the pariah, the "historical loser" who attains redemption: through the ceremony of flagellation for don Luis; in the form of eternal devotion to Parfaite in the case of Tincé; and in the affirmation of his paternity for Le Galeux. "La Folle amoureuse" may likewise be read as a story of redemption: the first Escolastica redeemed by the second and vice versa. But more important then their redemption, is that for which they are redeemed: don Luis for his collaboration with a Napoleon who in Morand's hands emerges as a thinly disguised figure for Hitler; Tincé for his involvement in a struggle against a Revolution committed at least in theory to the principles of freedom, equality and fraternity; and finally, doña Escolastica in her return to the fascists. How then is one to comprehend the relationship I myself have attempted to establish between Paul Morand, whose postwar works emerge as redemptions of fascism, and Walter Benjamin, who devoted his life to the struggle against the Nazis and died fleeing those whom Morand would redeem? One might argue, justifiably, that the practice of employing theory in a manner at odds with the intentions of its formulator is neither original nor, in our time, unfortunately, particularly shocking. And, I readily admit, at this time there exists no concrete evidence that Morand had read Benjamin or even knew of his ideas. I would again, in response, emphasize the purely speculative nature of such an association, one which arose from an impressionistic perception of certain similarities which, as they were affirmed by further textual examination, came to suggest the value of a comparison of certain of Morand's historical techniques to Benjamin's ideas on the philosophy of history. As a result, I am thrust into the position, and rightly so, of confronting the paradox of a seemingly apt description of these techniques by a marxist philosophy impregnated with a Judaic Messianism. A resolution to such a dilemma may prove impossible, but its further illumination may well lie in one of Morand's own works, the 1959 play *Le Lion écarlate*.

Le Lion écarlate dramatizes the love affair of Ferdinand Lassalle, the nineteenth-century German socialist, and Hélène von Dönniges, the seventeen-year old daughter of a Bavarian diplomat, whom Lassalle met in 1862. In a move consistent with his treatment of history, Morand compresses the historical events spanning two years in a period of several days in the play, all the while adhering surprisingly faithfully to historical accounts of the affair. The plot line of the play is relatively simple: Lassalle meets Hélène and they immediately fall in love, despite the probable hostility of her parents who support her engagement to Yanko Rakowitza, a Romanian of aristocratic lineage. Hélène defies her family and flees to Lassalle in his pension in Geneva, followed closely by her mother who has divined her daughter's intent. Lassalle rejects Hélène's offer to consummate their love and asks her to wait until he himself has persuaded her father to accept their marriage. She reluctantly returns home with the Baronne von Dönniges. Several days later, Lassalle, alarmed by his inability to penetrate the von Dönniges household, rallies his friends Rustow and the Comtesse de Hatzfeldt.

Aided by an envoy from the imperial court, they persuade the Baron to grant a private interview between Lassalle and Hélène. Hélène arrives and immediately rejects Lassalle, citing the position of her family and explaining her earlier passion as mere fancy. Lassalle is stunned and challenges both the Baron and Yanko to a duel. Yanko kills Lassalle and the final scene closes upon his funeral.

The basic structure of the intrigue appears strikingly familiar: Lassalle asks Hélène to wait and when they are finally reunited, she rejects him, citing her heritage as her principle reason. Is this not, in abridged form, the story of "La Folle amoureuse" in which Tobolsky asks the first Escolastica to wait; while their symbolic reunion in the encounter of doña Escolastica and the Russian Captain ends with doña Escolastica's rejection of her lover based upon the memory of her own ancestry? Viewed in their similarity of structure, the story of Lassalle and Hélène appears, in *Le Lion écarlate* as a perfect compression of "La Folle amoureuse," one which eliminates the spatial and temporal distance between the first and second part of the novella. If the play reflects a further compression of the earlier story, I would also venture that *Le Lion écarlate* constitutes a "rewriting" of "La Folle amoureuse" in more direct relation both to Morand's own political situation and to his particular historical method. Along another vein, this reworking also picks up distinct thematic threads from "Parfaite de Saligny" which, as we shall see, enable us to more accurately pinpoint the role that story plays in the elaboration of Morand's historical project. Most remarkable, perhaps, is Morand's choice of an actual historical figure as hero, thereby violating Lukàc's directive and his own previous practice of creating a fictitious protagonist occupying a relatively minor position in relation to the historical conflict, while keeping "world historical" figures well in the background as directing forces who, as personalities, do not directly appear in the story of the central character. Morand's focus upon Lassalle in this play enables us to perceive more clearly the ways in which Morand "customizes" history to his own purposes. Particularly evident are the techniques of historical displacement, observed in his previous historical works, effectuated by the insertion of an intertextual underpinning, at once historical, literary and mythological.

I would begin by examining the political situation of the play, which further evidences a link with "La Folle amoureuse." In that latter, it will be recalled, doña Escolastica swings between fascism and communism. A similar phenomenon, if not in its resolution then in its terms, is to be found in the figure of Lassalle himself. Lassalle's political position, both in history and in this play, may best be described as occupying a position between Marxism and imperial nationalism. Indeed, Lassalle's principal biographer,

Hermann Oncken, chose as his title: *Lassalle: Zwischen Marx und Bismarck*. Lassalle and Marx were for some time good friends, linked by their common opposition to bourgeois liberalism and Lassalle acted as Marx's publishing agent during the latter's exile in Britain (Footman 68-69, 75). Their break in 1862, ostensibly over a misunderstanding concerning a financial matter, more probably arose, as David Footman argues, from Engel's distrust of Lassalle and from a growing sense on the part of Marx that Lassalle was moving in a direction unacceptable to his principles (180). Furthermore, as Footman points out by citing a letter from Marx to Engels, Lassalle stood accused of appropriating the ideas of the two thinkers for his own purposes (180).

One of the "problems" with Lassalle's position, from Marx's perspective, no doubt lay in Lassalle's increasingly nationalist leanings. Lassalle's vision called for a worker's revolution culminating in the establishment of a centralized authority, elected by universal suffrage, which would oversee worker's concerns. This authority, however, came to take on authoritarian qualities, it was to be an elite regime composed of "men who understand your position... men, armed with the shining sword of science, who know how to defend your interests" (Footman 167). In the play, Morand clearly indicates exactly to whom Lassalle refers: "Bismarck, c'est le seul homme à la taille de notre avenir" (310). Bismarck and Lassalle actually did meet upon several occasions, and Bismarck's recollections of these meetings leave no question as to his perception of the socialist leader: "He was very ambitious and by no means a republican. He was very much a nationalist and a monarchist. His ideal was the German Empire, and here was our point of contact" (Footman 175). In the play, Lassalle's position vis-à-vis the monarchy is very clearly put in the following exchange:

> Journaliste - "L'autocratie repose sur la féodalité et il y a un fossé entre ouvriers et féodaux."
>
> Lassalle - "Non. Il n'y a de fossé qu'entre le prolétariat et la bourgeoisie libérale. Le socialisme vivra fraternellement avec un régime autoritaire...guidé par lui." (310)

The notion of a socialism guided by an authoritarian regime, here compared to a feudal system, takes on a distinct tone. The question of the relationship of Lassalle's program to that of the National Socialists in the mid-twentieth century escapes neither his biographers nor, as we shall see, Morand.

In the play itself, the difficulty of defining Lassalle is thematised on several occasions. Early in the play, two journalists engage in a comic "pas de deux":

- Un étonnant oseur!
- Ou un prodigieux poseur!
- Un héros de Schiller...
- ou un dandy d'Eugène Sue.... (309)

Later, the Comtessse Hatzfeldt intimates that such an inability to pinpoint his character arises from the contradictions of Lassalle himself. While explaining to Lassalle why he is unacceptable to so many, namely Marx and Engels, she focuses on the fact that he simply "doesn't belong," to anything or anyone but himself:

> Mon cher enfant, vous n'en êtes pas. Vous ne faites corps avec aucune catégorie connue. Vous êtes le champion du prolétariat et vous dînez en habit, vous êtes Juif et vous n'aimez pas vos coreligionnaires. (317)

Lassalle is the consummate outsider: a voice for the worker attired as an aristocrat, a Jew and an antisemite, a marxist and a nationalist.[4] But Lassalle's uniqueness is at once his greatest quality and the principal force behind his failure. The Comtesse continues her portrait:

> Vous êtes de la race maudite de ceux qui ont raison trop tôt, vous êtes l'artilleur qui tire trop loin. Aussi, vous prend-on toujours comme bouc émissaire. Mais consolez-vous, ô chef de la future Allemagne socialiste: les boucs émissaires sont les ancêtres des dieux. (317)

Lassalle is simply too early, his vision surpasses the comprehension of his era. Historically ignored by Bismarck and denounced by Marx, in his own time Lassalle failed to garner the support he felt he merited. Rather, he served as a weapon, a scapegoat, employed by both sides of the conflict to split the opposition (Footman 178). Lassalle joins the ranks of Morand's other historical losers who emerge as political pawns, sacrificed for having held a position untenable in the present but redeemed by the future. The Comtesse's closing maxim, "les boucs émissaires sont les ancêtres des dieux," nicely formulates the fate of all of Morand's pariahs.

But in the play, Lassalle's ultimate downfall emanates not from the political conflict which was nearing a climax spurred on by Prussian belligerance, but rather from his fight to win Hélène. Here again, *Le Lion écarlate* appears to conform to the practice of intersecting the political situation and the personal tragedy in such a way as to privilege the latter. Probably the most striking aspect of

---

[4] Lassalle's position as an assimilated and antisemitic Jew is little noted but certainly no mystery. See in particular his letter to Sonia Sonstev, reprinted in part in Footman, 118-120.

the relationship between Lassalle and Hélène as rendered by Morand, lies in the extent to which it is depicted as an almost mythological encounter on the order of classical tragedy. All the elements of Cornelian tragedy suggested by the story infiltrate the play: a heroine torn between duty to her family and love for a man who threatens to destroy that family, a hubristic hero, a chorus in the form of the Comtesse Hatzfeldt (322), a sudden reversal at the moment of denouement, and the death of the hero. Hélène's name obviously evokes one possible model, and her resemblance to Morand's other "antique" heroine, Parfaite de Saligny, would seem to suggest that both figure, to a certain extent, Helen of Troy. But, as in the case of Parfaite, the myth appears in *Le Lion écarlate* as curiously filtered through Giraudoux's version of Homer's tale.

In the scene in which Hélène meets the Comtesse Hatzfeldt for the first time, the resonances to Giraudoux's play are particularly strong. The Comtesse seeks to impress upon Hélène the gravity of her relationship with Lassalle and, at the same time, to discover the depths of the young girl's emotions. This scene recalls the interview between Andromaque and Hélène (of Troy) in *La Guerre de Troie n'aura pas lieu* (III, 8) in which Andromaque entreats Hélène to "love" Pâris so as to give meaning both to their alliance and to the impending disaster. Hélène von Dönniges clearly appears as a figure of destiny: "Pensez-vous que le destin m'ait choisie pour jouer un rôle dans la vie de Ferdinand Lassalle?" (321). The Comtesse, in her final judgment of Hélène, leaves no doubt as to what such destiny Hélène represents: "C'est une fille capricieuse, qui se laisse emporter par son imagination. Elle sera la perte de notre Lassalle et son oeuvre" (348). Lassalle seems to occupy the position not of Pâris, but of Giraudoux's Hector, whose political efforts are ruined by the "destiny" of that Hélène.

The linking of Hélène to the figure of Helen of Troy may have been suggested to Morand not only by a certain similarity between the two, but also perhaps by an anecdote related by Lassalle's American biographer. It seems that Lassalle, while decorating his home, had commissioned a fresco to be painted round the walls of his dining room: "but had not yet decided if it was to depict the Edda Saga or the Siege of Troy. But in any case the heroine - whether Helen or Brünhilde - was to be modelled on Fraulein von Dönniges" (Footman 190). The reference to Brünhilde is provocative, for if we would recall that Parfaite represents not only Helen of Troy but also France, might not Hélène von Dönniges doubly function as Helen and Germany, at least in the mind of Lassalle himself? But in Morand's play, I would argue, Hélène is just as representative of France as Parfaite. Among the subtle allusions in the play to Morand's other works, two in particular may aid us in pursuing this relation. First, when exchanging passionate words, Lassale and Hélène refer to one another as "lightning and thunder:

Lassalle - "Hélène, vos cheveux ont la couleur de la foudre."
Hélène - "N'êtes-vous pas la tonnerre?"

In Morand's first war-time chronicle, "Le Festin de pierre" (1941), a thinly veiled allegory drawn from the don Juan legend, the vengeance of France's decadence came in the form of "la tonnerre hitlérienne." Next, the Comtesse refers to Lassalle's project concerning Hélène as the ravishing of a virgin: "Vous voulez arracher une vierge à sa famille, après dix mots de conversation? Et l'enlever à son fiancé?" Now, in "Le Ravissement de l'Europe," another wartime text, Hitler appears not as thunder but as the minotaur kidnapping the virgin Europe. Lassalle later says: "Je rugis vers Hélène..." (346); he bellows like a bull. Europe, in Morand's earlier fable, displays a certain masochistic attitude toward her captor, just as does Hélène in explaining her ideal lover: "Il me faut être contraint, sommé d'obéir à une puissance qui me capture et me ligote" (322). There appears to be some basis for viewing Lassalle as a counterpart to Hitler and, along the same vein, Hélène as a figure for Europe/France. In addition, when responding to the Comtesse's accusation, Lassalle responds: "Je chasse un premier occupant, je prends sa place: c'est l'histoire de l'humanité" (319). This "first occupant' is literally Yanko, of course, but when viewed in relation to the "Le Ravissement de l'Europe," this occupier emerges as the old man standing guard over the virgin in Morand's allegory: Karl Marx (152). Thus Lassalle as Hitler would drive away Marx; Lassalle's position between marxism and nationalism would be, in a sense, overwritten by the victory of Hitler/national socialism over Marx/communism.

The simultaneous characterization in the play of Lassalle as a Marxist, as Hitler, and as Hector appears contradictory, but such a paradox is one of the distinguishing characteristics of Morand's historical heroes: don Luis is a lover both of France and Spain, Tincé emerges as a sometimes reluctant, sometimes enthusiastic participant in a conflict itself marked by indeterminancy. Morand's Lassalle combines the commitment to the proletariat of a Marx and the nationalist project of a Hitler, while at the same time evoking the pacifism of a Giralducian Hector. This multivalence, I would argue, serves not only to blur such distinctions in the play, but also permits Morand to develop a character whose position can ultimately only emerge as unique, independent of the political conflicts raging about him.

In *Le Lion écarlate*, perhaps more than in any of Morand's previous historical works, a strong parallel may be observed between the author and his hero. Again, both historical similarities and clues within the play argue for such a possibility. Let us begin by briefly enumerating several such allusions. Firstly Lassalle, like Morand, was a writer before entering into political life. In the play, Lassalle is described by a metaphor suggestive of the impact of his political noteriety on his literary career: "Au fond, il est comme ces écrivains que tout le monde connaît et dont personne n'achète les livres" (310). This description would equally apply to Morand's situation after the war; Morand, like Lassalle, was an historical loser. Secondly, just as Ferdinand loved Hélène, so Paul Emile Charles *Ferdinand* Morand loved Hélène Soutzo, a Romanian who, incidentally, had previously been married to a Romanian prince (Fogel, 73). Coincidence of names aside, perhaps the most compelling argument for Morand's identification with Lassalle comes from Morand's description, in his memoir *Venises*, of his own political trajectory:

> Je n'ai jamais aimé que la paix; cette fidélité m'a valu de curieuses infidélités du sort; elle m'a fait traverser, en 1917, une gauche fort avancée, pour me déposer en 1940 dans un Vichy maurrassien où je n'étais pas moins dépaysé. (85)

Morand thus describes himself as moving between the radical left and fascism, implying at the same time that even as he admits having participated in both the one and the other at specific moments, in reality he adhered to neither, citing his pacifism as the basis of his actions. Several paragraphs later, Morand performs much the same move when explaining his position in 1917:

> "Je crois au socialisme mais ne le conçois que national," dis-je innocemment à Bracke-Desrousseaux. (J'étais loin de me douter que ces deux mots, vingt ans plus tard, feraient sauter l'Europe) Il me répondit sèchement: "Impossible, le socialisme est, par essence, international." (86)

Morand here recounts a rejection by Bracke-Desrousseaux, a prominent radical socialist leader, which would parallel Marx's rejection of Lassalle for much the same reason. In claiming to have been both a socialist and a nationalist, Morand himself provides the link to Lassalle, and then adroitly manoeuvers himself out of the obvious combination of the two words by claiming innocence as to their eventual and deadly association. Morand presents himself as having been both a socialist and a nationalist, but never a National Socialist. Lassalle appears to be the ideal historical figure around whom Morand could construct a literary illustration of his own political position.

Along another vein, the dramatized love affair of Lassalle might equally be said to symbolically mirror Morand's relationship to France. Drawing from my argument that Hélène functions in the play to represent, on one level, France, her rejection of Lassalle's devotion, a passion for which he came close to sacrificing his political beliefs, would correspond in many ways to France's rejection of Morand after the Liberation. Morand adds an interesting twist to history in his play. After Hélène's rejection, Lassalle rejects her in turn: "Je me délivre de tout le mal que tu as fait entrer en moi. Tu n'étais pas un don, tu n'étais qu'un avertissement. Va, maintenant tu ne m'es plus nécessaire" (356). Lassalle's belief that Hélène was in true rebellion against her family, that is, against bourgeois liberalism, is shattered by her rejection of him. The sting is exacerbated by the revelation that his perception of her had based itself on illusory appearances. More importantly, his love for her brought him to the verge of betraying his convictions:

> J'allais tromper le Peuple. Le peuple toujours trompée... J'allais inscrire mon nom sur la liste des charlatans et des imposteurs de l'Histoire... Femme-piège, je te faisais cadeau d'une vie que ne m'appartenait plus; je l'avais donnée à mon parti, à mon oeuvre. Merci, Hélène, de l'avoir refusée. (356)

Is this play not Morand's own declaration that he himself does not belong on that ignominious list? For Morand too believed sincerely that his devotion to France had been betrayed by France herself after the Liberation. Repeatedly he invoked his fidelity to his nation and his love for France as the reason behind his participation in the Vichy government, only to find himself rejected by a France which must have appeared to him a reversion to its own bourgeois liberalism of the thirties which he himself had decried.[5]

Another historical "modification" proves equally illuminating. Whereas historically Yanko Rakowitza provoked the fatal duel with Lassalle, in *Le Lion écarlate* it is Lassalle who issues the challenge, giving as cause the question of personal honor: "J'avais revé d'un amour éternel, et je n'ai eu qu'une brêve trahison. Reste une affaire à liquider" (357). To Rustow, he explains his injury:

> Tu ne voudrais pas que je passe par profits et pertes le jeu abominable que l'on a joué avec moi? J'ai été moqué et bafoué, écarté du pied. Pour cet affront, il me faut réparation. Ne crains rien, tu dois voir que je suis maître de moi; j'ai une volonté glacée, solidifiée. La partie a été engagée: je la terminerai avec l'impassibilité d'un jouer d'échecs. (357)

The last phrase of this declaration falls like a bombshell upon a reader of "La Folle amoureuse" and indeed upon an examination

---

[5] See in particular his letter to Denise Bourget of September 13, 1944 in *Lettres du Voyageur*, ed. M. Burrhus, 23-27; and the partial reproduction of a pamphlet, written by Morand and circulated among the members of the Académie française in 1958, in Ginette Guitard-Auviste, 224-225.

of Morand's postwar historical works. For what does Morand do but seek to end his own story of perceived betrayal with the composure of a player of chess. Beneath the guise of the disinterested player, lies the very much interested Morand whose aim is to conceal his project of self-redemption under the mask of historical, and thus "impassive," fiction.

The mien of the dispassionate chess player thus brings us back to the Automaton Chess Player and so to Benjamin's "puppet called historical materialism." If we were to again modify the image of the automaton, in relation to *Le Lion écarlate*, Lassalle would be cast in the role of the puppet, with all the deceptive impassibility of the latter, while under the table Morand, armed with his own self-redemptive theology, pulls the strings.

And what more perfect figure than that of Lassalle in our paradoxical confrontation of Morand and Benjamin? Lassalle reunites all the contradictory terms of such a juxtaposition: a Marxist Jew who is also nationalistic and antisemitic, and yet who escapes all those epithets in Morand's portrayal of him as an individualistic outsider. Cast in a role approaching that of a mediator, Lassalle would reflect the grotesque and twisted aspects of Morand's "use" of Benjamin's philosophy.

III

FILMING THE EVENT

Fouquet ou le soleil offusqué

In his biography of Leonardo da Vinci, Sigmund Freud notes that biographers often choose their subjects "for personal reasons of their own emotional lives" (80). Freud here modifies Plutarch's declaration that the lives of great men "serve me as a sort of looking-glass, in which I may see how to adjust and adorn my own life" (Nadel 21). This passage from the prescriptive benefits of biography (Plutarch) to the projective (Freud) marks the increasing awareness in the twentieth century of the intimate interaction between the subject and the biographer. André Maurois, in a series of lectures presented at Trinity College in 1928, recounts the autobiographical motivations driving his choice of Shelley as subject:

> I had just left the lycée and was full of philosophical and political ideas which, *mutatis mutandis*, represented just those ideas which possessed Shelley and his friend, Hogg, at the time of their arrival in London.... Shelley had experienced such checks as seemed to me to be somewhat of the same nature as my own [...]. The pride and certainty of youth were succeeded in me by a lively need of pity and here too I discovered traces of Shelley as he was towards the end, after the loss of his children. Yes, in very truth, I felt that to tell the story of his life would be in some measure a *deliverance* for myself. (120-21) (my emphasis)

Maurois's first attempt at such a deliverance came in the form of a novel which, as he himself admitted, was not very good. He then turned to a biography of Shelley, equally flawed in his eyes but representative of his own view of biography as a means of personal expression (121). Maurois's movement from the novel to biography as a medium for the deliverance of his "self" may perhaps be pertinent to my continued discussion of Paul Morand's postwar prose as I turn, in this and the ensuing chapter, to his works of a biographical and autobiographical nature as they reveal a continued tension between their historical contexts and the contemporary concerns of the author. Like Maurois, Morand displayed a similar move from the predominantly fictional works of the forties and fifties to the practice of nonfiction, namely biography, which dominated the sixties and early seventies, interrupted by only one novel. Before turning to these works per se, let us briefly examine the "personal situation" of Morand during the late fifties, in particular one episode which, I believe, may have prompted his interest in biography.

In 1958, Paul Morand presented his name to the Académie française in his second bid for entrance, having failed in his first attempt in 1938. Several members immediately took offense and a bloc formed, led by André Siegfried, François Mauriac and Jules Romains, protesting that Morand's election would represent an affront to those members who had resisted the German occupation of France (Rousso 66-67). The bitter polemic which followed, one without precedent in the history of that august body, provoked a flurry of letters on both sides of the issue from a number of prominent writers. Morand failed to garner the necessary nineteen votes in 1958, but again stood for election in 1959. The "Morand Affair" came to an end only after de Gaulle, the new president of the Republic, threated to exercise his right of veto: "because of the partisan hatreds the writer would arouse within the Académie" (Rousso 68). Morand withdrew his candidacy and would not be elected until 1968.

The debacle at the Académie was not without effect on Morand's literary oeuvre. If the Second World War marks, as I have argued, a radical shift in Morand's focus from the contemporary to the historical, 1959 also appears to signal yet another, subtler displacement of attention from, as earlier mentioned, predominantly fictional works to historical nonfiction. In the case of Morand, his forays into historical nonfiction are all the more compelling because of his reputation as a primarily fictional writer. Before the war, Morand had published several noteworthy volumes of nonfiction, but limited himself to the genres of chronicle and travel writing. Both of these forms, while of historical interest, reflect Morand's early obsession with the contemporary. Works such as *Rien que la terre* (1926), *Paris-Tombouctou* (1928) and *New York* (1930), present the world in its state of "becoming," firmly anchored in the present and turned toward the future. A notable exception might be his *1900*, but even there the point of view remains firmly ensconced in 1931, the date of its composition. It was not until 1942 that Morand published his first major work of "historical" nonfiction, a biography of Guy de Maupassant. In 1961, Morand published *Fouquet ou le soleil offusqué*, a biography of the ill-fated Nicolas Fouquet, followed by *La Dame blanche des Habsburg* (1963) and *Sophie Dorothée de Celle* (1968); *L'Allure de Chanel*, an unfinished collection of anecdotes, was published posthumously in 1977.

Of these works, the best known is undoubtedly his biography of Fouquet, copies of which continue to line the shelves of the visitors shop at Vaux-le-Vicomte. *Fouquet ou le soleil offusqué* was also a personal favorite of Morand, as he himself stated in an interview with Stéphane Sarkany. The importance of this slim volume emerges as well in Morand's own reflections on his postwar prose:

> J'ai toujours aimé les causes perdues: Fouquet, Caillaux, Berthelot, Laval. Quand ils furent envoyés en forteresse, traînés en Haute Cour, mis ignominieusement à la retraite, attachés au poteau, mon affection pour eux a crû d'autant. [...] L'échec après le succès, ce devait être encore le thème de mes livres entre 1950 et les années soixante; après *Fouquet, Le Flagellant de Séville, Les Clés du souterrain, Le Dernier jour de l'Inquisition, Hécate*.... (*Venises* 84)

Indeed, what better description of his own post-World War II works that that given by Morand himself in this passage from his autobiography? His taste for "lost causes," here those of a quartet whose strange assemblage I shall later consider, is reflected in the historical situations he chose as settings for his later works: the Napoleonic occupation of Spain in *Le Flagellant de Séville*; the Inquisition in nineteenth-century Peru in "Le Dernier jour de l'Inquisition"; Russian trading settlements in nineteenth-century California in "La Folle amoureuse"; Europeon resistance during the Boxer Rebellion in "Fleur du ciel"; and the political projects of Ferdinand Lassalle in *Le Lion écarlate*. Furthermore, all his protagonists follow the prescribed trajectory of success followed by failure; the gallery of Morand's historical "losers" is large: Loup de Tincé, don Luis Almovar, don Esteban, to name just a few of his fictional heroes, not to mention the actual historical figures who appear as protagonists in his historical drama and as subjects of his biographies: Elizabeth of Bavaria, Guy de Maupassant, Sophie Dorothée de Celle, the entire Habsburg family and Nicolas Fouquet.

Morand's enumeration of his preferred historical figures and those of his books which conform to the model of "échec après le succès" privileges Fouquet as the initial name on each list. Of course, in the first instance, Fouquet is simply chronologically "first," but in the second, Morand explicitly violates chronological order by implying that after *Fouquet ou le soleil offusqué* came *Le Flagellant de Séville*, "Les Clés du souterrain," and so forth, when in fact the dates of publication of these works are 1961, 1951, 1956, 1946, and 1954, respectively. The only convincing explanation of such an order is that of a hierarchical arrangement according to the degree to which Morand felt each work meets the criteria put forth in this passage. As such, *Fouquet* would stand as the most explicit or most "perfect" example. Equally intriguing, *Fouquet* is the sole biography in this list of otherwise fictional novels and short-stories. Might this not be a signal that in his own eyes Morand's best representation of historical failure came in the form of nonfiction?

92 Paul Morand

In studying Morand's postwar prose, I have hitherto focused upon those fictional works which best reveal Morand's strategies of historical representation. But following Morand's own lead, it is perhaps through a nonfictional work, his self-nominated biography of Fouquet, that I might most profitably continue to explore the manner in which Morand approaches an historical subject. Such a proposition does, however, leave me on somewhat perilous ground as I prepare, implicitly, to compare Morand's techniques of fiction to those of his nonfiction. Fortunately, the way has been prepared for us by a number of contemporary theorists who have contributed to the weakening of the traditionally strict lines of distinction between fictional and nonfictional discourse. Among others, I would cite the work of Hayden White, Lionel Gossman, Dominick LaCapra and Paul Ricoeur as important to such an endeavor. Against the models of the early Annales group, these thinkers have argued for the inevitablity, even the necessity in the case of Ricoeur, of the transmission of history in narrated form, one which relies heavily upon techniques traditionally viewed as exclusive to the domain of fiction, and for the examination of nonfictional works through a lens normally reserved for fiction. Without engaging in an exhaustive review of such arguments, I would suggest that Morand's biography of Fouquet provides an excellent example of a highly stylized and "fictional" rendition of history, one which, when compared to his earlier works of historical fiction, serves to throw certain aspects of Morand's postwar prose into relief. I would thus propose the examination of the historical and artistic qualities of Morand's biography of Fouquet with an eye to the further illumination of Morand's conception of the relationship of history to art and to pursuing our study of Morand's use, both ideological and aesthetic, of history. I will begin with the study of the stylistic aspects of Morand's account of the life of Nicolas Fouquet: his extensive use of metaphor and metonymy, the insertion of a secondary biography, and his use of narration as a means of temporalization. Subsequently, the relationship between Morand's approach to biography and the ideological motivations driving his postwar works will be brought into focus through a juxtaposition of passages from *Fouquet*, Morand's own explanation to the Académie française of his involvement with the Vichy government, and an essay by Jean Paulhan.

Fouquet is brief, only 175 pages, quite short by traditional standards of biography and in view of the complexity of its subject. A relative measure of brevity, however, represents an inherent aspect of the biographical endeavor in general, one which might be termed its *partial* nature. For very practical reasons, a biography cannot contain every aspect, every detail, every movement of its subject, and as such, as in the case of historiography, necessitates a process of selection. Certain aspects are included, others rejected; the result is that biography can only be, at best, partial and therefore an essentially synecdochal genre. Some recent biographies reflect en extreme expression of this representation of the whole by the part in what Nadel terms "segment" biographies which analyze only a portion of the subject's life (196). *Fouquet* loosely falls into such a category in its restriction to the last twenty years of Fouquet's life, of which the period from March 9, 1661, the date of Mazarin's death, and September 5 of the same year, receives the lion's share of attention. Morand does frequently allude to and bring into focus aspects of Fouquet's earlier life, for example, his "apprenticeship" under Mazarin, but only as such aspects support his interpretation of Fouquet's fall from power. The core of the biography centers around this downfall: in its emphasis on Louis XIV's abrupt seizure of fiscal authority, in the description of the infamous soirée at Vaux-le-Vicomte, and in the highly dramatized narrative of the arrest of Fouquet. At the same time, this focus on the principal events of Fouquet's downfall, reflecting Morand's predilection for failure after success, in no way prevents the biography from providing a surprisingly "complete" picture of Fouquet despite several glaring omissions, notably Fouquet's family situation. Morand leads the reader on a whirlwind tour of the last years of Fouquet in the course of which he manages to evoke not only Fouquet's earlier life but also the era. This "compression" of textual space, while at times dizzying, reveals Morand's stylistic hand at work on his subject while pointing to, as we shall argue, a continuation of the compression of temporal space between the historical moment and Morand's present. One way in which he effectuates such an operation is through his extensive use of highly figural language manifested in the frequency of "turns of speech" or tropes.

The use of tropological structures in nonfiction has been thoroughly explored by White and Ricoeur, drawing on Kenneth Burke's identification of four "Master Tropes": metaphor, metonymy, synecdoche and irony.[1] I have suggested that biography itself functions as a synecdoche, in its establishment of a signifying relation between a part of the subject's life and its totality. In *Fouquet*, Morand establishes such a synecdoche between not only the account of Fouquet's downfall and Fouquet's life but also between this episode and the phenomenon of Louis XIV's "century." As we shall see, Louis XIV's obsessive pursuit of Fouquet marks the advent of his absolutist regime and explains its raison d'être. Metonymy, a trope related to synecdoche (some

---

[1] See in particular White, *Metahistory*, 31-38 and Ricoeur, *Rule of Metaphor*.

would hold it indistinguishable), also plays an important function in the "construction" of *Fouquet*. As the expression of contiguity, it permits representation of the whole by its constitutive attributes, of the effect by its cause, or of the agent by the act. As Nadel points out: "metonymy makes the tasks of the biographer, selectivity and synthesis, possible" (166). Morand employs Fouquet's ancestry, his relationship to Mazarin and his Jesuit upbringing in just such a way.

But it is Morand's use of metaphor which provides the clearest opening to his stylistic approach to his subject. The most striking metaphor in *Fouquet* is the extended theatrical metaphor sustained throughout the biography. In the opening chapter, the involvement of Fouquet's father, François Fouquet in the condemnation of Henri de Tallyrand count of Chalais, a twisted affair machinated by Richelieu and the Duchess of Chevreuse, becomes the tare of Fouquet's trajectory:

> Comme dans ces tragédies antiques où apparaît la punition du père reportée sur le fils, le surintendant sera à son tour victime d'une juridiction d'exception, composée de juges serviles, et l'on verra surgir à nouveau, fatale à Fouquet, cette même duchesse de Chevreuse, fatale à Chalais. (13)

Foreshadowing Fouquet's destiny, this passage inaugurates the series of dramatic metaphors used to describe Fouquet; here he emerges as a tragic hero and the events of his downfall as tragedy. Both such designations are extended in the biography by numerous other allusions and metaphors. Fouquet does not possess "la taille de son destin," like the tragic hero he is a priori unable to measure up to his fate. Louis XIV is a "personnage shakepérien"(74), ruthless and impenetrable. The chapter devoted to the king's usurpation of the power formerly held by Mazarin is entitled: "La Face du théâtre change." Fouquet's encounter with Lauzun in the prison at Pignerol is described as a "coup de théâtre" (162) and an "Entrée de clown dans un drame élisabéthain" (163); Lauzun himself is "comme Sganarelle" (171). Such metaphors function not only to describe the particular individual but also to represent the way in which Morand interprets and presents Fouquet's story as an incident itself suggestive of such metaphors. The following remark a propos of the infamous evening at Vaux-le-Vicomte demonstrates just such an operation:

> [...] ce fût le décor d'une réussite parfaite, qui n'a duré qu'une seule soirée, celle du 17 août 1661. Aucun dramaturge n'a réalisé pareille unité de lieu et de temps: le 17 août, à six heures du soir, Fouquet était roi de France; à deux heures du matin, il n'était plus rien. (87)

The events of that night themselves are seen as provoking a natural comparison with classical theater, relating in microcosm Fouquet's descent. Morand's interpretation of his subject extends to its presentation. The entire biography loosely bases its structure on a dramatic model in its focus on four very specific moments: the death of Mazarin, the soirée of Vaux-le-Vicomte, the arrest of Fouquet, and Fouquet's encounter with Lauzun. The first two events serve as clear preparation for the climactic arrest of Fouquet, with the fourth functioning as an ironic and tragic twist on the dénouement of Fouquet's death.

Morand's choice of theatrical metaphors, of tragedy in particular, offers a glimpse of the ideological motivation behind not only his choice of subject but the manner of its representation as well. In depicting Fouquet as a tragic hero, caught in the unfolding of a preordained destiny fashioned by others, notably by Louis XIV and Colbert, Morand effectively rejects the responsibility for Fouquet's debacle onto the "hubris" of the hero and onto destiny itself. In much the same way as Morand's other historical losers, Fouquet is redeemed by the displacement of his "crime" from a political to a literary (romanesque for the former, tragic in the case of Fouquet) order.

The second major group of metaphors is drawn from the tradition of bestiaries and from nature. The former serve to strengthen the crucial opposition between Fouquet and his arch-rival, Colbert; the latter, notably the sun metaphor, stage the struggle between Fouquet and Louis XIV. From the beginning, the radical divergence of Fouquet and Colbert is expressed metaphorically:

> Il y a des êtres émergés de la nuit, dont la poussée vitale est celle d'une fusée serpentine: ainsi Colbert. D'autres s'épanouissent goulûment au soleil du bonheur, étendent joyeusement leurs frondaisons: tel Fouquet. (14)

Night opposed to day, dark to light, a serpentine spindle ever spiraling inward versus the joyous expansion of foliage, Colbert and Fouquet are set in polarity. "Serpentine" relates this description of Colbert to his designation as a snake, suggested by his blazon: a "couleuvre" or grass snake whose misnomer as it represents Colbert is quickly remedied by Morand: "Ses armes sont à la couleuvre (Coluber = Colbert) en pal tortillé d'azur. Non pas une couleuvre, mais un terrible serpent au dard perçant, dressé sur sa queue" (63). In reinterpreting Colbert's heraldry, correcting, as it were, the species of the snake, Morand subtly signals his own reinterpretation, fitting his schema, of the individual.

Fouquet's blason, "l'écureil (en breton, le fouquet)" (90), likewise serves to describe:

> Buffon a fait du souple animal un portrait qui semble dessiner involontairement la figure du Surintendant: "vif, alerte, industrieux, fin, le corps nerveux, très réveillé, allant par bonds... il construit adroitement son nid." (90)

The images of the snake and the squirrel as designating Colbert and Fouquet do not originate with Morand, of course, and he openly cites a popular ditty circulating after Fouquet's condemnation:

> Le petit écureuil est pour toujours en cage.
> Le lézard (Le Tellier), plus rusé, joue mieux son personnage,
> Mais le plus fin de tous est un vilain serpent (Colbert).
> Qui s'abaissant s'élève et s'avance en rampant. (156)

Of interest, rather, is Morand use of these metaphors in his own stylistic rendition of the Fouquet/Colbert opposition. A particularly striking example occurs during Morand's description of the "financing" of the splendor of Vaux-le-Vicomte:

> Le Surintendant a pu penser qu'il importait peu qu'il ait dépensé paille et blé, que le Trésor public fût devenait le sien, puisque, ce soir, la France était servie, ses artistes célébrés et son art triomphant. Il fallait l'étroitesse d'esprit du reptile Colbert pour s'indigner de ce que la dette privée devînt la dette publique, et que l'Ecureuil, le plus rongeur des rongeurs, rongeât l'Etat. (91)

This is far from an ironic statement on the part of Morand, following as it does the enumeration of the artistes who contributed to Vaux and in the midst of a biography which constantly situates Fouquet as the patron and financier of the arts in France, a position, among others, that Louis XIV coveted and brutally usurped. At the same time, however, Fouquet's methods are presented as less than scrupulous. There is no denial of his misuse of public moneys, superbly imaged by the qualification of Fouquet's squirrel as "le plus rongeur des rongeurs rongeât l'Etat." The "crime" however, if one there be, seems to lie in the failure of the reptile Colbert to view such "nibbling" in the proper context.

The antithesis between Fouquet and Colbert is largely represented as a difference in personality, in particular in their respective attitudes towards the administration of their duties expressed in the "work ethic" attributed to each: "Colbert et sa maxime de l'ordre, opposée à la maxime de la confusion de son ennemi" (64); "il (Colbert) besognait dans les bureaux, Fouquet travaillait chez lui en s'amusant" (65). Their individual styles are again taken up metaphorically, this time in likenesses drawn from literary models:

> Fouquet est un personnage de Stendhal. "On lit dans Beyle qu'il eût aimé de traiter les grandes affaires en se jouant..." "Un Etat qui n'a pas quelques improvisateurs en réserve est un Etat sans nerfs" (Paul Valéry). (65)
>
> Colbert est un héros de Balzac: "Courage incroyable devant ces montagnes de dossiers... Ces monstres de besogne... de cupidité, de sécheresse, d'hypocrisie et d'envie..." (Paul Valéry). (65)

The description of Fouquet as a Stendhalian character, on the one hand, and of Colbert as Balzacian on the other is of particular interest for several reasons. The evocation of Stendhal in relation to Fouquet echoes Morand's sustained predilection for that writer and his fictional heros, perceptible in Morand's works as early as 1925, and evident in his historical works. Certainly many of Stendhal's characters fit the schema of "échec après le succès," Fabrice and Julien Sorel in particular. Likewise, the monstrous characters of Balzac, such as Vautrin, always succeed, like Colbert. We would also note the doubly anachronistic quality of these metaphors as Morand compares seventeenth-century historical figures to nineteenth-century literary heros by employing descriptions of the latter made by Paul Valéry in the twentieth century. Not only does Morand's operation displace Fouquet and Colbert from history to literature, but also projects them across not two but almost three centuries, a point to which we shall return in regard to the "present-ness" of Morand's biography.

If Colbert's hatred of Fouquet emerges as based upon a discordance of personal character and style, the rivalry of Louis XIV, on the other hand, is strikingly material in its representation. Put simply, Fouquet has what Louis XIV wants: Vaux-le-Vicomte, artists, writers, paintings, power and money. This obsession and its relation to Louis XIV's destruction of Fouquet is perhaps best expressed in the use of the sun metaphor, announced in the title and employed throughout the biography.

The sun, as Morand repeatedly stresses, was first used to describe Fouquet: "Sur les murs de Vaux, Le Brun lui donna le soleil pour emblème; Fouquet est un soleil qui se disperse en rayons, mais ses rayons ne brûlent pas" (14). Morand returns to Le Brun in his description of Vaux-le-Vicomte:

> Le roi avait fort goûté les peintures de Le Brun qu'il appellera bientôt à Versailles; moins goûté peut-être que l'une d'elles, *L'Apothéose d'Hercule*, représentait le Soleil (allusion à Fouquet). Louis XIV lui reprendra même cet astre! (91)

The confrontation of Louis XIV and Fouquet may be described as revolving around the question of who will personify the sun, as both metaphor and symbol. The outcome is known: Louis XIV forever holds the appellation of "Roi-Soleil." The sun of the title, the hidden, obscured, masked sun would thus refer to Fouquet who was imprisoned, hidden away at Pignerol, and reputedly locked behind the Iron Mask. At the same time, however, it is by no means certain that the "soleil offusqué" refers to Fouquet alone. Morand himself proposes another possible referent:

> Il est interdit de... c'est la devise des autocraties. Il est avant tout interdit, quand on n'est pas le roi, de vivre de manière souveraine. Au suprême de bon goût, il n'y a de place que pour un seul homme, comme sur le trône. L'éclat de Louis XIV, à mesure qu'il s'élève, s'offusque de l'élévation de ce Surintendant à qui l'on donne du Monseigneur. Vaux n'est pas un château, c'est un palais; ses fêtes obscurcissent toutes les autres. Est-ce en pensant à Vaux que Massillon dira un jour: "Tout ce qui brille plus que nous, nous blesse; tout ce qui nous efface nous trouve inexorable" [...] Louis se venge de n'avoir, un moment, été que l'ombre de Fouquet ou, comme disait Chamfort, que son clair de lune. (73)

In light of this passage, might not the "soleil offusqué" refer equally to the king, whose rising star found itself eclipsed, darkened by the brilliance of Fouquet? Whose vengeance for having been rendered nothing more than shadow was indeed inexorable? The problem of Morand's title, or perhaps its genius, is centered around the richly suggestive adjective "offusqué" as a derivative of the verb "offusquer." In its first definition, offusquer means "empêcher l'effet de la vue" (Littré), "cacher à la vue" (Larousse), hence the idea of Fouquet hidden at Pignerol, as well as the notion presented in this passage of effacement (tout ce qui nous efface) in regard to Louis XIV. Its second definition, "empêcher de voir en éblouissant," taken literally, would render the title "the sun blinded," an allusion first to Fouquet's failure to "see" the inevitability of Louis' usurpment of power, a theme which runs throughout the biography. At the same time, it might also refer to Louis XIV's rage, his reason as blinded by Fouquet's sun. In this instance, the fourth definition given by Larousse, "obscurcir l'esprit," to obfuscate or stupefy, comes into play. Larousse's third definition, "masquer l'éclat de quelqu'un ou quelque chose" likewise permits a double postulation: the sun (Fouquet) obscured (by Louis XIV) and, in this passage, the (rising) sun (Louis XIV) obscured (by Fouquet). The images of this passage in particular support the latter formula: the galas at Vaux obscuring all others (those of Versailles); Louis XIV as the shadow or "clair de lune" of Fouquet. Pulling all these suppositions together is the statement: "L'éclat de Louis [...] s'offusque de l'élévation de ce Surintendant [...]" in which the pronominal form of the verb may be read either reflexively as avoidance of the passive (is obscured) or idiomatically (takes offense, is scandalized). Morand presents the Sun-

King as conscious (overly) of the dimness of his persona beside the brilliance of Fouquet and enraged by this comparison.

How then are we to interpret the title? Does the "soleil offusqué" function as mere apposition? Or, on the other hand, does it designate Louis XIV? To accept the latter would be to read the title as "Fouquet ou Louis XIV," to imply that for Morand Fouquet's story is also that of the King. Indeed, this inference may well prove to be founded on more than the slippage suggested by the title. Many parts of the biography, particularly those describing Louis XIV, more than suggest the synonymity of Fouquet's downfall and Louis XIV's ascension. Furthermore, these passages, along with those devoted to Colbert, at times prompt one to momentarily wonder exactly whose biography one is reading.

Morand's intertwining of the lives of Fouquet, Colbert and Louis XIV somewhat resembles what has been rather awkwardly described as "group biography," a term used to loosely designate biographies with multiple subjects. Group biography, as one theorist puts it, stands as a response to modern skepticism of pure individualism and to growing emphasis on communal interaction, noting that: "implicit in group biography will be the notion that the individual is less than the whole, that the sum is greater than any of its parts" (Peters 41). While one hesitates both to recognize such techniques and assumptions as specifically modern, recalling as only one early example Strachey's *Washington and Jefferson*, and to relegate Morand's biography of Fouquet to a corresponding sub-genre of biography, the notion of the illumination of one life via another figures prominently in Morand's endeavors as a biographer. Indeed, two of Morand's other biographies offer even more radical examples of the consideration of multiple lives. *La Dame blanche des Habsbourg* (1963) traces the lives of the members of the Habsburg family as they are reunited not only by their family ties but also by the mysterious woman in white allegedly seen by each shortly before his or her death. Like Morand's other historical works, emphasis is placed upon the eventual downfall of the Habsburgs, here attributed to the strange curse of the "white lady." Decheance likewise constitutes the primary focus of *Ci-gît Sophie Dorothée de Celle* (1968), the biography of Sophie Dorothée, the unfortunate wife of George of Hanover, later George I of England. As in *La Dame blanche des Habsburg*, multiple lives are examined as the story of Sophie's life unfolds: those of her mother, Eléonore d'Olbreuse; her husband; and her mother-in-law, Sophie of Osnabrück.

There exists, of course, a thin line between a "portrait" of an individual who plays a role in the life of the biographical subject and a "biography" of that person. Morand's treatment of Colbert constitutes the former in its description of a personality designed to bring into focus, in its difference, that of Fouquet. In the case of Louis XIV the same is true, but Morand here signals another intent, one concurrent with and yet slightly distinct from his biography of Fouquet:

> Ici, Louis ne sera examiné que par rapport à Fouquet. Mais que cet angle est lumineux! "Nous ignorons tout de sa vie intérieure" disent ses biographes; voilà ce qui excite l'esprit. Ce monarque cadenassé nous laisse entrevoir son secret. (70)

While limiting his examination of Louis XIV to the latter's relationship with Fouquet, thus proposing that Fouquet's drama is thereby illuminated, Morand also more than suggests that the reverse is equally true: Louis XIV is "explained" by his involvement with Fouquet. Just as Morand earlier proposed to offer a "correction" of the received view of Fouquet, here he promises to accomplish that of which Louis' previous biographers were incapable: the revelation of his "vie intérieure," the unlocking of this "monarque cadenassé," by situating such a pursuit in relation to the "affaire Fouquet."

Morand describes Louis XIV as having been, in the beginning, a "grand timide," constrained by Mazarin and his own pudeur in his desire for women, and marked by a perception of the "inferiority" of his ancestry:

> S'est-il jamais dit que les Bourbons sont de moins bonne race, ou plutôt de moins pure descendance, à cause de la tache Médicis, celle de l'apothicaire florentin, que les Lorraine, les Rohan, les Habsbourg, les Wittelsbach? (70)

All these factors combine to create an untenable position for the proud young king, prompting the king to create an alternative identity:

> Le sang espagnol de Louis ne supporte pas cela; cet orgueilleux fabriquera donc très tôt son personnage; il commence par couvrir son embarras d'un air aisé. [...] Louis est un personnage faustien, devenu apollinien à la force du poignet. Déjà avec Marie Mancini, il se déguise en cavalier de *L'Astrée* et en homme du bel air. (71)

Morand here suggests that the Louis XIV of history is in fact a carefully fashioned persona, the king as an actor playing out a role created by and for himself. Louis XIV essentially represses his own mediocrity, hiding it behind an "appollinien" demeanor but without being able to eradicate it entirely. This, Morand offers, is particularly revealed in Louis's involvement with Fouquet, an incident during which the true nature of the king emerges:

Filming the Event 101

> La colère est un révélateur unique: Louis XIV, enfant, entrait dans des rages folles; ensuite, le sens de la mesure, l'horreur du scandale furent les plus forts. Toujours sur ses gardes, Louis le Grand ne se livrera plus; mais dans l'Affaire Fouquet il laissera pour la dernière fois éclater son courroux et se montrera lui-même. (71)

For Morand, the eruption of Louis's anger, anger all the more intense because of its repression, constitutes an expression or breaking-through of the "true" Louis XIV. The promised revelation of the "padlocked" king is here exemplified: Fouquet functions as a catalyst, playing upon all the fears, desires, and sexual insecurities that the monarch has hitherto been able to bury. Fouquet's wealth, the sumptuous Vaux and his way of life are played against Louis XIV's need for money to assure not only the expression of his power, but also the remediation of his own sense of inferiority: "de l'argent, pour ses maîtresses, pour les guerres, pour Versailles naissant, pour donner confiance, pour avoir confiance en soi" (71). The "true Louis" is timid, proud and suffering from a acute lack of self-confidence.

The psychological tenor of Morand's treatment of Louis XIV becomes explicit later on when the king is described as possibly suffering from a sort of unresolved Oedipal complex:

> A-t-il eu le complexe freudien du meurtre paternel, inassouvi envers Mazarin, reporté sur Fouquet? Le Surintendant appartenait à la génération qu'on déteste, simplement parce qu'elle vous précède. Louis XIV voit en lui un rappel du cauchemar de sa jeunesse: la guerre civile. (81)

Far more provocative than the idea of a simple generational rebellion, the suggestion of an oedipal conflict is supported by numerous other allusions. Not only does Morand situate the confrontation of Fouquet as a challenge to the authority of a symbolic father, but also explicitly underlines the sexual component of the conflict. The true father figure, as Morand implies, was Mazarin, not an uninformed choice since Mazarin was publicly understood to be the lover of Anne of Austria, Louis XIV's mother. Fouquet also emerges as Louis's amorous rival in the account of the intrigue of Mlle de la Vallière, Louis's young mistress, to whom Fouquet was accused of making improper gestures. The nightmare of Louis's youth might be read not only as that of the Fronde, but of the struggle with Mazarin for his mother and thus for the authority of the father, now displaced onto his rivalry with Fouquet.

The oedipal rivalry of Mazarin/Louis XIV and then Fouquet/Louis XIV plays itself out on yet another level: "Qu'il ait été l'amant ou l'époux morganique d'Anne d'Autriche, peu importe: Mazarin est l'amant de la France; il a joué sa vie sur elle et il a gagné" (55). With Mazarin dead, such a role, in Louis's eyes, naturally passed to Fouquet who, in a very concrete sense did "possess" France, perhaps more so than the Cardinal himself, and of which Vaux stands as the most powerful symbol. Morand repeatedly insists upon what Vaux represents: not only the money of France, but her best architects, painters, sculptors and artisans as well: Le Brun, le Nôtre, le Vau. Fouquet enjoys the favors of her artists and of her writers: "Scarron l'appelle le Patron" (31). Morand even suggests that Fouquet, in continuing the work of the Hôtel de Rambouillet, is responsible for the development of French literature: "C'est à Fouquet qu'on le doit, tant il sait agréablement et finement rétribuer le talent" (89). The gallery of this talent attests to Fouquet's "acquisition" of French letters: Molière, La Fontaine, Scarron, Pellisson, Loret (88); Bussy, La Rochefoucauld, Retz, Saint-Evremond, Corneille, Mlle de Scudèry (89). The displacement of the figure of the father from Mazarin to Fouquet, when coupled with the image of Mazarin as not only Anne d'Autriche's lover but France's as well, invites us to extend the latter analogy to Fouquet.

But if Louis XIV emerges as an oedipal figure à la Freud, with Mazarin/Fouquet as the father figure, on another level Fouquet himself is depicted in terms recalling the mythological Oedipus. We would recall the link drawn at the end of the first chapter between François Fouquet's participation in the condemnation of Chalais and the eventual condemnation of his son: "Comme dans ces tragédies antiques où la punition du père reportée sur le fils [...]" (13). Just as the punishment of Laius's crime is tranferred to the destiny of his son, so is Fouquet's downfall tied to the crimes of his father. And like Oedipus who misinterprets the oracle, Fouquet also exhibits a singular inability to interpret the "signs" of his destiny.

> Pas un instant, il n'a deviné, dans le jeune monarque, le Grand Roi; il n'a pas pressenti la révolution du pouvoir, la mutation de l'axe français de Paris à Versailles, l'extraordinaire déplacement d'équilibre dont il sera brusquement la victime. (45)

> Confiant et aveugle; n'ayant su ni percer à jour la Reine-mère; ni qualifier Mazarin, ni juger Colbert, ni prévoir Louis le Grand. (15)

Fouquet remains blind to the event of Louis XIV, a destiny which determines his own. Morand attribues this disillusionment to a variety of sources, some more speculative than others. For one, Fouquet no doubt believed himself to be protected by his financial situation: "Fouquet a dû croire que tout s'achète, même le destin" (15). Morand also suggests that Fouquet also may have possessed secret information compromising to the king: "Détenait-il des secrets qu'il ne pouvait pas rendre publics, dont il ne doutait pas qu'ils fussent propres à retourner l'esprit du roi?" (79). Finally Morand touches upon another possible motive, that of self-destruction, in another nod to Freudian psychoanalysis: "Il y a chez les hommes une tentation de se détruire, qui peut primer le besoin de se conserver. Fouquet a-t-il cédé à ce vertige?" (79). Although highly provocative, Morand does not pursue such an hypothesis, offering neither explanation nor illustration of this death drive. What remains is an oedipal-like failure to discern the playing-out of a series of events which Morand clearly endows with a mythological character of destiny.

After his trial and condemnation, the description of Fouquet at Pignerol continues the link to Oedipus. High in the prison, Fouquet is transformed into an almost sacred figure, echoing the sacralization of Oedipus at Colonneus in Sophocles' play: "[...] sa hauteur d'âme naturelle s'éléva vers le ciel" (155). Lest the allusion escape us, the biography closes on the evocation of Fouquet's loss of his daughter (to Lauzun), mirroring Oedipus bereft of Antigone and Ismene just before his "disappearance."

This repeated invocation of both the psychoanalytic and mythological figures of Oedipus continues the technique identified in *Le Flagellant de Séville* of a periodic "lifting-out" of the protagonist from his historical context, a strategy which permits Morand to "freeze" linear history for an instant and to interpret that instant in a highly literary manner. This is, of course, exactly the operation effectuated by metaphor as it momentarily disrupts linear narration in a movement of substitution which lifts one term into the context of another in an explicitly interpretive move. Morand's interpretive strategies play out, as we have attempted to demonstrate, on several metaphoric planes: dramatic, emblematic, literary, psychoanalytic and mythological. This multiplicity of displacements lays bare the hand of the writer, both in terms of his aesthetic concerns and in the analysis of his subject evident in the nature of his comparisons. Let us now examine Morand's use of another figure, metonymy, as it functions in much the same way to illustrate Morand's techniques of stylistic presentation.

To return to Vaux-le-Vicomte, we would note its function as a double metonym evoking, on the one hand, all France's glory, a metonym created by the terms of the biography, and, on the other, Fouquet himself. Morand displays a predilection for what one might term "geographical" metonyms. Fouquet's residence at Vincennes, Saint-Mandé, expresses his care to remain close to the center of power while carefully dissimulating his own:

> Partout, en homme avisé, le Surintendant s'est installé à l'ombre du pouvoir; pas autant que Mazarin, qui couche chez le roi et chez la reine-mère, mais presque. A Paris, Fouquet a acheté une maison derrière le palais de Mazarin; [...] La maison est assez grande pour que le roi, Mazarin, Monsieur, frère du roi, y aient été reçus, ainsi que Christine de Suède, mais c'est le contraire du tape-à-l'œil de Vaux, monument à sa gloire, édifice de propagande. A Saint-Mandé, il a conservé une vieille façade modeste, le chaume du côté où le roi regarde, les tuiles et la plus belle façade du côté invisible; ainsi à Bagdad, pour ne pas effrayer le calife, les maisons en torchis ne laissaient rien deviner de leurs trésors. (24-25)

While Vaux stands as the expression of Fouquet's flagrant display of his wealth and of his love of pleasure, Saint-Mandé represents another Fouquet, careful of appearances and living in relative modesty surrounded by his books. Perhaps most important is the emphasized opposition between Vaux and Saint-Mandé. Morand continues, offering an explanation of the difference and suggesting (again) why Vaux so attracted the ire of the king:

> Son souci de modestie, si près de la Cour, est évident. Saint-Mandé n'est pas une terre, comme Vaux qui confère la noblesse à son propriétaire; ce n'est pas une terre noble, mais une "roture." (25-26)

Fouquet dares not reveal himself so close to the king; Saint-Mandé confirms the fiction of his position as vassal. But Vaux, as a true "terre," bestows nobility and thus power in what may be an oblique reference to the Fronde, the resurgence of which Louis greatly fears.

As Vaux and Saint-Mandé represent the two "sides" of Fouquet, Louis XIV is similarly designated by his "site": Versailles. The king's inferiority complex is superbly translated by the inferiority of Versailles placed next to Vaux: "Vaux bat Versailles de cinq ans. Fouquet n'est-il pas un Louis XIV prématuré?" (87); "Le château, 'montagne d'architecture,' qui nargue Versailles" (90); before the fountains at Vaux: "Louis XIV, avec amertume, pense à Versailles qui n'a pas d'eau" (96). If on one level we have observed the conflict between Fouquet and the king unfold as a struggle for the metaphor/symbol of the sun, here Morand stages a metonymic battle between Vaux and Versilles, between the wildly successful Fouquet and the insecure, childish king.

But if Vaux, on that fateful night in 1661 represents Fouquet's triumph, for posterity it remains the emblem of his folly:

> Vaux, palais des illusions.
> Chacun vit d'illusions, mais rares ceux qui les projettent dans une oeuvre visible après trois siècles. [...] Vaux, énorme échec pétrifié; mais ce n'est pas

l'échec d'un fou, ce fut le décor d'une réussite parfaite qui n'a duré qu'une seule soirée, celle du 17 août 1661. [...] Vaux ou le songe d'une nuit d'été. (87)

Vaux, his most prized creation, is also the expression of his biggest mistake, an error shining in its success and an irony perceptible three centuries later. Fouquet's dream palace provides Morand with fertile ground for his rendition of history, enabling him to make full use of literary tropes. I would recall Morand's use of theatrical metaphor which described the ill-fated evening at Vaux as a perfection of the classical unities of time, place and action. The same evening functions as a synecdoche of Fouquet's fall from power. Vaux, I have also argued, is a metonym for Fouquet and here, in the above citation, the space between the "réussite parfaite" and the "énorme échec pétrifié" creates irony.

The ultimate "échec," the outcome of the clash of Louis XIV and Fouquet, furnishes yet another site synonymous with Fouquet: Pignerol, the prison high in the Piedmont where Fouquet spent the last fifteen years of his life. Early in the biography, Morand evokes the contrast intended between Fouquet, host to the king, and Fouquet, abject prisoner:

Il faut toujours chercher dans un personnage ce qu'il a d'extrême. En Fouquet, ce qui est intéressant [...] c'est enfin, la soudaine et pathétique antithèse entre Vaux et Pignerol, entre le palais et le prison, entre la lumière des salons et les ténèbres de l'*in-pace*. (47)

If Saint-Mandé expresses the diplomacy of Fouquet and Vaux his triumph and illusion, Pignerol, this "prison noire à l'intérieure d'une prison blanche," is his failure.

Up to this point, our discussion of *Fouquet ou le soleil offusqué* has been centered around Morand's use of rhetorical figures and his insertion of a sub-biography, that of Louis XIV. Such an emphasis, besides being, in my opinion, justified by the text, points to a major aspect of Morand's approach to history, namely his techniques of compression. Biography, as we earlier pointed out, resembles the enterprise of historiography in that it normally entails the sifting through and selection from an overwhelming amount of information. Tropes provide one means of reducing such overabundance, permitting the biographer to express maximum meaning in a minimum of words. Synecdoche and metonymy, as agents of condensation, constitute the most obvious figures for such an operation. Morand describes Fouquet as "issue de la grande bourgeoisie de la robe" and as "le type même de l'élève des Jésuites parisien," the era is "la Fronde finissante," conjuring up all the images of the civil war. The contrast between Paris and the country is augmented by the comparison of the latter to the paintings of Callot: "Cette France-là, c'est celle de Callot," that is, the misery, starvation, brigandry, etc., depicted in Callot's work.

Metaphor, in its expansion of meaning via substitution, also affords Morand an economy of description. The period is "cet immense cage tournante, tourbillante, où l'écureil Fouquet apprendra l'agilité"; Mazarin is "le Tentateur," a "facchino" and a "polichinelle"; Colbert emerges as "le plus tartufe de tous." Fouquet's judges are "les pions de Colbert" and his condemnation that of "la mort lente." Morand's metaphors at once expand meaning and, as we noted in regard to his use of dramatic metaphor, aid in the structuring of his particular interpretation of Fouquet all the while "liberating" Morand from a tedious laying-out of fact after fact.

The insertion of the sub-biography of Louis XIV functions in much the same way, situating the king's hatred of Fouquet within a psychological profile of the young king. Fouquet's downfall, seen from this angle, becomes the necessary condition of Louis' self-affirmation. At the same time, the reverse appears equally true: Fouquet's arrest and imprisonment are the immediate effects of Louis's takeover. Morand locks the two events in a relation which by force of its chiasmic cause-effect structure becomes almost metonymical in nature.

The process of condensing and compressing the multitude of events, players, ambiguities and contradictions of the Fouquet affair is also evidenced by many other aspects of the biography. Morand makes liberal use of his own predecessors in the long line of commentators on Fouquet's life; almost every page contains a reference or quotation from a previous biography, history or contemporary account. By constantly situating his work in relation to these others Morand legitimatizes the biography, giving added weight to his own assertions, and places himself in the company of some very illustrious names: Retz, Scarron, Saint-Simon, Choisy, La Fontaine, Mme de Lafayette, and Voltaire, to name just a few. Many of the direct citations are purely illustrative: "Sa bonne tête est capable de contenir tout le soin d'un Etat (Sévigné)" (21); the king is "un homme dont 'l'esprit est au-dessous du médiocre' (Saint-Simon)" (50); on Mazarin, "grand saltimbanque de son naturel (Retz)" (22); and "Vaux ne sera jamais plus beau qu'il ne le fut cette soirée-là (La Fontaine)" (93). Others express interpretations close to Morand's own: "Tout le monde faisait des affaire, le tort de Fouquet fut d'en faire plus qu'un autre, avec profusion, avec scandale (Saint-Beuve)" (125). Perhaps the most remarkable quotations, if only for their length, are of Brienne, himself a player in the intrigue, and Mme de Sévigné. In both instances Morand relinquishes his narration, allowing their voices to continue the story. Brienne's account of the events immediately leading up to Fouquet's arrest consists mainly of his record of conversations with both Louis XIV and Fouquet on September 3 and 4, 1661. These transcriptions give a vivid and concise account of the state of mind of each and provide a summary of the king's motivations, permitting Morand to concentrate on the succession of events without being obliged to render the psychological profile of its players. The series of letters written by Mme de Sévigné describing the trial of Fouquet likewise provides important background. Not only does she describe the physical demeanor of Fouquet but also her own emotional response, one obviously intended to represent the collective reaction of society.

We would also note the numerous citations of contemporary literary works, including Mlle de Villedieu's play about Fouquet, *Le Favori* (145), Corneille's *Le Menteur* (88), and Molière's *Les Fâcheux*, the latter written for and performed for the first time at Vaux before the king. La Fontaine is extensively quoted, in particular his poem "Elégie aux nymphes de Vaux" and Morand singles him out as "à jamais l'historien de cette nuit enchantée" (100). Mlle de Scudéry's *Clélie* is quoted four times, once accompanied by the remark that the only portion of this novel still read is that describing Vaux (89). Morand's use of such passages lends his biography a distinct literary tone, one already established by its highly figurative language. In addition, the preponderance of literature devoted to Fouquet, or in which he figures, attests to the extent of literary society's involved in the affair and of the almost unilateral rally of literature to his cause, an important point in Morand's work to which we shall return.

The compression at work in *Fouquet ou le soleil offusqué*, visible in Morand's use of figurative language and his recourse to direct quotation, finds its best expression in Morand's lightning-fast style. Passages such as the one cited below attest to the fact that Morand very much remained in 1961, the modern stylist of his earlier fame:

> Brillant, insinuant, mondain, maître en compromis, casuiste, imbattable en vers latins, amateur de devises ingénieuses, attiré comme un papillon par les girandoles de toutes les fêtes, Fouquet est le type même de l'élève des Jésuites parisien (en province, c'est une autre affaire: les Jésuites de Rheims donneront Colbert). Cette montée en volutes, ces lignes plus courbes que le dos des courtisans, ces arabesques en porte à faux comme la morale d'Escobar, et, pour finir ce grand arc brisé, c'est bien l'architecture jésuite, c'est la vie même de Fouquet. (22)

The terse firing of first adjectives and then epithets reaches a crescendo with the comparison to a butterfly attracted to the deadly candelabrum, a perfect expression of Fouquet's fatal inability to resist pleasure and show.[2] The tension eases for an instant in the anticipated metonym of the Jesuit student and then begins again, its movement figured in the upward spiral of a baroque cathedral. The tortuous nature of the edifice: "montée en volutes," "ces arabesques," "lignes plus courbes," along with the sensation of suspension in mid-air, "en porte à faux," conveys the impression of a magically supported structure, hung from above with no foundation beneath. Indeed, Morand pulls out any such base in the comparison of the "curving lines" to the spine of a courtesan. That this fragile, self-supporting and corrupted architecture functions as a metaphor of the Jesuite ethic is confirmed first by the reference to Escobar, whose name at the time served as a perjorative denoting a self-serving hypocrite, and then by the synthesis of "c'est bien l'architecture jésuite." In these two sentences Morand offers a pronouncement on Jesuitism and a tracing of its deleterious influence on Fouquet. He even offers a commentary on his own style: "et pour finir ce grand arc brisé," a reference at once to the architectural metaphor and to his own construction of the same. Morand's stylistic economy entails no sacrifice of meaning.

I would now turn to the mechanics of the narration of Fouquet's disaster, namely to the temporal structure of the biography which reveals patterns of reduction similar to those visible in his style. We recall Morand's focus on four distinct instants: Mazarin's death (March 9, 1661); the evening at Vaux (August 17, l661); Fouquet's arrest (September 5, l661); and his encounter with Lauzun (not precisely dated in the biography but which occured sometime in early 1672 (Dessert 277)). The narration of Fouquet's story begins with the first, the death of the "petit" cardinal, and the subsequent events are presented in proper chronological order. As such, Fouquet belongs to the traditional form of the genre, one into which Morand himself inserts the book in the first paragraph, defending his decision to include a brief overview of Fouquet's ancestry:

> Les biographies ont coutume de débuter par l'étude de la famille et des aïeux du héros. Malgré l'ennui de ces préliminaires et pour ne pas déroger à la tradition, il faut dire deux mots des Fouquet à travers les âges. (9)

Morand signals that Fouquet not only is a biography but also that he has consciously adopted a customary form.

---

[2] The image of a butterfly drawn to a deadly light is prevalent in Malraux's novels, another link between the two. On insect imagery in Malraux, see Thomas Jefferson Kline, *André Malraux and the Metamorphosis of Death*.

But this "form" turns out to be rather peculiar. Let us take, as example, the narration of the events of the first "moment," the morning of Mazarin's death, which begins on page twenty-four: "Fouquet traverse son jardin de Saint-Mandé, lequel touche au parc du château de Vincennes." Fifteen pages later, he is still in his own garden: "Par ce froid matin du début de mars 1661, dans son potager de Saint-Mandé [...]" (39). On page fifty-seven, Fouquet finally exits his own property: "Ce matin de mars, le Surintendant entre, confiant, dans le parc de Vincennes, [...]" then "Le donjon de Vincennes grandit à mesure que Fouquet en approche [...]" (59), and finally, "Fouquet lève la tête, devant lui, il aperçoit le jeune Brienne [...]" (61) who informs him of Mazarin's death. In the course of this prolonged stroll, Morand "freezes" linear progression at several points, making numerous forays into the past, notably to Fouquet's apprenticeship under Mazarin and even farther back in his description of Mazarin's own rise to power and in a detailed explanation of the revenue system in place before Fouquet assumed control. Detours into the future also mark this portion of the book: allusions to Louis XIV's cementing of power, to the evening at Vaux, to Fouquet's arrest and trial, and to Pignerol. This non-linear form falls into what Tzvetan Todorov has identified as a narrative of substitutions, one which "constantly, though surreptitiously, turns back on itself" and, I would add, turns forward on itself, in what emerges, to use another of Todorov's terms, as a "retrospective future" narrated from the biographer's perspective (134-35). The synchronic narration in Fouquet serves several purposes. For one, it allows Morand to provide background information necessary to the comprehension of Fouquet's position at the time he sets off for Vincennes. The expansion of each of Fouquet's steps, as it were, also prepares the way for the "main event" of that morning: Louis XIV's declaration that he now controls the state's finances, centering attention on the meaning of that action as both repudiation of the past and preparation for the future.

The narration of the morning of March 9, 1661, does not, however, end upon Fouquet's encounter with Brienne. Rather, its focus shifts from Fouquet to Louis XIV, witness to Mazarin's death. After another detour, this time to descriptions of Colbert and Louis XIV, including the highly biographical passages on the king, the biography returns to Vincennes and to the meeting of the ministers convoqued by Louis XIV. This day, which "contient tout l'avenir, y compris la ruine de Fouquet," finally comes to an end in the biography with the King's declaration that "La face du théâtre change [...]" (76), fifty-two pages after it began, taking up roughly a third of the biography. But pages well spent, for within the magnification of one day, indeed of one morning, Morand essentially compresses Fouquet's entire life by digressing both toward the past and the future.

The same operation of condensation of textual space is perceptible from exactly the opposite angle in much of the remainder of the book. Morand again focuses on a very specific period when giving the account of Fouquet's arrest, for example, but the events of September 4 and 5, 1661, succeed one another in rapid succession with few detours over only ten pages. His trial, which lasted three years, consumes twenty-two pages; its narration is remarkable for the virtual absence of figurative language and of digression, with the exception of the pages reproducing Mme de Sévigné's letters and literary reactions to the trial.

The combination of synchronic and diachronic narratives in Fouquet relieves what Park Honan calls the tedium of "naming," the enumeration of events arranged on the horizontal axis of time (116). By intersecting the diachronic line of chronologically ordered narration of the events of the life of Fouquet with synchronic narratives which relate particular moments to others occuring at other times and which provide background information, Morand also achieves what Honan terms "historical present-ness" (118). This present-ness, for Honan, is the result of a successful recreation of a historical "present" such that the biography renders an experience of the past as a present, rather than as a retrospect. By this Honan does not imply that the biographer should seek to recreate the past moment as an isolated unit, that is, to pretend to an objective and complete "return" to the past. Indeed, such an effort would be both impossible and quite uninteresting in that it would leave no potential for interpretation. Rather, this "present-ness" holds the biograhy "on the edge of time," mediating the encounter of the historical subject and biographer's interpretive relationship with that subject (117). Honan cites Proust's *A la recherche du temps perdu* as the crowning fictional achievement of this "consistent illusion of the historical present" which permits one to experience "presents-that-were, and ways of feeling that are not normally our own" (115-16).

This "present-ness," Honan continues, is reached largely through the presence of the biographer's "persona," perceptible in his or her exploitation of style, particularly in use of metaphor which, Honan argues, itself occurs at the point of intersection of the diachronic and synchronic planes. This persona also, and perhaps most obviously, manifests itself in the role of the narrator and the degree to which the narrator is involved as interpreter and analyst of his subject.

Morand, on one level, succeeds admirably in creating a "historical present" in Fouquet. His use of the present tense, for one, contributes to a sense of immediacy, even as the retrospective nature of the narration is kept in focus by allusions to the end of Fouquet's drama and by interpretation of past events in light of this "future." The use of tropes and digressions, such as the sub-biography of Louis XIV and the detours made during Fouquet's walk to Vincennes, likewise develops the sense of a "total" historical present, one rounded out by feelings, motivations, anecdotes, etc., while at the same time revealing Morand's interpretive relation to his subject. The narration flows smoothly from factual accounts to quotations of letters, commentaries and literature, and overtly interpretive statements. The only "breaks" in the biography occur when Morand explicitly alludes to his own present, the time at which he writes Fouquet. The expression of a consciousness of the biographical "moment" is both desirable and, as many theorists and biographers themselves argue, necessary to a successful biography. But in Fouquet, Morand's references to his position, or rather to his era, strike one as highly anachronistic interruptions of the "historical present."

We have already noted two such anachronistic interventions. First, the evocation of Vaux as seen in 1961: "En 1961, Fouquet n'a pas encore cessé de transmettre son message de 1661" (87). Such a reference, as it situates the biographical moment in 1961, also transforms Vaux into a sort of document, one to be analyzed just as are written documents. As such this reference does transmit an awareness of the biographer's position and also somewhat justifies, by the dates, Morand's focus on the year of 1661 by marking a sort of tri-centennial homage. The second, we would recall, involves Morand's use of Valéry's remarks on Stendhal and Balzac as illustration of the comparison Morand makes between, on the one hand, Fouquet and the "Stendhalian hero" and, on the other, Colbert and Balzac's protagonists. This operation not only underscores the literary tone of the biography, but also, as we noted, connects Fouquet to Morand's other "Stendhalian" figures of his postwar works.

Other passages, however, function quite differently. Morand compares Fouquet to "[...] ces gentilshommes en fourrure qui traversent la vie entre des haillonneux tendant la main, qui hantent les planches de Callot" (39), and then provides a striking metaphor:

> Cette indifférence, cette coexistence des extrêmes, c'est l'époque; l'Occident d'alors, c'est l'Orient d'aujourd'hui où l'on voit côte à côte la masure et palais, la Cadillac de l'émir pétrolier et l'octogénaire pliant sous son couffin de crottes de chameau séchées. (39)

Through the process of the metaphor, Fouquet suddenly materializes behind the wheel of a Cadillac. Rather than a procedure used to harmonize the distance between 1661 and 1961 in what one might call the "duet" between the biographical moment and its historical subject, such a brusque comparison strikes a discordant note. Or does it? Let us consider yet another example:

> Il existe, de Colbert, trois notes qui règlent, minute par minute, le programme de l'arrestation prochaine du Surintendant. Rien de plus émouvant: c'est le film de l'événement avant l'événement, tel que pourrait le voir un démiurge de l'autre côté de la vie. Tout y est prévu, comme sur ces plateaux où le régisseur dessine à la craie le contour d'un corps, et où le metteur en scène commande: "Vous, l'assassiné, vous tomberez ici." (108)

To read these notes of Colbert is compared to seeing a film, that of Fouquet's arrest, before the fact. Morand continues the cinematographic metaphor in the image of the "régisseur," or production manager, who stages the scene before its filming. The comprehensive detail of Colbert's staging gives rise to the metaphor in much the same way that the evening of Vaux-le-Vicomte "naturally" evokes the unities of classical drama and Fouquet's story reflects antique tragedy. All three instances emphasize the highly dramatic quality of Morand's presentation and interpretation of his subject.

This passage reflects Morand's biographical endeavor in yet another way. If Colbert, on one level, is the "démiurge" and "régisseur" of Fouquet's arrest, both the creator and the orchestrator, on another, Morand himself occupies this position. For what does he, as biographer, do but animate a world seen like a demiurge from the "other side of life," from beyond its subject's death? If the demiurge can "see" this world because he has created it, if the production manager visualizes the scene before it is acted, Morand, likewise, organizes the account of Fouquet's downfall before it is narrated. In fact, the comment "Tout y est prévu" more aptly describes Morand's biography up to this point than Colbert's outline. That which Colbert's notes cannot contain: descriptions of his and Louis XIV's "true" motivations, of the reaction of others, of Fouquet's thoughts, and of the eventual outcome, indeed forms the content of the first one hundred pages of *Fouquet*. One might even hazard to say that the first two-thirds of the biography constitute the real "film de l'événement avant l'événement," particularly in the way in which the "event," Fouquet's arrest, is clearly spelled out from the beginning and then carefully prepared and organized again and again.

Thus, in one way, anachronistic metaphor in Fouquet may be absorbed into the representation of the biographical process. And yet, the images of the Cadillac and the chalk outline of a body underscore rather than integrate the temporal distance between 1661 and 1961. Why does Morand interrupt, however briefly, this

Filming the Event 113

"illusion" of a historical present so carefully constructed, in order to make such leaps into the future, and a highly technical one at that? Perhaps, and here I make an equally daring leap, perhaps the answer lies in yet another anachronism, this time a single word.

Early in the biography, Fouquet's future is described as follows: "Il va être pris dans un étau, entre deux orgueilleux, secs, prudents, dissimulés, *épurateurs* impitoyables" (15) (my emphasis). To a reader of this study, my interest obviously falls upon the term "épurateur" used to describe Louis XIV and Colbert. To begin, the use of this term to describe someone involved in a political purge or reorganization, according to Robert, did not enter the language until 1792, during the Reign of Terror. Indeed, "épuration" was not given its meaning of political act until 1835. Beyond this, references to the French language are unanimous in declaring that after 1944, "épurateur" acquired the particular connotation of one engaged in the purging of those who had collaborated with the Vichy governement and/or with Nazi Germany. Not only does this term not "belong" in Fouquet's era, but, for Morand and the reader, designates a role firmly anchored in the latter half of the twentieth century.

Let me state plainly my argument. If *Fouquet*, in large part, functions as the "film de l'événement avant l'événement," that is, as a staging of the event before its actual narration, might not the entire biography be seen as a similar preview of *the* event, the "épuration" of 1944? *Fouquet*, as the account of a purge, would thus stand as a dress rehearsal, situated in turn "de l'autre côté de la vie," on the nether side of the denouement of the Liberation. In order to clarify such a hypothesis, I now propose to compare three passages: the first from *Fouquet ou le soleil offusqué*; the second from one of Morand's rare accounts of his activities during and after the war as they relate to his involvement with the Vichy government; and the third from Jean Paulhan's essay "De la paille et du graine" (1944), written in protest of the National Committee of Writers' handling of the "literary" purge at the end of the Second World War.

The first passage comes from an explanation of Fouquet's position in relation to the abrupt seizure of power by Louis XIV:

> Plus haute encore, on trouvera en Fouquet l'opposition éclatante de deux époques, la Fronde et la monarchie absolue; la mort de Mazarin faisant la frontière. Avant mars 1661, tous vivaient, pensaient, agissaient, dilapidaient comme Fouquet. Tout d'un coup, dès la fin du printemps de cette même année 1661, tous vécurent, pensèrent, agirent à l'instar du Roi. Aucun acrobate ne sait basculer comme une foule; conversion et convertissement. L'idiote, l'innocente opinion publique fait ses rétablissements en un clin d'œil, avant même que les plus diligents *retourneurs de veste* n'aient réussi à dégager le bras

de la première manche de leur habit. C'est pour ne pas avoir eu ce flair que Fouquet, l'homme le plus habile, le plus expérimenté et le mieux informé de l'époque a été pris. Et puni, rétroactivement. Les punitions rétroactives sont peut-être les plus justes: condamné pour manque de flair. (46) (my emphasis)

The central argument of Morand's biography of Fouquet is encapsulated in this sweeping delineation of Fouquet's place in regard to his era. We find Morand's repeated emphasis on the suddenness and totality of Louis' takeover, as well as the notion of a "reign of Fouquet" prior to the crucial month of March, 1661. But perhaps at no other point in the biography does the "event" of Louis XIV receive such a schematic formulation. Mazarin's death serves as "frontier" between the era of the Fronde (Fouquet) and that of the king's absolutism; this cross-over is reflected in the change of verb tenses: "Avant mars 1661, tous vivaient, pensaient, agissaient, dilapidaient comme Fouquet"; the same verbs reappear in Louis' "era," but this time in the simple past tense rather than the imperfect. This grammatical leap is mirrored in the leap of faith made by public opinion: "conversion et convertissement." Fouquet's "crime" lay in his failure to predict and perform this syntactic acrobatic. The Surintendant, the most agile of all, suddenly lacks a flair for fashion, for the changing vicissitudes of power. Already in "Parfaite de Saligny" (1946) Morand had sketched a portrait of society tyrannized by whimsy; Parfaite, we would recall, engages in the futile and ultimately ridiculous attempt to remain "comme-il-faut," even as that standard changes almost daily in the context of the later years of the French Revolution. The image in the *Fouquet* passage of the "retourneurs de veste," those who change political positions as easily as they change coats, revives the fashion metaphor and leads us directly to the second text under consideration.

In 1958, in the midst of the controversy over his candidacy to a seat in the Académie française, Morand circulated a pamphlet among the members of that body, denying the rumor that he had associated with a particularly offensive Nazi officer, the General von Stülpnagel, during the Occupation. In closing, Morand describes his position during the war:

Je n'ai choisi d'être fonctionnaire qu'une seule fois, en 1912. Je suis entré par la grande porte. J'ai servi jusqu'en 1944 le gouvernement légal de la France. Souvent sollicité de me rallier à un gouvernement depuis lors légalisé, je suis resté fidèle au serment prêté; je n'aime pas prêter serment, mais quand j'ai donné ma parole, je la tiens; disposant de *plusieurs vestes*, je n'ai eu à *retourner* aucune. (Guitard-Auviste 224-25) (my emphasis)

Without forcing the issue, this document, which appeared two years before *Fouquet ou le soleil offusqué*, reveals a great deal about both

Morand's view of the purge of 1944, as its expression is itself situated in the context of the Académie's own "purge" of Morand in 1959, and his transferral of such an angle into his biography of Fouquet. Several of the issues central to his analysis of Fouquet's situation are found here in rude form: the schema of a radical split between two eras divided by a date-frontier, the succession of one legitimate government by another effectuated by an abrupt change of authority and, perhaps most obviously, the subtle allusion to the changing of political alliances as the turning of one's coat. Morand here refers to those who, by following popular sentiment and by becoming supporters of de Gaulle in mid-stream, placed themselves in a favorable position at the time of the Liberation. But one wonders as to Morand's particular handling of this metaphor. By preceding his disclaimer of having been a "retourneur de veste" with a reference to the several "coats" at his disposal, he lays open the image of his donning successively the coat of a Vichy ambassador and then that of a wrongly accused patriot, a "quick-change" performed in the course of the pamphlet itself.

A contemporary view of much the same scenario is found in Jean Paulhan's 1946 essay "De la paille et du grain." In this work, Paulhan accuses the members of the Comité National des Ecrivains (le Céné) of a "singular hypocrisy" in the drawing up of their black list of writers alleged to have collaborated during the Occupation. Paulhan points out that those who would sit in judgment in the name of France not so long ago themselves railed against the very idea of allegiance to the nation, quoting passages written before the war by Julien Benda, Paul Eluard and Louis Aragon, the principal players in the Céné's action (344-46). The chiasmus is neatly formulated:

> Quelle étrange aventure: la France a failli être ruinée par des hommes qui priaient chaque matin la déesse France; elle a été sauvée (entre autres) par ceux qui jetaient chaque jour l'armée française au panier. (353)

Paulhan all but labels the latter as turncoats themselves, without, however, diminishing the fact that they were among those who did indeed rescue France. Instead he subtly suggests that they have, in turn, deified the goddess France in the name of their own cause, much as did those whom they would now prosecute. The essay bases its polemic upon the argument that words are, by their very nature, unreliable. Language, Paulhan suggests, is incapable of representing once and for all, ideas and actions, citing as example the word "patrie" which means different things for different people at different times (346; 349-50; 352-53). Following Paulhan's line of reasoning, the Céné's use of this word to justify their actions would represent their own appropriation of the term to describe their endeavor, to the exclusion of all others. In a sense, the problem returns to a question of who has the right to call himself or herself a true patriot, a true Frenchman or woman.

This problem is not without resonance to *Fouquet ou le soleil offusqué*. Fouquet is repeatedly described as quintessentially French: "Fouquet est l'homme le plus vif, le plus naturel, [...] le plus français" (15); "sa figure si française" (158). The opposite holds for his ennemis, in particular Louis XIV: "[...] les Bourbons ('cadets chanceux' écrit La Varende) sont de moins bonne race, ou plutôt de moins pure descendance, à cause de la tâche Médicis" and "Il est plus espagnol que français, plus Habsbourg que Bourbon [...]" (80). Mazarin, more obviously, is also "less" French: "Ce fils d'un maquignon de l'Italie méridionale a le petit génie local du paysan italien [...]. l'Italien est un être de manège et de manoeuvre: c'est l'Oriental de l'Occident. Italien d'origine, Espagnol de nationalité, Français d'adoption, Mazarin sera l'homme-frontière [...]" (54). Colbert, in recompense for his lowly birth, invents foreign ancestry: "Il s'invente des ancêtres écossais, les Kolbert, venus d'Ecosse au XIIIème siècle [...]" (63), and then proceeds to live up to his imagined origins: "Le célèbre mot de Mme de Sevigné le résume entier: Colbert, c'est le Nord" (65). Fouquet emerges as persecuted by those whose claim to authority as representative of France is belied by their birth and, more importantly, by their comportment. In Morand's interpretation, Fouquet is victim (as are those on the Céné's black-list) of a purge machinated by figures whose claim to the "patrie" is historically tenuous at best.

Another factor, the role of literature itself, appears as a thread uniting these three passages. After the account of the sentence passed on Fouquet, perpetual imprisonment and not execution as Colbert and Louis XIV hoped and expected, Morand makes the following observation a propos of the effect of the involvement of literary figures on the trial:

> En vérité Voltaire a raison: "Ce sont les gens de lettres qui lui sauveront la vie." C'est de son procès que date un phénomène qui surprend toujours l'étranger: l'importance qu'a la littérature, ou du moins les gens de lettres, pour la politique, sinon en France, du moins à Paris. (151)

Morand's insistence upon the literary world's support of Fouquet, both before and after Louis XIV's taking of power, suggests that these writers are not to be grouped under the rubric of "retourneurs de veste," at least where Fouquet himself was concerned. In addition, this literary support itself is of great historical importance, according to Morand, as it signals the beginning of the "phenomenon" of literature's involvement in politics in France.

But while such an involvement has a positive effect in the biography, that is, in 1661, the reverse is true of the situation described by Paulhan. In fact, Paulhan stresses that the literary purge following the Liberation itself constitutes a "new" phenomenon, one in stark contrast to the absence of such persecutions following the First World War. Those who failed to "purge" Romain Rolland, for example, in view of his anti-French writings during that war, now would enthusiastically expel from their ranks writers who had committed what Paulhan judges to be much the same crime (329; 332-37). Paulhan seems to be admonishing the members of the Céné for turning on their own, signalling that literature is in danger of adopting its own form of censorship, one which might well come back to haunt it later.

As for Morand himself, was he not in fact facing a (second) literary purge in 1958-59, before the Académie Française, a punishment carried out as in the case of Fouquet retroactively? And could one not consider *Fouquet*, published in 1961, as an admonition levelled against that body and the other writers who had spoken out against him for having violated the tradition, inaugurated three hundred years earlier during the "affaire Fouquet," of literature's support of one of their own? Indeed, such an accusation of hypocrisy echoes that of Julien Sorel before his judges at the end of *Le Rouge et le noir*, in another link to Stendhal's fictional heroes. Such a reading of the biography, while somewhat limiting the scope of appreciation of its many other aspects, does permit its ideological situation within the context of Morand's other postwar historical works. Fouquet, as handled by Morand, reflects the prototypic figure of the historical loser redeemed, first in his fictional works and now in a work of nonfiction, by Morand's practice of transcending history via highly artistic maneuvers. And, as in the other works we have considered, such a displacement of his protagonists and their historical contexts inevitably brings to bear an analogy to the events surrounding their contemporary counter-part: the Second World War in France and its aftermath. The repetition of these themes and narrative strategies in work after work takes on a quality of compulsive obsession, that of the replaying of a particular event over and over. Along this vein, one might hazard to identify Morand's description of Colbert's scheming as the "film de l'événement avant l'événement" as an apt metaphor for the majority of Morand's major postwar works as they focus on specific historical situations which, by virtue of their representation by Morand, come to stand as historical "previews" of the Occupation. Likewise, these works themselves constitute the re-staging of that period, a series of "films of the event *after* the event," exploiting all the potential for retrospective correction even as they ground themselves in a prospective era.

What judgment, then, is one to pass on *Fouquet ou le soleil offusqué*? That it is yet another installment in a series of repetitions which runs the risk of tedium, or that it represents yet another of Morand's fascinating and engaging observations of history? To separate these two possibilities amounts, in my opinion, to stripping away the true locus of interest in these works. For it is within exactly the combination of a persistent echo of 1944 and the varying "voices" of history that the true impact and originality of Morand's later work is best heard. The danger of boredom inherent in repetition is allayed by the constant movement, visible from work to work, through history. From Revolutionary France, Morand carries his story to Napoleonic Spain, to the Russian/Spanish confrontation first in California and then during the Spanish Civil War, and to the "grand siècle" of Louis XIV. To such a rich range of historical material we would add the variety of genres: novels, short-stories, plays, essays, biographies and finally autobiography. Morand's only contemporary rival in the domain of historical fiction, Jean Giono, produced similar transpositions of the Occupation into historical contexts, but with neither the breadth of perspective nor the flexibility of form displayed by Morand.[3] Morand's talent lies in creating and sustaining a viable historical past, one consonant with and expressive of the period, while at the same time permitting a detachment which renders a transhistorical experience with the present. The accomplishment of such a feat, already difficult in fiction, takes on an additional burden in Morand's nonfiction where to the constraints imposed by history is added knowledge of the actual subject's life. The stripping away of the potential for creative invention does not, however, rob the writer, in this instance the biographer (or rather, auto-biographer), of ground for imaginative construction. Indeed, textual strategies in a sense become more clearly perceptible when "fact" is clearly identifiable as such and thus "separable" from invention. As I have attempted to show, Morand's techniques of representing history in fiction differ little from his approach to the problem in *Fouquet*, indicating that beneath the changes of historical contexts and genres, there runs a deeper link, one which may be identified, to borrow Maurois' term, as a deliverance if not of himself, then of the figure of the pariah which so haunts these works. If there exists a development or evolution in this series of variations on a theme, it lies, as we noted at the beginning of this chapter, in Morand's recourse to biography during the last decade of his literary

---

[3] See in particular Jean Giono, *Le Hussard sur le toit* and *Ennemonde*, an epic story of Provence.

production. For what better way to redeem or release the historical loser than by practicing such on operation on an actual person, one such as Fouquet whose credentials for such an election are well established. At the end of *Fouquet ou le soleil offusqué*, Morand suggests that while by all appearances Colbert won the battle, in reality he lost the war:

> Mais Fouquet a sauvé sa vie profonde, laissant Colbert condamné à ramer sur la galère mondaine, avec des gants parfumés. (178)

Is it not rather more correct to say that, in this work, it is Morand who has saved Fouquet's "vie profonde" by subjecting it to the corrective forces of his artistic rendition of history? In the following chapter, I shall examine a similar procedure carried out on yet another "real" subject, this time Morand himself.

IV

POSTCARDS FROM VENICE

> Toute existence est une lettre postée anonymement; la mienne porte trois cachets: Paris, Londres, Venise; le sort m'y fixa, souvent à mon insu, mais certes pas à la légère. (8)

In all its provocative ambiguities, the initial sentence of Paul Morand's autobiographical portrait of the city of Venice, *Venises*, signals a deliberate confusion of one of the traditional suppositions governing the genre of autobiography. Morand compares every existence, every life, and thus his life, to a letter mailed anonymously, a letter sent without return address. There is, then, no indication on the envelope, nor perhaps on the letter inside, of to whom that existence belongs. In contrast to the assurance of identity characteristic of more traditional autobiographies, life, or rather the task of representing one's own, here emerges as an experience of depersonalization whose process and product forbid the attachment of a name: its author and/or subject's name.

At the same time, a deeper issue seems to be a stake. The anonymity may also refer to an unknown: existence as a letter written or sent by an unidentifiable other, by someone or something else. This reading of Morand's sentence is supported by the reference to a destiny (*le sort*) which operates without Morand's knowledge (*à mon insu*). He would thus claim to a certain innocence of or blindness to not only the workings of destiny but the purpose and meaning of his existence as well.

But Morand's letter does bear an identifying mark, three in fact, in the form of the postmarks of three cities: "la mienne porte trois cachets: Paris, Londres, Venise." Morand seems to suggest that the only name affixed, the only signature, is that of a city or cities. That the postmark might be called upon to stand in for the signature of the sender and/or author, is supported by Morand's use of the term "cachet." In the modern age, this word refers primarily to the mark affixed, either by hand or by machine, to an envelope in order to indicate the place and date of its mailing. A "cachet" also, however, denotes what may otherwise be described as a "seal," an imprint bearing the insignia (e.g. coat-of-arms) or initials of its sender. In Morand's phrase, the modern, technological practice of the postmark does the work of its ancestor, the seal: the place and time of the postmark replace the seal as the "sign" of the sender.

In Morand's book *Venises*, however, it is a question not so much of the replacement of the one by the other as of a metaphorical substitution such that an implied tautology is created, on one level, between Morand and the city. For if Morand proposes to talk about his life by revealing, in essence, selected excerpts of the letter, he does so in a work which is as much a portrait of a city as a self-portrait:

> 'C'est après la pluie qu'il faut voir Venise' répétait Whistler: c'est après la vie que je reviens m'y contempler [...]. Venise, ce n'est pas toute ma vie, mais quelques morceaux de ma vie, sans liens entre eux; les rides de l'eau s'effacent, les miennes pas. (9-10)

Then, immediately following this statement of autobiographical intent, "I return there to contemplate myself" Morand continues with a phrase belonging more to the genre of travel writing or city-portrait:

> Je reste insensible au ridicule d'écrire sur Venise à l'heure où même la primauté de Londres et de Paris n'est plus qu'un souvenir, où les centres nerveux du monde sont des lieux sauvages: Djakarta, Saigon, Katanga, Quemoy, [...]. (10)

It is fitting that Morand should choose to write about his life by writing about a city. All of his literary works, in one way or another, are about travel: voyages across space, in his earlier works, and voyages through time, in his postwar prose. He himself spent the greater part of his life traveling. Indeed, his life and works might be characterized as one long travelogue. The form of *Venises* itself reflects this itinerant tendency: "Venise, ce n'est pas toute ma vie, mais quelques morceaux de ma vie, sans lien entre eux" (10). The book is composed of a series of fragments, each bearing a notation of place and date, as if imitating entries in a travel journal.

Morand's purpose, as I shall demonstrate in this chapter, is to tell the story of his life and to attempt to identify or attach meaning to his existence in and via the city of Venice. The initial gesture of disassociation from or depersonalization of his existence opens the way for his exploitation of the postmark of the city. *Venises*, then, may be read not only as a travel journal, but more specifically as a letter, or a series of letters from Venice, autobiographical in nature, each fragment of the text bearing its own "postmark" in the form of a time and place notation. Or perhaps one should speak of post cards from Venice, depicting, on the one side, scenes from Venice and, on the other side, scenes from a life. Jacques Derrida's comment "je suis une carte postale" may, if not in its philosophical implications for Derrida's reading of Freud, at least in its structure, repeat Morand's gesture (41).

Equally, Derrida's explanation of his attraction to post cards is not without resonance to Morand's project: "Ce que j'aime dans la carte postale, c'est que même sous enveloppe, c'est fait pour circuler comme une lettre ouverte mais illisible" (16). Gregory Ulmer, in reviewing Derrida's book, speculates on what Derrida's terms, in general, mean:

> The post card and the signature (the proper name) share the character of being both readable and unreadable - the post card circulates, its message exposed to anyone who looks, but, whether because of the excess or the poverty of the message, it is meaningless (without interest) to all, even to the signer and recipient, who understand it to say no more than "I am here." (42)

Without pretending that such an explanation exhausts all possible elements of what would no doubt be labelled today a "post-card theory," the idea that one motivation for sending a post card is merely to say "I am here," that is, literally, that "I am in the place depicted on the 'front' of the post card," is highly relevant as regards Morand's text. Such a description parallels Morand's evocation of the anonymity of existence in that there is no meaning or explanation of existence except in the message (the cachet) that "I am (was) here." What Morand proposes to do in this book is to explain or describe the "I" in terms of the "here," such that the "here" provides a meaningful structure to the "I." "I am here" takes on a totalizing reflexivity and the post cards from Venice become, for Morand, as tautological as the signature.

While we have by no means exhausted the semantic possibilities of this very rich first sentence, it is time to move on, although we shall return over the course of the pages which follow to the "cachet" deployed by Morand and to his invocation of an unknown destiny, "le sort m'y fixa." In these pages, I shall center on Morand's use of Venice as a vehicle for autobiographical revelation, first commenting on the notion of a depersonalization or disengagement of not only the author but of the subject, Morand, as well. Next, I will take up the thread of *Venises* as a series of post cards or snapshots and the way in which Morand represents the city in response to his autobiographical project. Finally, I will examine the particulars of Morand's self-revelations, especially the manner in which he constructs his life story within the parameters of his city or cities of Venice as he maneuvers those revelations into a means of both construction and concealment, primarily concealment of one particular part of his life, the years between 1939 and 1951, a period entirely absent from the book and one which spans Morand's involvement with the Vichy government and his years in semi-exile in Switzerland. My conclusion will be that Morand, as he paints a picture not only of himself but of the city as well in a highly motivated attempt to pinpoint the "author" of his existence, ultimately offers a commentary on one way of looking at and writing about the past, that is, about history.

The first five paragraphs of *Venises* constitute a sort of "autobiographical pact," to borrow Lejeune's term which he uses to describe the often implicit promise made by the autobiographer to the reader concerning both the parameters of what will be revealed and the degree of congruence between the identities of the author and the hero of the book. These paragraphs do delineate Morand's intent, as we noted, to write his life in and through the city in a series of fragments arranged chronologically, although Morand does permit himself, as we shall see, a measure of chronological freedom within certain fragments. What is curious about this pact is that the relation it describes between Morand and his existence, the subject of the book, emerges as a link predicated on the lack of any such relation between Morand and the world he seeks to recollect. As we saw earlier, Morand opens the book by positing existence, or the force behind existence as anonymous: "Toute existence est une lettre postée anonymement." In the next sentence, he employs a similar metaphor of lack:

> Venise résume dans son espace contraint ma durée sur terre, située elle aussi au milieu du vide, entre les eaux fœtales et celles du Styx. (9)

This highly refined phrase, the first of its kind to exploit the physical situation of the city, demonstrates Morand's subtle technique of establishing a metaphorical relation between his life and Venice, even as it contributes to the motif of the void underlying each term. Morand binds the two together in a sweeping identification of the spatial and the temporal, reminiscent of the time/place notation of the postmark, and then launches both into a void representing life as an empty space between birth and death. The literal and figurative exploitation of the image of the waters of Venice, "les eaux foetales et celles du Styx," as both the actual waters feeding and draining the lagoon and the symbolic waters of birth and of the mythological river of Death, situates Morand's metaphor in a sort of watery limbo, neither "here" nor "there." To this displacement from, in a sense, his existence, he adds a disengagement from the world: "Je me sens décharmé de toute la planète, sauf de Venise, sauf de Saint-Marc [...]" (9). While one immediately tends to read the adjectif "décharmé" as "disillusioned," it might also be read quite literally as "released from a magical spell," and thus as released from a sort of mystical bond uniting human existence to the earth. But neither "décharmé" nor its presumed corresponding verb is to be found in any of the major dictionaries of the French language. Absent from the language, the adjective joins Morand and Venice in the "vide." And to add just one more example of such a disjunction, I would again cite

Morand's declaration of intent: "c'est après la vie que je reviens m'y [à Venise] contempler" (10). Morand, though obviously not yet dead, places his perspective outside (after) his life.

On one level, such a detachment may be seen as a necessary corollary to an approach to the autobiographical project. In this way, Morand would here set himself apart from his existence at the moment he picks up his pen in order to transfer his attention to a previous existence: that of the young Morand whose life he intends to recount. And yet, as one progresses through *Venises*, it becomes apparent that this initial gesture of disassociation from both himself and the world is not only a device of recollection but also the expression of a profound sense of alienation which not only haunts the various periods in question but also, and more importantly, characterizes his vision of himself and of his life at the moment he writes. Early in the book, Morand explicitly places himself in a position ever at odds with his century:

> Est-ce la destinée, ou est-ce ma faute: j'arrive toujours quand on éteint; dès le début c'était terminé; j'ai vu la fin du XIXe siècle; celle d'un enseignement secondaire qui durait depuis toujours (1902); celle du service d'un an (1906); la disparition de l'or (1914); j'ai vu mourir plusieurs républiques et un Etat; et deux empires expirer; sous mes yeux disparut un troupeau de renommées solides ou déraisonnables, et quelques gloires. Je suis voué à ce qui finit; ce n'est pas seulement le fait d'un grand âge, mais d'une fatalité dont je me sens le poids. Je suis veuf de l'Europe. (14)

The final phrase of this passage is perhaps the most quoted line from all Morand's works, and yet to separate it from the preceding avowal invites its partial misreading. For when Morand states that he is the widower of Europe, he points not only to his position in 1971, faced with the death of Europe as he once knew it, but to a succession of such "deaths," of lights going out in 1900, 1902, 1906, and so on. In a sense Morand has always been a "widower," confronted at every turn with his separation from a Europe he had only just begun to experience and in which he had just arrived. Hence, perhaps, Morand's notorious obsession with velocity: fast cars, fast trains, fast women and a fast-paced literary style, all of which earned him the epithet of "homme pressé" long before he created the fictional character in his 1942 novel, *L'Homme pressé*. The sensation of always lagging behind, of the imperative of catching up or of going ever faster in order to keep pace is palpable in his earlier works and, interestingly enough, remarkably absent from his postwar books.

Morand's position is here attributed not only to his age but also to a certain "fatalité" or fate, as anonymous here as in the initial sentence of the book. Morand's insistence upon the role of destiny in his life creates a sense of the arbitrary and the accidental. In addition, this passage illustrates a particular way of representing Time as a series of ruptures which successively close off certain eras, many "deaths," and, at the same time, as a force transcending those deaths, permitting Morand a bird's-eye view from which to witness a certain evolution or progression of time. We shall see how Morand's use of the city of Venice mirrors this technique as the physical structures function in much the same way as does Morand's perspective in this passage.

But, to return to my argument, the isolation of the terminal sentence constitutes only a partial misreading, for if Morand posits this essential state of being ever "out of sync" with the world as descriptive of his life's trajectory, this sense of being left behind or left out coincides even more dramatically with the sentiment not of mere solitude but of an intense alienation at the end of his life, the point from which he writes:

> Ce monde d'hier, je le regarde sans ressentiment, ni regret; simplement il n'est plus; pour moi, du moins, car il continue, sans gêne, sans embarras [...]. (170)

> Malhabile à servir, je n'ai plus rien à faire ici-bas, sinon à faire de la place. (171)

> J'ai été absent trop longtemps; chez moi se parle une langue étrangère que je n'entends plus; d'ailleurs il n'existe pas de dictionnaire. (172)

Significantly this alienation emerges as neither painful nor nostalgic but rather as a mere statement of separation. Morand experiences his existence as an absence, he quite simply does not exist in the world surrounding him. This position receives its summary formulation at the end of *Venises* when, in the closing paragraphs of the book, Morand describes himself standing before the mausoleum in Trieste where he will be interred after his death: "Là, j'irai gésir, après ce long accident que fut ma vie" (215). Morand symbolically effectuates the impossible, the description of his own death, and becomes "absent" before our very eyes. And this cemetery, toward which the entire works tends, becomes the ultimate metaphor of that life whose eventual end it has already absorbed. Morand will be buried in Trieste, in the tomb of his wife's family, because there is no room in his own: "[...] comme il n'y avait plus de place, là-bas, dans le caveau de famille où j'aurais voulu dormir, j'ai accepté l'asile que m'offrent mes cousines par alliance [...]" (214). Morand has no place in France, with his family; eternal asylum is granted in Trieste, a place itself con-demned to remain outside Europe: "[...] sorte de pendu oublié au haut de l'ogive adriatique [...]" (214). In this stunningly macabre image, Morand joins Trieste on the gallows, a forgotten "pendu" or "hanged man." His death is as solitary and as mysterious (who is the hangman?) as his existence.

This brings me back to the question of Morand's initial evocation of anonymity in the form of the letter and of the void in which existence is situated in the opening pages of *Venises*. Morand's account of his life quite appropriately, we now see, begins with the absence of a correlation between his self and his existence because that (absence) constitutes that which the entire work will describe and explain: his experience of alienation at the end of his life and at the end of the book. Thus, on the one hand, Morand's "absence" runs as a thematic thread throughout the book. But, we would also recall that Morand's proclaimed intent in these pages is indeed not to "tell" his whole life, but only those parts relating to Venice: "absence" constitutes his method as well, figured by the fragmentary structure of the book in which the blank spaces reflect this partial and sporadic intent. From time to time throughout *Venises* there appear reminders of this restriction, particularly at points where Morand quite consciously violates this intention:

> Raconter le Paris d'alors n'est pas mon propos; il ne s'agit ici que d'un tête-à-tête avec Venise, ces pages n'ayant d'autre mouvement que celui de la vie sur ses flots. (90)

> Venise n'est que le fil d'un discours interrompu par de longs silences, où de temps à l'autre, divers pays l'emportent, comme ils m'ont emporté [...]. (105)

Such statements, which one might term reaffirmations of Morand's autobiographical pact, come at junctures where Morand does indeed "raconter Paris" and does focus on the moments which "fill in" the interrupted conversation with Venice. They function to pull the narrative back into alignment by redirecting attention back to the city just as it threatens to swerve off (and indeed does) into forbidden territory. By constantly resituating *Venises* within the confines of Venice, Morand assures that certain holes or "vides" remain intact as his autobiography is reabsorbed into the city. Thus a literal notion of absence, here absence from Venice, serves a structural purpose and, as we shall see, one particular absence from Venice during and after World War II, a period itself absent from *Venises*, will furnish a link between the thematic and structural functions of the notion of alienation.

In much the same way, Morand plays upon the notion of plurality signalled by the title of the book as a means of assuring, paradoxically, both the presence of the autobiographical subject/city and the possibility of selected "absences." Plurality, in *Venises*, exists on many levels: the book is not only a city-portrait but a self-portrait as well; Venice is not one city but many, as seen across time; Morand is likewise presented as a series of Morands depicted in various "Venices"; the Venice of *Venises* is not only that seen by Morand but by his predecessors as well; and finally, the fragmented form of the book illustrates the effect of multiplicity. Such an insistence on what might be seen as a surplus of affirmation also works as a negation as it effectively provides Morand with a means of avoiding a singularization of his own life. Morand's play on his literal absence from the city mirrors the figurative absence of the force behind his existence. What appears to be a strategy of reproducing the incertitude of his destiny in the form and style of *Venises*, a strategy aiming at a reconstruction or an attempt to understand the why, if not the who, may ultimately be used as a means to further mystify. The terms of the autobiographical "pact," both plural and partial, promise an abundance and deny totality at the same time. Much of this effect depends upon Morand's exploitation of the figure of Venice. Let us now turn to the city and its role both as itself an "empty" space and as a means of assuring presence to the autobiographical subject as it constructs the post card effect of "I *am* here."

In his 1980 book, *Miroirs d'encre*, Michel Beaujour makes the following observation a propos of Vuillemin's *Le Miroir de Venise*:

> Jules Vuillemin prend pour *fonds* de son "essai" la ville de Venise dont le nom seul (peut-être parce qu'il nous parvient à travers les évocations de Ruskin, de D'Annunzio, de Barrès, de Proust ou de Mann) suffit à susciter chez le lecteur l'attente d'une richesse inépuisable liée à une poignante mélancolie, comme d'une île Saint-Pierre humanisée, civilisée, susceptible de fournir à un homme d'Occident épargné par la radicale misanthropie de Rousseau l'exact miroir où déchiffrer son image engendrée par l'histoire et vouée à l'engloutissement. (162)

Like the isle of Saint-Pierre, the site of Rousseau's *Fifth Promenade*, a site which, as Beaujour points out elsewhere, represents a public domain insofar as it is a landscape accessible to all rather than a private site to which access is limited to the writer's own personal recollections, Venice evokes universal recognition due not only to its own history but to literary history as well. Morand recognizes this debt as a sort of ceremonial duty:

> Les canaux de Venise sont noirs comme l'encre, c'est l'encre de Jean-Jacques, de Chateaubriand, de Barrès, de Proust; y tremper sa plume est plus qu'un devoir de français, un devoir tout court. (33)

The erotic overtones of Morand's act do not escape Beaujour, whose sole reference to *Venises* is a citation of this passage as example of the erotisation of Venice (160). It seems appparent that Beaujour's title, in some respects, plays on Morand's image of the inky waters of Venice, for what does the writer see as he bends over the canals but both the image of himself and the reflections of the city and those writers who before him had responded to a similar sense of "duty"? Thus Venice, as represented by its canals, serves as a generative mirror, one which provides its observer with a historical source in which to situate and there construct his own image. Morand certainly avails himself of this "inexhaustible richness" as Venice emerges across his life in what Beaujour terms the "fonction génératrice de la topologie," engendering the image of Morand via the artistic, literary and above all, as we shall see, structural aspects of the history of the city (146).

But if Venice provides a plenitude of mirrors and is itself a mirror for Morand, on another level, the mirror seems curiously empty. Perhaps the most striking feature of Morand's Venice is that it appears strangely uninhabited. Morand refers to many people in Venice, but practically none are Venitian. There are no descriptions of life in Venice amongst its own people; in fact, the only natives evoked are the gondoliers, and then only as part and parcel of an institution as physical as the Grand Canal itself. Many of his images of Venice present a vacant city: "La ruelle était deserte" (34); "l'image d'une Venise presque déserte, où, cachés dans l'angle des campi, quelques rares marques donnent l'échelle" (49); and: "Trois heures du matin. A cette heure-ci, Venise est un Guardi, sans personnages. Plus de funiculi..." (140). No "funiculi," no cordons of life: a city detached from the living, such is Morand's Venice. This is not to say that no one inhabits the city, but those who do are dead, appearing only in the form of statues, tombs and inscriptions. In the single crowd scene described, a masked ball, one slowly comes to realize that those present represent the "dead"; the parade of costumed figures is nothing more than a "défilé des morts," a procession of figures from the past: Marco Polo, Catherine II, Louis XIV, etc. (163-64). Indeed, this scene doubly emphasizes the title of the section in which this fragment is situated: "Morte in Maschera" or "Masked Death," for not only have the historical figures passed from the realm of the living but the people behind the masks as well. Morand emphasizes their "deadness" by interjecting: "elle n'est plus"; "morts tous deux"; "dort maintenant dans la paix du cimetière"; "à jamais éteints."

Morand empties the city of beings so as to repopulate it, not only with Venetian ghosts, but with his own phantoms as well. Many pages are devoted to the description of foreigners: literary tourists and expatriates alike, many of whom came to Venice long before Morand. Nearly every description or observation of Venice is doubled by a reference, either via direct citation or allusion, to another, previous observer of the city. Among others, Morand cites Montaigne, Rousseau, Ruskin, Byron, Goethe, Balzac, Stendhal, Browning, Taine, Gautier, Proust, Barrès, Corvo and D.H. Lawrence. The effect is the overwhelming impression that one has before one's eyes not only Morand's Venice, but all the Venices of literary history. Morand is acutely aware of the tradition of writing about Venice and his knowledge of the literature of Venice is striking: he goes so far as to quote the earliest known description of Venice in the French language by the abbé Commynes. One function of these cameo appearances is obviously to confer authority to Morand's portrait of the city, much as his use of Goya in *Le Flagellant de Séville* served to validate his new role of observer of history.

Such references function in yet another way, as a means of situating Morand's life through identification with past writers. Morand's use of his predecessors' voices often emerges in illustrative comparisons:

> Bagués et roucoulants comme les pigeons de Saint-Marc passaient les pédérastes; Venise, "cité contre nature" (Chateaubriand), les avait toujours accueillis; [...]. (39)

> Les cyprès ont grandi, roussi au vent de mer, les Frères melchites, "couleur barbe de météores" (Byron), ont blanchi; [...].(120)

> Enserré dans les *rii* de Venise comme un signet entre les pages; certaines rues si étroites que Browning se plaignait de n'y pouvoir ouvrir son parapluie. (133)

Chateaubriand, Byron and Browning are here quoted as illustrations of Morand's Venice, as though Morand adds to his own vision by layering onto it other Venices or, more precisely, by situating it in relation to the others. The third passage, revelatory not only of the relationship of the book as a whole to Venice, but also of this "layering," presents the observer "pressed in the streets of Venice like a bookmark between the pages." Morand, is likewise pressed between his own pages, those of *Venises*, just as Venice hems in or contains both his life and this book. The reference to Browning and his umbrella expands this metaphor by introducing another Venice: that of the English poet. Thus Morand would be within not only his book, but pressed between the pages of the larger book comprised of all visions, literary and other, of the city as well.

At the same time, a direct link is established between Morand and the earlier writer as he positions himself in his place, a maneuver made possible by their purely spatial coincidence. He observes the same "scene" as did the past figure:

> Goethe, Taine ont, d'ici même, décrit ce survol; ils ont vu ces tables du café Quadri posées devant les Procuraties comme des dominos. (179)

The coincidence of site functions as a structure which superimposes two different times on a single point. Michael Riffaterre, commenting on Chateaubriand's use of monuments, argues that: "Chronological impossibility and artificiality as far as taste and esthetics are concerned are non-existant on the plane established by the monument" (131). Similarly, the context of Morand's comparisons is natural: the remembering, inspired by a site, of a quote, or an image; its effect is, in reality, highly artificial as it collapses temporal distance.

Furthermore, this remembrance, this pointing backward, resembles Chateaubriand's monuments as described by Riffaterre, in yet another way. Riffaterre opposes the affective memory (that Proust expands upon) in Chateaubriand to the latter's evocation of memory founded upon a monument. Affective memory, he argues, effectuates a disappearence of the present as it is absorbed into a total immersion in the past:

> A present-day detail evokes its earlier analogue, which destroys it and takes its place [...]. This echoing of repetition of analogous elements from the present to the past then summons up the unique experience in the past. (139)

Such a form of memory only serves to further isolate the individual, as it is unavailable or unintelligible to anyone else. Monumental memory, however:

> [...] is a memory shared by all mankind [...]. It enables anyone who contemplates it to find his counterpart, contemplating the same monument, and to find in his counterpart similarities to himself. These form a basis for an affinity and put an end to solitude. (131)

This affinity, it must be added, is also an affinity between the past and present. The present remains intact, as a crucial component of the memory. This is definitely the case in Morand's citations or rememorations of his predecessors whose past observations are invariably coupled with a specific observation made by Morand in the present. If Goethe and Taine observed the same tables in front of the Café Quadri, it is Morand who supplies the image of the dominos in the above citation.

Perhaps even more illustrative of this technique is the following observation in which Morand merely enumerates his predecessors:

> Le Burchiello était jadis le seul moyen de transport, celui de Montaigne, du Président De Brosses, de Goethe, de Casanova. (106)

This boat, the "Burchiello," which for centuries has carried passengers from Padua to Venice, is at once one vessel and five: the four employed respectively by Montaigne, the Président De Brosses, Goethe and Casanova, and the one observed now by Morand: "[...] (le) Burchiello d'aujourd'hui, qui n'a plus rien de commun avec son ancêtre ('le petit-fils du Bucentaure' disait De Brosses)" (107). Whether or not it is a question of the same boat is irrelevant. Each "saw" a different boat and yet in Morand's evocation all collapse, as it were, into one multi-layered image. This image gives expression to a certain tension between Morand's invitation, on the one hand, to read history "across" the centuries and, on the other, to consolidate specific moments in a collapse of temporal distance made feasible by a spatial coincidence, in what resembles, borrowing Benjamin's expression, a constellation, here comprised of five "stars." Let us now examine the manner in which this technique of consolidating the past and the present, here in the form of literary references which bolster Morand's feeble sense of his present existence, functions in much the same way in Morand's exploitation of the city of Venice.

From the beginning, Morand describes his relationship to Venice in uniquely spatial terms:

> Venise jalonne mes jours comme les espars à tête goudronnée balisent sa lagune; ce n'est, parmi d'autres, qu'un point de perspective; [...]. (10)

Venice delimits his life, just as the buoys of the lagoon mark its channels and indicate the limits of its passageways. A limited perspective, certainly, but one which lends a spatial dimension to his life. Venice proves to be the perfect place to situate a life, to give physical dimension to the temporal. This is nowhere more evident than in a passage quoted above: "Venise résume dans son espace contraint ma durée sur terre [...]" (9). And Venice is the perfect city in which to tell a life, situated itself between "les eaux fœtales et celles du Styx," between birth and death. Even the physical structures of the city contain within their architecture an allegory of life:

> Une vie ressemble souvent à ces palais du Grand Canal, commencés en bas par un appareil de pierres orgueilleusement taillées en pointes de diamant, leurs étages supérieurs hâtivement achevés en boue séchée. (132)

One sees here a concrete image of the collapse of temporal distance earlier observed in relation to Morand's evocations of his literary predecessors. Duration cristallizes around a site as the palaces serve as a metaphor for life in its various stages. The physical structure emerges as a point of anchorage as it demonstrates a physical exteriorisation of existence, a sort of skeleton which serves as an organizing principle for what is, from Morand's perspective, unorganized. This, I would argue, is the principal function of the city in this book: a means of giving shape and, by extension, coherence to Morand's life.

Morand very subtly inserts himself into the city, or rather inserts a certain image of his self:

> A Venise, je pense ma vie mieux qu'ailleurs; tant pis si je montre le nez dans un coin du tableau, comme Véronèse dans *La Maison de Lévi*. (33)

Morand "paints" himself into the city as a figure in the scene, as an observer of the scene, and, like Veronese, as its creator. If "toute existence est une lettre postée anonymement," Venice itself is not only the postmark, indicating origin, but also the envelope, the container, while Morand's life is the "contained," to borrow terms used by Beaujour to describe ideal mnemonic spaces (Beaujour, 149). Much the same image recurs later in the book, this time with an interesting twist:

> De même qu'en 1917, j'avais vu Venise enfoncer son coin d'ombre dans ma vie exilée [...]. (170)

Here it is Venice which inserts itself into Morand's life, as if into a painting of the latter, becoming in turn that which is contained or represented. If Morand is a witness and a figure in the tableau of Venice, the reverse is equally true. As much as Morand "tells" Venice, the city "tells" Morand:

> Je veux en avoir le cœur net; surmontant mon peu de goût pour moi-même, j'ai donc pris Venise comme confidente; elle répondra à ma place. (33)

Venice emerges as a sort of surrogate charged with the task of speaking for Morand, of telling the story he himself cannot and will not recount. The two *Venises*, the city portrait and the autobiography, thus emerge as two sides of the same coin, or rather, of the same post card. By "writing" Venice Morand simultaneously writes himself, as he is in turn written by the city, each supplying both the image and its reflexive narration, thereby situating the temporal within the spatial and vice versa. At the same time, Venice functions not only as a mouthpiece but as a reflective other, one which lends its structure and comprehensibility to Morand's existence.

As noted above, Morand places a great deal of emphasis on the physicality of the city, evoking its physical structures as metaphors of the life process. In this way, these edifices function as a means of providing a concrete spatial dimension to duration, which often has the effect of collapsing temporal distances within that duration. This technique also emerges in the manner in which Morand invokes particular sites as grounding points which testify to the passage of time. One such structure is the train station in Venice:

> La gare de Venise à jamais est restée pour moi une entrée triomphale; celle d'alors n'était pas celle d'aujourd'hui [...]. L'ancêtre, c'étaient trois arcades verdies d'humidité, culottées par la fumée de charbon. Ce qui n'a pas changé, c'est la coupole de bronze vert de San Simeone Piccolo; les bombes de deux guerres, visant la voie ferrée, l'ont épargnée. (33)

The two structures in this passage, the station and the neighboring church's cupola, attest in their juxtaposition to the passage of time. The station, seen in its "original" state (1908) and simultaneously in its contemporary form (1971), reflects time's mutations, while the bronze dome of the church stands as a sort of unchanging observer or eternal witness to such changes. These two structures are also used to mark Morand's own story. The above passage is situated in a fragment dated 1908, roughly Morand's first encounter with Venice. In a 1918 fragment, both landmarks reappear in an entirely different context, marking another important visit to Venice immediately after the first World War:

> La vieille gare de Venise se débarbouillait aux éclairs projetés par les torpilleurs franco-anglais qui surveillaient l'Adriatique [...]. M'est restée présente l'irréalité de cette nuit d'automne, où le dôme de San Simeone Piccolo - toujours lui - surgissait, avant de repiquer une tête dans le Grand Canal. (75)

The station, illuminated by the search lights of the torpedo boats, again provides an indication of the era while the church dome remains temporally fixed: "toujours lui." Thus, over the course of the book, Morand presents basically three "scenes" of the station: 1908, 1918 and 1971 (by reference to the contemporary edifice), all linked by the presence of the unchanging church dome functioning as a static point of reference against which temporality may be both perceived and arrested.

A more pronounced instance of this illustration of temporality occurs later in the book in a fragment dated 1908-1970, qualified by the notation: "Les trois âges de l'homme." Morand again takes as his point of perspective a physical structure, the Procuraties, more precisely the arcaded buildings which line two sides of the Piazza San Marco: the Procuratie Veccie to the north, and the Procuratie Nuove to the south:

> Que d'années, de mondes, de modes, de fois, d'espoirs, j'aurai vu passer sous ces Procuraties, parmi ces promeneurs de l'après-dîner [...]. (182)

Morand then proceeds to elaborate on just what he has seen paraded beneath the arcades: namely change, over time, curiously symbolised by modifications in military uniforms. Morand treats the reader to a sort of fashion retrospective unfolding on the Piazza: from the uniforms of the Triple Alliance (1913), to those of World War I and the twenties, next remarking the passage from "le style mussolinien" from around 1935 to the "étoffe hitlérienne" and then noting, "pour suivre l'Histoire en courant," the American influence of the Liberation culminating in today's version of the "relaxed" soldier. Aside from the comic relief of this inventory of the history of military taste, the entire passage demonstrates the technique earlier seen with regard to the train station/church dome. A particular physical or spatial site functions to illustrate, via its own fixity, temporal change. The Procuraties work, much as does the cupola of San Simeone Piccolo, to illustrate time by providing a fixed focal point before which time itself is paraded, a procedure recalling the photographic practice of documenting a particular locale over a period of time. Certain central landmarks remain unchanged even as the surrounding decor, from clothing styles to modes of transportation, serves to situate each image in a particular era. The superimposition of the individual images reveals a tension between the repetition of the static figure(s) and the difference perceived in the temporal mutations of its surroundings. This "photographic" method, as practiced by Morand, produces a series of "Venices" clustered around a single site, a sort of constellation formed by the freezing of time in space. This technique echoes that illustrated by the passage in which Morand evokes his life as a series of lights going out (14). In that passage, we would recall, there is a simultaneous evocation of destruction (death) and of preservation (remembrance). Like Chateaubriand's monuments, which represent both death and victory over death, the Procuraties, as well as the other structures of Venice, recall both the absence of the past and its presence (Riffaterre, 131).

Morand underscores the centrality of this technique in concluding his "fashion show" by situating it in relation to his enterprise as a whole:

> J'arrête ce défilé des fantômes de la place Saint-Marc, n'étant ni Carpaccio; ni Saint-Simon qui cependant écrivait: "Ces bagatelles échappent presque toujours aux *Mémoires*; elles donnent cependant l'idée juste de tout ce que l'on y recherche." (183)

Saint-Simon's phrase, appropriated even as Morand protests that he does not fit into the category represented by the memorialist, provides a justification, even an explanation, not only of this passage in particular but of the book as a whole. Morand seems intent upon seizing these "bagatelles," these seemingly unimportant details, which, as Saint-Simon declares, escape from his own work and which nevertheless represent the true essence of the memorialist's endeavor. Morand, in a passage filled with such trivialities, signals his desire to continue where Saint-Simon left off by constructing his book in and around those very observations which, although seemingly random, translate his true intent. But, following the strand of my argument concerning the emphasis placed upon the architecture of Venice and the use to which it is put, Morand's "bagatelles" are neither random nor unimportant as they consistently point to an attempt to spatially depict duration even as the passage of time is itself emphasized.

The other reference in this passage, to the fifteenth-century Venetian painter Carpaccio, proves equally revelatory. By his own account, Morand is no Carpaccio, but perhaps, I would suggest, he is a Veronese. One recalls Morand's earlier reference to this painter, often considered a less gifted descendant of Carpaccio, and to his painting *Feast in the House of Levi* which Morand cites as an illustration of his own relationship to Venice: as Veronese painted himself into his painting, so Morand inserts himself into his depiction of Venice. Now, Morand having borrowed one painterly device from this artist, a brief examination of two other, far subtler techniques which link Morand to Veronese may not be without interest as regards the Procuraties passage in particular. Discussing the theatrical structures of Veronese's art, David Rosand comments:

> Time is indeed another coordinate in the complex structure of Veronese's art, functioning in two ways: as historical reference and as narrative sequence. One of his major means for establishing the parameters of historical reference is costume; variations in fashion are juxtaposed to create a series of temporal allusions ranging over wide stretches of geography as well as chronology [...]. (167)

This method of creating a montage of period costumes, and we would note the presence of military dress in *Feast in the House of Levi*, coincides with Morand's parade of such "fashion" beneath the Procuraties in which, à la Veronese, a range of temporal allusions coexists, creating a network of historical reference within the same space. One might immediately object that whereas Veronese constructs a simultaneous juxtaposition, Morand presents a succession of historical moments. However, Morand assures a significant degree of immediacy by situating his parade of fashion within a unified site: the arches of the Procuraties. Interestingly enough, this "site" proves to be quite similar to that employed by Veronese. *Feast in the House of Levi* is dominated by three arches which divide the painting into three distinct scenes with the figure of Christ, in accordance with the traditional form of the triptych, dominating the central tableau. The action of the painting unfolds under these arches, much as Morand's retrospective passes beneath the arcades of the Procuraties. Veronese's use of such forms in general serves, according to Rosand, a very specific function: "The tripartite structure of compositions like the so-called *Feast in the House of Levi* offers an architectural means of isolating moments in the reading of the picture" (162). Now, while Rosand develops his argument to include the notion of narrative, and thus temporal, sequencing in reference to later works such as *Supper at Emmaus* and the *Rape of Europa*, he does not comment on such a sequencing device in *Feast in the House of Levi*. While the former paintings do present a clear narrative chronology, the latter seems to imitate the fixed structure of the religious triptych where the perspectives of the two outside panels focus upon the center panel. This would be true, were it not for the figure of the artist himself, situated in front of the pillar supporting and separating the first and second arches. Veronese is here depicted in a peculiar stance, turned toward the left, arm raised beckoning to an invisible figure in the "wings," to borrow from Rosand's theatrical vocabulary. Given the natural movement of the (Western) eye from left to right, Veronese's gesture to a figure outside the painting, that is, to the spectator, would be interpreted as an invitation to "read" the painting as a narrative sequence rather than as a traditional iconographic act of self-reflection. In this way, the arches would function to provide a structure for the narrative of the painting. Veronese's painting creates a tension between these seemingly contradictory ways of "reading" its compositional struction: as a static fixed form (a triptych) and as a narrative both spatial and temporal in its dimensions. To relate idea of tension back to *Venises*, the arches of Procuraties similarly furnish a narrative space in which the passage of time, represented by Morand's retrospective of military fashion, may be depicted while the spatial coincidence (the Procuraties) collapses the intervals. Indeed this technique is characteristic of Morand's overall use of the physical structures of Venice which serve as a compositional device for ordering the narration of Morand's life. Morand subtly invites the reader to follow, across the various manifestations of Venice, the progression not only of history but of the autobiography as well, to "read" the series of post cards from Venice which, when superimposed, constitute the image of his life. This tension mirrors that of the structure of the book as well, which displays both narrative (continuous) and fragmented forms. In addition, the presence of Veronese in his painting as both a figure and its creator, mirrors Morand's position in his own "canvas" representing the Procuraties and, on a larger scale, that of his relationship to Venice.

He stands as witness, much as the physical structures themselves provide testimony. It should be noted that this fragment occurs late in the book at a point where Morand himself becomes a sort of physical monument, one as representative of the past as the Colleone, a tranformation to which we shall return. Let us now turn to the more purely autobiographical element of *Venises* as it both invokes the city as a structure of meaning and reproduces the tension created by Morand's manipulation of temporal duration.

Morand divides the book into four parts, each representing a period of his life: "Le Palais des Anciens" - adolescence; "Le Pavillon de quarantaine" - maturity; "Morte in maschera" - old age; and "Il est plus facile de commencer que de finir" - death. After the initial evocation of Venice as the guiding principle of the account of the life which follows, Morand declares: "A Venise, ma minime personne a pris sa première leçon de planète, au sortir de classes où elle n'avait rien appris" (10). Venice, then, is to be the site of the young (minimal) Morand's "education." But he has not yet gone to Venice, nor does he here reveal the nature of the lesson eventually learned. Instead, after creating a rather Proustian horizon of expectation, he retreats to just that schooling which taught him nothing, enumerating the failures of the traditional system to provide him with an adequate basis for the formation of his self:

> Les auteurs classiques ne me parlaient pas... Commencer la vie par Bérénice! Aimer Bérénice à treize ans? (11)

> La philosophie de ma jeunesse n'était que l'annexe d'un triste hôpital psychiatrique; la géographie ne m'offrait qu'un catalogue de golfes et d'îles, un inventaire de cimes et de fleuves... quant à l'Histoire, ses cassures artificielles, ses fameux "tournants" [...]. (12)

One quickly gets the picture. This lack of "relevance" perceived between the subject studied and the reality of the minimal Morand, attenuated by the long list which follows of the "omissions," from prehistory to Hugo and astronomy, resulted in a general lack of curiosity: "Je n'avais faim de rien" (13).

To this apathy, Morand adds what he terms a "pessimisme originel," fostered by the books of the family library: "le Renan d'après la défaite, Schopenhauer, Zola, Maupassant, Huysmans, leurs grincements de dents, leur rire noir" (13). Indeed, Morand attributes much of this pessimism to his family and to his father in particular who repeated to the young Morand: "Souviens-toi de te méfier" and "Tes amis peuvent être un jour tes ennemis."

Interestingly, it is the father who plays the larger familial role in the book. Morand devotes only one paragraph to his mother in a sympathetic portrait which describes her as so tied to his father, so lacking in her own identity and so "perfect" as to furnish no extraordinary example of maternity when compared with "la mère d'un Proust ou celle c'un Gide" (15). It is his father, rather, with whom he most identifies:

> L'aimais-je, ou moi en lui? Je n'arrive pas, même aujourd'hui, à faire le départ. Tout enfant, j'avais le sentiment que mon existence dépendait de lui, que, s'il disparaissait, la maison s'écroulerait. (14)

All indications point to what one might obviously term an early and successful resolution of the Oedipal complex: identification with the father, acceptance of his authority, surrender of the mother.

Morand's identification with his father and through him with the family, at once pleases and frustrates: "Je ne connaissais pas encore mon temps; ce que je vivais, c'était le temps des miens, l'air que je respirais, c'était leur air" (20). This time, and this "air," which constitute the young Morand's only world, are preeminently those of the past, or rather, of a certain attitude toward that past:

> Les Anciens, on leur devait tout, sans jamais les égaler; on leur devait, d'abord, reconnaissance: j'avais toujours vu mon père éviter de marcher sur le tapis persan de l'atelier par respect pour un objet de haute époque. (20)

This familiarity with the past, translated as a duty of respectful recognition, at the same time contains its own interdiction forbidding any prospect of a relation other than one of veneration. The effect of this fetichism of the past on Morand's early years is clearly delimited when, in what is perhaps the central image of this section, Morand describes his youth in the first of many metaphors drawn from the physical structures of Italy:

> Il existe à Padoue, un très vieux palais, datant de 1252, qu'on appelle encore le *Palazzo degli Anziani*: c'est l'image même de mon adolescence; je vivais hier; j'habitais au milieu d'hommes d'autrefois; j'en étais même arrivé à ne plus regarder le monde qu'à travers les Ancêtres. (19)

This palace, from which this section takes its title, haunts the entire first part of *Venises* and figures the way in which the past, experienced as an immersion, functions both as a way of living and a way of seeing or knowing in the present. Morand's milieu, his family and their way of living, epitomize this sense of existing in the past: the ritual dinners at his grandmother's house; his father's "mercredis d'hiver" à la Mallarmé; the parade of late nineteenth-century musicians, artists and writers. This sense of seeing the world through the lens of the "Ancients" persists throughout Morand's acount of his youth, ever deferring the "education" of Venice anticipated by the opening citation.

There are moments which hint at or initially promise to serve as the sort of epiphany projected early in the book. At Caux in 1906, high above the Rhone, the young Morand seems to undergo a certain transformation:

> Je n'ai plus jamais oublié cette brusque entrée dans l'universel. Jamais je n'avais existé autant [...]. Bien plus tard, je devais comprendre mon émerveillement devant ces cimes vierges; grâce à elles, je m'évadais d'une prison; mais de quelle prison? (24)

This "liberation" from, as Morand next explains, the "dark Paris of Zola" of his upbringing, promises to release him from the influence of the past and to allow him to experience his world: "Je me trouvais soudain au centre de moi-même" (25). But if he declares his freedom, the language used to describe the panorama which so liberates and indeed the manner in which he expresses this revelation, ultimately reveal the extent to which he continues to regard the world through "the eyes of the Ancients." Take, for example, the image of the morning:

> Ce matin-là, tout avait gelé [...] les cygnes qui s'étaient endormis se réveillaient les palmes prises dans la glace [...] une sorte d'été blanc, dont la stérilité insultait à l'autre été tout agité de rivières et de moissons. (24)

He transforms the scene into a Mallarméan winter, complete with swans, their wings frozen in the ice, and a white sterility. His exclamations of plenitude, in the former citation, of the sentiment of existence and of entry into the universal echo those of Julien Sorel in the "gorge" scene from *Le Rouge et le noir*, as much as the notions of evasion and of prison recalls another Stendhalian hero, Fabrice del Dongo.

Along the same line, his long-awaited descent into Italy, stopping in Lombardy before going to Venice, is marked by his stop in the forest of Tremezzina, among the chestnut trees:

> Je n'ai jamais oublié l'odeur de cette châtaigneraie de la Tremezzina, de cette même forêt que traversait Fabrice en route pour Waterloo [...] châtaigniers comme ceux que *La Nouvelle Héloïse* situe à Clarens. (30)

Even as he approaches Venice and intimates transformation, Morand employs images which maintain the young Morand squarely within the "Palais des Anciens."

Perhaps one of the most interesting characteristics of this first part is the curious reversal of the search for origins common to many autobiographies. Particularly in the case of autobiographers whose origins are uncertain, one thinks especially of Mary McCarthy and Sartre, such a quest often dominates life-histories. In the case of Morand, there seems to be no such lack; indeed, one might speak of an overabundance of origins:

> Une tradition d'origine très lointaine assurait à toute chose, à moi-même, une place prédestinée. J'entrais dans la vie pour toucher mon dû: Titien, Véronèse n'avaient peint que pour se faire admirer de moi, ils m'attendaient; l'Italie se préparait depuis des siècles à ma visite. (27)

Aside from the obvious irony of this passage, the sentiment of already always belonging assures the young Morand of a fixed point of departure. This "surplus" of ancestry condenses into a single origin: the past, which continues to determine Morand's early self as he becomes successively the observer of a Mallarmean scene, a Julien Sorel, and a Fabrice. The much expected departure for Venice produces no change in Morand's immersion in the past. The factories of the new industrial Italy hold no interest: "Je vivais le dos tourné à l'avenir; l'avenir pouvait-il être autre chose qu'un passé immanent?" (31). Nor does his first stay in Venice itself redirect his interest: Morand's "first" Venice, "1908 Venise dans le rétroviseur," is above all the Venice of the past. His wanderings in the city emerge as nothing so much as a series of promenades through the pages of his predecessors. The constant "parade" on the Grand Canal is "'ce registre de la noblesse vénitienne', comme dit Théophile Gautier" (34); the less respectable neighborhoods provoke references to Balzac, Jean-Jacques, and le Président de Brosses (36-37); "c'était encore l'Italie du jeune Beyle" (37); the pederasts and homosexuals are seen through the lens of Chateaubriand and Proust. The extensive use of citation throughout this section mirrors this process of filtration through the Past. At this point, the young Morand's future, his destiny, does not appear at all arbitrary or accidental, nor is the "sender" of his existence anonymous but rather plural. The abundance of origins is itself cast in the role of fate: Morand's destiny is determined, set into motion by the Past. His youthful rebellion may be no more than an adolescent revolt against a perceived determinism, a possibility we shall further explore later.

The familial milieu in Venice differs little from that of Paris. The "Français de Venise," as Morand describes his father's guests, are reunited in their taste for the past: "Pour nos convives, le passé, c'était le présent" (44), and "Nos amis ainsi remontaient vers le passé, vers plus d'oxygène, comme la truite saute les barrages, vers l'amont" (44). But this circle, indeed the whole of Europe represented in Venice, totters on the edge of becoming itself part of the past which they so admire. Increasingly the tone of this section marks a watershed and projects forward to the great change which lies ahead:

> Entre les cafés Quadri et Florian toute une société européenne vivait à Venise ses heures dernières. Et pas seulement des Français, François-Joseph, le vieil arbre de la forêt, allait tout ensevelir dans sa chute. Les seigneurs autrichiens [...] l'Angleterre [...] l'Allemagne bismarkienne [...] l'Italie [...] les Balkans. (47)

The effects of the First World War on Morand are neatly summed up at the beginning of the second chapter in the initial fragment dated "Début 1918": "Le Palais des Anciens menaçait ruine" (75). Quite appropriately, this fragment recounts Morand's stop in the train station at Venice after a diplomatic visit. This station, we earlier observed, functions as a spatial and temporal marker, here reappearing in the context of his first visit to Venice after the war. Morand only hints at his role of non-combatant and of the ravages of the war, Venice itself "tells" the story:

> A Venise, à travers la coupole percée de Santa Maria, on apercevait le ciel bleu; l'Arsenal avait été touché, le Palais des Doges crevassé, Saint-Marc était étouffé sous cinq mètres de sacs de sable retenus par des madriers et des filets d'acier; disparus les chevaux de Quadrige! Roulés les Titiens; canaux sans gondoles, les pigeons, mangés. (80-81)

The damage to the physical city, that is, to the edifice of the "Palais des Anciens" corresponds clearly, in this passage, to the ruin of all that the palace metaphorically evokes: the milieu which immersed the young Morand before the war. Much of this fragment is devoted to Morand's observations of the political and moral ruin of the "old guard": "Une année à Paris venait de faire de moi le témoin stupéfait de la faillibilité des dirigeants [...]. Chaque jour les vieilles générations perdaient de leur prestige" (76). He details the compromise of one "grand Français" after another: Briand, Ribot, Berthelot, Poincaré, Clemenceau, and describes the corruption and fatal indecision of the makers of policy, and the schisms of opinion observed even among family members, citing the rivalry of the Daudet brothers, Léon and Lucien. The war wreaked more than physical damage, it signalled the end of one era and the start of another: "Un âge d'or finissait; un autre se levait, ourlé de noir" (80). Morand specifies the moment when, for him, the remains of the golden age began to tarnish:

> Je notais, à ce moment, aux dernières pages de mon *Journal*, à la veille de partir pour Rome, l'impression que la guerre, au tournant de 1917-18, faisait

soudainement sur moi: "Cela a une autre odeur, c'est une conjuration luciférienne." L'Europe commençait à sentir. (78)

The title of this section, "Le Pavillon de quarantaine," a reference to the signal flag flown by ships to warn of contagious illness on board, reflects this sentiment of infection, degradation and contamination.[1]

But if this period is described as one of putrefaction, corruption and ruin, it also signalled, for Morand and his generation, a liberation not entirely understood and a bit daunting in its expectations: "'Cette honteuse période de 1914-1918', osait écrire Larbaud [...] nous apparaissait, dès 1917, comme une obscure libération" (76). Morand seems finally to have found his liberty, not within himself, but within the era, one characterized by its radical distance from the past: "ce miracle, renouvelé de 1798, de n'avoir personne devant nous; père et grand-pères avaient décampé, se faisaient oublier; tout était vide, béant, offert" (91). Morand escapes the "Palais des Anciens," but not without a certain pang: "Je me désolidarisais des anciens, à partir de 1917, sans cesser d'accepter l'héritage; le déchirement de l'affranchi" (86). After this rather ambigious declaration of independence, the succeeding fragments focus on the phenomenon of the postwar avant-garde: Picasso, Massine, les "Six," Max Jacob, Radiguet, etc. Morand's place among these figures appears to him as a rather fortuitous accident:

> Comment me trouvai-je précipité du séjour chez les Anciens dans les rangs avancés, comment une jeunesse de stylite m'avait-elle placé dans l'avant-garde? Je me le demande encore. Etait-ce la vague des générations qui m'élevait dans son flux? (92)

Rather than a direct result of his disengagement from the "Anciens," this privileged place in the ranks of the avant-garde is depicted as accident. False modesty? Or perhaps symptomatic of Morand's practice of describing his involvement in art as in politics, as an accident, much as his literary protagonists of the postwar (WWII) period experience similar strokes of fate. The invocation of destiny made in the first sentence of the book: "le sort m'y fixa, souvent à mon insu," may well refer not only to Morand's presence in Venice but to his role in history as well.

Morand's youthful revolt against the destiny represented by the Past, manifested, despite himself, in the heady experience of the twenties, results in nausea:

---

[1] This is most evident in his 1925 collection of short stories *L'Europe galante*. For a perspective on Morand's political stance see van Noort, "Sleeping with Europe."

> Une photo, souvent reproduite, montre, à la Foire du Trône, les Six musiciens, Valentine Hugo et moi-même, dans un de ces bateaux peints sur la toile d'un photographe forain; penché sur le bastingage je dégobille, et Valentine me tient la tête; c'est l'image même de ce que je ressentais en 1925; l'après-guerre me donnait soudain envie de vomir. (102)

Just as the golden age gave way to the "conjuration luciférienne" of the war and its aftermath, the sentiment of liberation found in the avant-garde turns into an urge to vomit. In an interview given in 1971, Morand explained his seeming revolt against the avant-garde by remarking: "J'ai vu que le feu d'artifice était tiré; alors il ne fallait pas continuer à vivre, mais élargir son horizon" (Archives, 75). Morand refers to this explosion in *Venises* while noting the gentrification of the avant-garde, symbolised by the relocation of the "Boeuf sur le toit" to the "beaux quartiers" (103). Paris had come to symbolise the "fausse vie" at a time when the city was losing what he termed "the moral control of the world" which it never recovered (103). The nausea provoked by this spectacle was suppressed only by another attempt at evasion, this time in Morand's literal flight from Europe between 1925-1933, during which time his numerous travels and pseudo-diplomatic missions kept him away for significant periods.

Interestingly, this withdrawal of Morand from the nauseating spectacle of Europe corresponds to an increasing withdrawal of himself from this section of *Venises*. At the beginning of the chapter, as we noted, Morand explicitly cast himself in the role of a witness to the events of the war. This position increasingly comes to be that of a detached observer after his decision to leave Europe. In the second half of "Le pavillon de quarantaine" Morand isolates himself from the description of the years between 1925 and 1939. The narrative focuses rather on Venice, countering the very autobiographical tone of the first half by retreating, as it were, into the city. At the same time, and as a result, the autobiographical threatens to slip into memoir, privileging scattered observations about Venice and the era over the account of Morand's life and activities during this time. Long passages describing the Brenta river and one of the villas, the Malcontenta, lining its shores, followed by a brief analysis of Proust's encounter with Venice, are succeeded by a series of impressionistic notations and anecdotes, highly impersonal in content and tone:

> Jadis le *Gazzetino* de Venise publiait la liste des gens tombés à l'eau dans la journée; cette rubrique a été supprimée. Choit-on moins? (129)

> Midi, personne ne parle plus; les Vénitiens ont des spaghetti plein la bouche; ils y ajoutent tant de fruits de mer que les nouilles deviennent algues. (131)

> Au XIVe siècle, pendant deux heures, le Grand Canal s'est trouvé à sec, après un tremblement de terre. (134)

> Le dialecte vénitien s'illustre par sa lettre Z; le Grand Canal lui-même forme un Z. (136)

Morand continues this withdrawal throughout the fragments of the 1930s, relating the events of that decade in a terse manner reminiscent of historical annals:

> Mort de Stavisky, appris à Venise. L'U.R.S.S. entre à la S.D.N. Mort du roi Albert, assassinat de Dollfuss. Nuit de Longs Couteaux. Hindenburg. Hitler maître de l'Allemagne. Publication de *L'Armée de métier*, par de Gaulle, avec préface de Pétain. (137)

The rise of fascism, the mobilisation under Mussolini, the ascension of Hitler, all are evoked not by Morand's reactions but by Venice:

> Le 24 septembre 1930, je me trouvais, assis sur un banc de pierre, face à la lagune. Là où mouillaient jadis le *Bucentaure* [...] dix torpilleurs gris sont alignés. Le ciel d'automne tremble sous l'avance triangulaire des hydravions de métal; des drapeaux blanc-vert-rouge descendent jusqu'à terre. (144)

> Je regarde autour de moi, j'aperçois des êtres blonds descendus, genoux nus, du Tyrol, sur la place Saint-Marc. Ce qui apparaît dans le monde, ce qui commence à faire entendre sa grande voix, c'est la jeunesse de 1930, l'Allemagne qui ne lit plus *A l'ouest rien de nouveau*, qui parle "de guerres véritables, qui font cesser tout espèce de plaisanterie"; âge ardent qui n'a pas connu la souffrance [...] "Nous entrons dans une période tragique, annonçait Nietzsche, époque catastrophique." (145-6)

The images of the torpedo boats, the flags and the blond heads on the Piazza San Marco represent the great changes taking place. Morand's position is eminently that of a passive observer as he abdicates even the role of interpreter of these signs to Nietzsche. Morand's only "involvement" in the last part of the second chapter comes in its final fragment where he describes his participation, at Bled in 1939, in "une des Commissions du Danube [...] notre mission: surveiller, techniquement et un peu politiquement, le Danube, de l'Allemagne à la mer Noire" (154). But Morand's description of this Commission "très pacifique" serves only to launch a meditation on the history of the often troubled relations between Venice and the Slavic countries: "Ces souvenirs ne servent qu'à évoquer, à la veille de la guerre, la tête-à-tête des Slaves et de Venise" (155). Far more important than the ironic confluence of this mission and history is the geographical encounter of Venice and Slovenia

The spectacle of Morand's confrontation with his era during the early twenties, central to the first half of "Le pavillon de quarantaine," cedes to the spectacle of Venice's confrontation with the unfolding of history in the 1930s. Morand progressively disengages himself, as the city becomes the recorder of experience, and disappears, in a sense, into the city as he disappears from *Venises*. One might attribute this to a corresponding sense of a loss of stability vis-à-vis his existence. We have observed him swinging from one "destiny" to another: the Past, the avant-garde, the voyage, none of which seems as yet a sufficient cadre for his self. Morand seems both to signal the inability of the story of his life to provide its own structure and to give over this function entirely to the city.

This drawing-back culminates in his complete withdrawal from Venice at the end of this chapter which closes upon a final symbolic vision, "seen" from afar, of the city: "du haut de l'Alpe dinarique, le vieux lion de saint Marc vivait les derniers jours de sa grandeur adriatique" (155). Morand signals not only the catastrophe that lay ahead but also his impending separation from Venice, concluding this section by stating simply: "Je n'allais plus revoir Venise pendant douze ans" (155). Morand takes leave of Venice and *Venises* on the eve of the war. He will not return until 1951, nor will he pick up the "discours" of *Venises* until that date. But before turning to the resumption of his relationship with Venice, let us briefly examine the twelve-year absence, of Venice and of Morand, symbolically contained in the blank pages separating the second chapter from the third.

Morand has clearly prepared the suspension of his narrative between 1939 and 1951 by repeatedly emphasizing the partial nature of *Venises* and by reiterating the motif of absence. His project, it is recalled, is to present those fragments of his life which are vitally linked to Venice: a tête-à-tête, a discourse interrupted only by his absence from the city. Morand here remains faithful to his word. However, this is by no means Morand's first exile from Venice. One might argue that the period encompassing the First World War is also absent, "occurring" between the first and second chapters. But, as earlier observed, Morand comments extensively on his activities during the years 1914-17 after the fact. Equally, the years of his military service (1910-13) and the absence occasioned by his world travels (1925-33) are tied to Venice by his discovery of a series of "Venices" in Paris, London, and Bangkok. Thus, while there are other instances of a suspension of actual contact with Venice, none are accompanied by the silence marking his absence from Venice during and after the Second World War.

This is not to say that Morand entirely ignores this period, but the rare allusions to it are not in their proper place in the chronological unfolding of *Venises*. Early on he refers to Rome in 1917 as "déjà la France de 1940" (81), and, when describing the sudden liberty of the early twenties, notes: "Tout s'offrait, tout espérait être cueilli; tout le fut; les gros obstacles nous attendaient vingt ans plus tard. Autre histoire... Le temps n'est pas venu de la conter" (96). This time has not come, neither here, in this 1921 fragment, nor indeed in *Venises* itself. The author of *Tais-toi* (1965) has learned to hold his tongue. The sole direct allusion to Morand's life during the war comes in a passage describing his political position in 1917: "cette fidélité (à la paix) m'a valu de curieuses infidélités du sort; elle m'a fait traverser, en 1917, une gauche fort avancée, pour me déposer en 1940 dans un Vichy maurassien où je n'étais pas moins dépaysé" (85). If Morand claims a "dépaysement" or an alienation, this reference is equally misplaced, twenty-three years and pages before its time. The notion of blind fate, here temporally distorted, is again at work in his account of his place in history. Morand even situates himself in Vichy during the war, again, in terms of the chronology of *Venises*, years before the fact. After a passage describing the tension between his career as a writer and his diplomatic service (interrupted in 1927) he remarks:

> Lorsque je rentrai dans les "bureaux", cette ancienne patrie, à la vieille de la dernière guerre, je ne retrouvai pas ce que j'avais laissé, douze ans plus tôt; la politique, l'esprit syndicaliste après 1936, l'intellectualisation des services, l'entrée des Normaliens dans les cadres, ce n'était déjà plus tout à fait la même âme; les derniers vestiges d'autrefois, je les rencontrai parfois, perdus dans les chambres d'hôtel de Vichy. (100-101)

Although this passage comes from a fragment dated 1921, the use of the simple past (passé simple) to describe not only his reentry into the service occasioned by his appointment in 1939 to the "Ministre de la guerre économique" in London, but his presence in Vichy during the war as well, underscores the chronological violations observed with respect to the latter period. While avoiding an explanation of why he found himself in these same hotel rooms, Morand places himself there long before the "proper" moment in *Venises* to recount such a presence arrives.

Morand refers to the years after the war spent in Switzerland in a passage, dated 1908, cited in part above, concerning the chestnut forest of Tremezzina:

> Je devais vivre encore dans une châtaigneraie en 1944; durant trois années, à Montreux, je me suis nourri de châtaignes entassés avec leur bogue dans une baignoire inutilisable, faute d'un abonnement au gaz; la châtaigneraie de

Maryland dévalait de la villa abandonnée jusqu'aux premiers toits de Territet, avant de s'enfoncer dans le Léman. (30)

Again, the verbal tenses reveal a great deal about the positioning of this recollection. From a prefiguration of the future: "je devais vivre encore," Morand switches to a retrospective stance: "je me suis nourri," recalling the switch in verbal tenses in *Fouquet ou le soleil offusqué* used to mark the frontier between Fouquet/Mazarin and Louis XIV. It seems that all leads us up to this point (to the war) and then that all turns back to it with the "void" of the twelve years from 1939 to 1951 constituting the pivotal juncture. In light of these passages and those which follow, this particular absence from Venice functions as a fulcrum around which the entire book revolves, tending first prospectively and then retrospectively toward this period, underscoring the centrality of this silence to the rhetoric of the book. If I have argued that Morand uses Venice as a structure of existence, one which permits him to both describe his life and to attempt to understand it, Venice must also be seen as a structure of denial, of an evasion of a totalization of both his life and its meaning. We have seen how many of Morand's literary techniques create tension: between the passage (distancing) of time and the collapse of temporal distance; between a narrative of seamless form and a fragmented form; and between an integration of existence and a fragmentation of that existence. This tension is made possible through Morand's focus on the city of Venice as a monument à la Chateaubriand. I would suggest that the ultimate import of the twelve-year gap in Venises lies in its announcement of a shift in the locus of tension from Venice to Morand himself, such that he is transformed into a sort of monument. A fundamental rupture has taken place, as we shall see, which more squarely situates this gap as a modification in the relationship of the past and the present, a modification represented by the figure of Morand himself. In order to explore such a hypothesis, let us now turn to what does comes next: Morand's return to Venice and to *Venises*.

As after the First World War, Venice is again called upon to fulfill its role of surrogate, filling in a highy restricted portion of all that had transpired historically since 1939:

Maria P..., une amie vénitienne que je questionnais sur la fin de la dernière guerre, à laquelle elle assista, me disait: "Cet hiver 1945 fut celui d'une Venise sinistre [...]. J'entendais les bombes démolir Padoue. Plus d'électricité, les *vaporetti* sans combustible; aux murs, des affiches décrivent des tas d'engins mortels qui tombaient du ciel, auxquels le public ne devait pas toucher. (159)

Even as Maria P... narrates, it is Venice who "tells" the story in a series of predominantly visual images.

When Morand picks up the narrative himself, in the second fragment of the third chapter, it is to describe a masked ball at the Palazzo Labia, given by his friend "B." in 1951, organized around the theme of Marco Polo's return to Venice.[2] As earlier noted, the true impact of this parade of costumed figures lies in its representation of the "dead" who are not only the historical figures but the people behind the masks as well, themselves long gone, hence one signification of the title of this chapter "Morte in maschera" (Masked Death). But it is not only the masked revelers who have passed into another realm but Morand as well:

> Il serait ridicule de parler de cette dernière soirée comme une fillette de son premier bal, mais dès l'arrivée je savais que je venais faire mes adieux à un monde; ermite par nécessité, seul depuis onze années, du haut de mes glaciers, je tombais tout à coup dans une échauffourée de plaisir, dans un glas de l'imaginaire. Un bal? Un bal en Italie, comme dans Stendhal! (160)

Morand's return to Venice emerges as a sort of farewell appearance not to the city but to a world from which he has already withdrawn. Rather than a triumphal Marco Polo, Morand is little more than a ghost, taking his place among the represented figures already on the other side of life.

The two fragments which follow likewise present scenes of symbolic "deaths." A Giorgione exposition provides the impetus for a meditation on the relatively marginal position to which the painter, after a period of acclaim, had been relegated. Giorgione, to whom all had been attributed at the turn of the century, now stands dispossessed, his influence discounted: "Dans la préface du catalogue, Pietro Zampetti cache mal sa déception. Que reste t il de Giorgione? Trois portraits! Quel soir de champ de bataille! [...] Giorgione s'éloigne" (166). In the next fragment, Morand describes the auction of the contents of the Labia, a fourteenth-century palazzo and the last of its kind in Venice to "dégorger ses richesses":

> -A cent mille lires, plus personne?
> Sous les voûtes nues, en marbre d'Istrie, se répercutait: Plus personne... Funérailles d'une vie, non pas de grand collectionneur, mais de grand amateur... L'Italie n'en est pas à un camposanto près.... (170)

---

[2] Morand's friend "B." was the Mexican millionaire Don Carlos de Bestegui who had purchased the Labia in 1949 for half a million dollars and spent almost a million in restoration. Of this infamous evening, the Aga Khan was reported to have said it was the best celebration of the coronation of King George in 1911 (Hibbert).

This "amateur" is none other than Morand's friend "B.," and the Labia, the site of the masked "ball of the dead" earlier noted. The fragments comprising this third section all repeat, through various images, the scene of a radical and terrible rupture between the present and the past, one which, for Morand, is as definitive as death itself. We have observed Morand describing his alienation as an absence, as a fundamental split between his self and the present in which "se parle une langue étrangère que je n'entends plus; d'ailleurs il n'existe pas de dictionnaire" (172). This expression of linguistic discord echoes a passage in "Parfaite de Saligny" (1946) in which the protagonist, Loup de Tincé, imprisoned for suspected counter-revolutionary activities in 1792, meditates on the new France being born, one which a priori excludes him: "Une France nouvelle qui déjà avait une autre figure, portait d'autres habits, parlait une langue neuve" (199). The rupture, whether "style" 1792 or 1944, effects an unbridgeable distance. In the same fragment, dated 1964, Morand describes, one after another, examples of this schism: from the way the barber cuts his hair to the use of first names, dodecaphonic music and the sacrament of the Eucharist, every encounter, every day-to-day activity measures the breadth of the gap.

Bruno Thibault suggests that the hallmark of *Venises* centers around just this notion of a radical divorce between the past and the present (125). *Venises* certainly is one variant of what Thibault terms an "écriture du désastre," but the catastrophe, according to him, is that of 1918, whereas the structure of the text itself suggests, in its radical thematic and structural partition, that the real disaster was 1944 (124).[3] This is also an "écriture de mélancolie," of nostalgia for the past, but one is hard put to identify which past (124). The past of the Belle Epoque? The Roaring Twenties? Or perhaps, it is a past which understood the Past as destiny, a fate which Morand resisted, but one which remained comprehensible to him.

Thibault goes on to argue that Morand's choice of Venice as the site of his literary testament is grounded on a perceived similarity between the trajectories of the city and of Europe as a whole across history, dual passages from grandeur to decadence (125). For Thibault, the central metaphor of *Venises* is as much the resemblance of the fates of Venice and Europe and those of Venice

---

[3] In using the expression "écriture du désastre," Thibault evokes, consciously or not, the book of that title by Maurice Blanchot in which Blanchot situates such "writing" as belonging to and as a result of the Holocaust. It is perversely ironic that Thibault should make, like Morand, such an historical "error" by using the expression in a seemingly innocent way and by failing to attribute if not its origin, then in modern connotation.

and Morand, and he goes so far as to suggest in the former case a synechdocal relation: Venice (for Morand) is *the* European city, her death represents that of the whole. One would be quick to point out that in the last section of Venises, "Il est plus facile de commencer que de finir," that Morand does present images of a dying Venice. Numerous passages deal with the physical sinking of the city, and Morand details the history of the lagoon as well as the hydrological efforts to reverse the effects of nature and man. Many argue that the dying of Venice provides Morand with an apt metaphor of his own end in these final pages. Such arguments generally base themselves, however, on two phrases taken from a single passage in a fragment dated September, 1970:

> Parfois je cherche à me faire saigner, en m'imaginant que Venise meurt avant moi, qu'elle s'engloutit, n'ayant finalement rien exprimé, sur l'eau, de sa figure. [...] Venise se noie; c'est peut-être ce qui pourrait lui arriver de plus beau? (201)

Morand's masochistic rendition of Venice's potential plight becomes a poignant echo of the death of the author. What more terrible fate for a writer, Morand seems to ask, than to die never having expressed anything, never having left, on the surface of his or her medium, any trace. But are we not witnessing Morand's trace, itself etched onto the very waters of Venice? In addition, it is vital to note, between the initial and final phrases of this passage, phrases quoted above, the development of a phastasmagoric image of a Venice which, having "drowned," does not sink to unfathomable depths but only a few feet below the surface. The city remains visible and viable, to the hordes of future tourists peering from their vaporetti at the submerged city. Even commerce continues as frogmen comb the vaults of the Grand Hôtel in search of the jewels of some long-departed American *touriste*. It is not difficult to perceive an analogy between this still visible city, sunken under the water of time and scrutinized by future spectators and the book *Venises*. Venice is drowning, but in Morand's image of its fate it is a death intimately linked to its existence and one which paradoxically, preserves the city.

But this passage is the whole neither of this chapter nor, indeed, of the book. Morand's begins the final section by asking: "Qui recommencerait Venise?" (183) and then immediately offers the example of one man who attempted such an endeavor: Volpi, whose efforts began in 1917 to industrialize and reenergize the city. A futile enterprise, perhaps, but one which gives Morand an opportunity to signal the adaptibility of Venice and its people:

152 Paul Morand

> Les Vénitiens offrent un bois dur, à l'épreuve des déluges. Ils s'en sortent toujours; leurs maisons ont toutes deux issues, une sur l'eau, l'autre sur terre. (190)

There is a sense of certitude, in Morand's text, of the durability of the city: "l'Italie a un siècle; Venise en a quinze; l'adage reste vrai: Veneziani, poi Christiani! (Vénitiens d'abord, chrétiens ensuite)" (191). Rather than a Venice in its agony, Morand traces the cyclical nature of its trajectory across history: ruin and renewal, albeit renewal marked by the passage of time. Life goes on, he states, in a constant juxtaposition of the past and present: "Dans un vieux décor, la vie continuait, un peu comme une pièce de Beckett jouée dans les arènes de Nîmes" (198). It is simply that Morand has no role in this new "comedy."

Thibault's determination to justify Morand's choice of Venice as a metaphor for the death of Europe is laid bare in yet another example of the dangers of partial citations of this dense book. When Thibault offers the following example as proof of Morand's insistence on Venice's (and thus Europe's) illustrious past, his omission of the first part of the sentence misleads the reader:

> Venise a été "une sorte de Manhattan, de cité prédatrice, excessive, hurlante de prospérité, avec un Rialto qui était le Brooklyn Bridge de l'époque, un Grand Canal, sorte de Cinquième Avenue pour doges milliardaires". (Thibault, 125)

What Thibault omits is the all-important initial qualification: "Venise redevenait ce qu'elle avait été au XVe siècle [...]" (198). While Thibault's citation suggests a pessimism based upon the demise of the city, the passage read in its entirety offers an image of Venice undergoing a process of "rebecoming," or at least of refashioning in the present, that which it once was: an energetic and vital center of modern life. Thibault seems to imply that Morand's musings on Venice belong to a tradition of melancholic meditations on ruins; if this is so, however, the ruins of Venice appear, in Morand's hands, to be endowed with a certain re-generative power, or at least, to be in a state of evolution.

Should one, then, recognize in Morand the symptoms of an eternal optimist? Certainly not. Morand carefully refrains from speculating about a future which has no relevance for him in these pages. If Venice is "in evolution," Morand is not. Only the dialogue between himself and the city, between past and present, has a place in *Venises*, and it is the latter "conversation" which comes to dominate the final pages of the book, as it has dominated the bulk of his writing after the war.

Let us now turn to an example of this dialogue which demonstrates the transformation of Morand into a "ruin" or monument. In a 1969 fragment, Morand describes his encounter with a group of hippies, three young men and a woman who have come to rest in this place described as a sort of net in which are caught up all the undesirables of History: "Une vraie nasse, ce fond de l'Adriatique... Tous les réfugiés de l'Histoire; elle berce dans ses bras lagunaires un éternel *exodus*" (194). (Morand's italics). Morand's description of these latest "rôdeurs de l'Absolu," a depiction so "realistic" that one can sense only too well the foul odor which first attracted Morand's attention, culminates in the question:

> Que pouvaient contenir ces êtres: quelque Bonaparte se trompant de siècle, un Chateaubriand qui n'écrirait jamais, un Guatamelata sans destinée, un Lope de Vega sans manuscrit? Se les imaginer à quatre-vingt ans faisait froid dans le dos. (195)

The "real" question is less concerned with the potentiality of these beings than with how to situate them, even negatively, within History. Morand also cleverly positions them in regard to his own history, for to imagine them at eighty is to imagine them at his own age in 1969. Such an identification sends chills down his spine, but also prepares the tone of his next meeting with the same group on Crete, a year later.

From a mini-bus which "rendait l'âme" in front of a café at Candi, emerge three men who Morand recognizes as the hippies of the previous summer in Venice. In a gesture he deems appropriate to his age, he invites them to lunch and launches into a meditation on his own "hippie days":

> Les amants de la grand-route, je les jalouse souvent; ils solidifient des rêves épars, ce que Balzac nomme: "la vie de mohican," ils me rappellent notre 1920, nos insultes à la société, notre besoin de destruction, nos défis sur papier d'affiche, à l'heure où le traité de Versailles assassinait l'Europe; ils me font revivre notre "feu à tout," "feu sur tout." Ceux-ci, que feront-ils quand ils auront fini d'errer au bord de l'inexistence? Je les moque, je les plains, je les envie. (206)

Rather than emblems of a decadent, pre-apocalyptic society, as Thibault maintains, these hippies provide Morand an image of his former self, 1970's style (123). Much as life in Venice resembles Beckett played in a Roman venue, the encounter of Morand and these young *révoltés* at once throws temporal distance into relief and abolishes this same space in the broad sweep of identification effectuated in this passage. Morand mocks their present, but both envies and pities their future, a future denied him at this point in his life, but one which he knows only too well.

Perhaps more importantly, the introduction of these beings, at once so firmly rooted in the present and yet evocative of the past, permits Morand to enter himself onto the rolls of History as representative of a type, a sort of paradigm, that may now be held as a model against which the contemporary can be compared. Morand himself becomes a monument of the past in the present. Certainly, on more than one level, *Venises* is the account of a passing into History. It has been remarked that *Venises* is dated, "démodé," that it represents a private world no longer accessible in the present. But far from a weakness, this is exactly the point. *Venises* is less an attempt to recapture the past than a means of historicizing that past. As Michel de Certeau comments, a line of demarcation must be drawn, a death must be declared in order for history to be made, or rather, written (3-4). We have seen Morand, in the opening pages, posit his own death: "c'est après la vie que je reviens m'y contempler" (10), a declaration which permits him to order and interpret the events of his life, much as a historiographer works on historical events. And yet, after advancing into the second half of the book, it becomes clear that the "after-life" from which vantage point he writes coincides not so much with his own literal although imagined death, as with the symbolic death figured by his alienation from the postwar world. The break occasioned by Morand's absence from Venice from 1939 to 1951 historicizes all that precedes and, strangely, all that follows the gap in the pages of *Venises*. If Morand's use of the physical space of Venice permits him to posit the city as a measure of both change and permanence, he himself, in the final chapters, comes to occupy this role. Nowhere is this more evident that in the "hippie passages" where Morand himself functions as the marker, the monument, through which time and timelessness may be perceived.

All this depends on the revolving door of the twelve-year absence: he goes in as a figure of the present (though, as we have seen, he progressively withdraws in the preceding fragments), and emerges as a figure of the past. His subsequent self-condemnation to a living after-life would not be possible were it not for this period, one almost sacred in its silence, which performs such a transformation. As a result, it may be misleading to unrestrictively label the hiatus an "absence." While it does represent a veritable absence (Morand's from Venice) in the structural scheme of the book, this gap also emerges as a presence at work throughout *Venises*. To put it slightly differently, these years, and the events that fill them, overdetermine both that which precedes and that which follows, as perceived, for example, in the use of verbal tenses in the scattered allusions to Morand's activities during the war. That which is seemingly suppressed, silenced, turns out to be the most powerful of presences, permeating the entire work.

A similar phenomenon is visible in Henry Adams's third-person autobiography, *The Education of Henry Adams*. Adams's work resembles *Venises* in several ways. First, in its focus on a very specific location, the steps of the church of Santa Maria di Ara Coeli in Rome as a marker of his own intellectual life: "The church of Ara Coeli seemed more and more to draw all the threads of thought to a center, for every new journey led back to its steps" (67). Adams's work also demonstates an extreme disassociation of the author from the life he depicts, accomplished foremost in his text by his use of the third person in its narration. The intended distance is pursued in yet another, far subtler, way which resembles Morand's work. Like *Venises*, *The Education* contains a gap, a void of twenty years which, in both its "content" and its relationship to the work as a whole, bears an uncanny and perhaps instructive resemblance to the twelve-year gap earlier noted in Venises. Within Adams's gap, from 1871 to 1892, occur two very important events: his career as historian and the suicide of his wife. By omitting the crowning achievement of his nine-volume *History of the U.S. during the Administrations of Jefferson and Madison* and the death of his wife, events ocurring during the gap, Adams further distances himself from his self-portrait. *The Education*, it would appear, is about neither Adams as historian nor Adams as man. However, as John Paul Eakin points out, Adams himself states the intention to use the story of his life not for the revelation of his self but rather for "the study of the relation between the human mind and history" (*Touching*, 150). Viewed from such an angle, the twenty-year gap appears quite differently. Eakin argues, in a passage not without relevance to our study of *Venises*, that:

> [...] the twenty-year gap in the record, canceling both history and personal history, becomes instead the narrative's most striking symbol of the relation between the two, of the accelerating pace of change that is its dominant theme, for Adams insists throughout on the mismatch between his "eighteenth-century training" and the disorienting reality of the "twentieth-century multiverse." (*Touching*, 151)

Eakin's argument is quite provocative: the "gap" becomes a symbol for that which it excises, the relationship between history and personal history, and, at the same time, marks a sort of rupture symbolic of the accelerating pace of change. This change, it seems, represents a modification of the relationship itself, in the way in which man relates to the past. The discontinuity between Adams's eighteenth-century sensibility and his twentieth-century reality is clearly set forth by Adams himself: "He saw before him a world so changed as to be beyond connection with the past. His identity, if one could call a bundle of disconnected memories an identity, seemed to remain; but his life was once more broken into separate pieces" (209). Adams's phrase offers perhaps one of the best descriptions of Morand's *Venises*, capturing the effect, in the latter, of discontinuity and of ambiguity or plurality of identity, as well as the idea of a critical breaking point, all traits easily recognizeable in Morand's text. In both works, these issues are marked by their coincidence with their respective periods of silence, each of which points to what Eakin terms the cancellation of history and personal history. As in Adams's work, Morand's gap serves to suppress a similar yet radically different story of the personal and the historical. For if Adams's "untold story" is that of his relation to history as an historian and of personal tragedy, Morand's "story" is likewise that of his all-too-personal encounter with history during the Occupation of France, but as an active participant. In Morand's case, the hiatus points to a radical rupture between the past and the present situtated in the event of the Second World War and, more specifically, within the Occupation of France. One might equally speak of a radical disjuncture not unlike that opposing Adams's "eighteenth-century sensibility" and the reality of the "twentieth-century multiverse," transposed from the event of the turn-of-the-century to the postwar and, by extension, post-1968, era.

But while in the case of Adams, sensitivity to this rupture leads to his eventual elaboration of a theory of history based upon a mechanical model of material acceleration, Morand offers no explicit formulation of the relation in his work of the past and the present other than the demonstration that such a relation no longer exists, or at best, exists only in a radically different form. By positing himself, in the second half of the book, as a figure of the past or of History itself, Morand plays upon generational difference in a way which underlines the "non-existence" or absence of that past in the present. At the same time that he solidifies his existence as a sort of monument, that monument has, ironically, become unreadable, for, as we noted before, the present speaks a language incomprehensible to Morand and, by extension, cannot itself understand the language of the past.

Were one to look for a historiographical model which reflects this view of the past as illustrated in *Venises*, the work of those historians loosely identified as "third-generation Annales" proves illuminating. Pierre Nora's monumental work, *Les Lieux de mémoire*, both theorizes the "crisis" in history of the past two decades and offers, in its contributions by eminent French historians, new ways of reading and writing history. Nora's editorial preface describes the current trend of "présentisme" visible not only in the discipline but manifest in popular culture as well. He situates this trend as the result of a dissolution of what he terms "mémoire-histoire," or "memory-as-history" and its replacement by "pure" history. In the past, Nora argues, memory and history coexisted and were even congruent to the point of virtual synonymity. History, along the lines of Halbwach's notion of collective memory, was as alive to people as personal memory and as an instrument of identification played a vital role in the unifying force of institutions such as the state and family and community units. According to Nora, the twentieth-century emphasis on the individual rather than the collective, as well as the increased dissemination of information which, rather than strengthening a sense of collectivity, hastened the fragmentation of society, resulted in the divorce of history and memory, or rather, the transformation of the idea of memory. This transformation had its seeds in what Nora terms the "conversion definitive à la psychologie individuelle" of the turn-of-the-century, heralded by the major role consecrated to individual memory by Bergson, Freud and Proust (Nora, xxix). Memory passed from the historical to the psychological, from social to individual, from transmitted to subjective, in the course of which our perception of the past has been radically altered. Whereas formerly perception of the past might by characterized as a lived past, that is, the past was not considered to be truly past but a vital part of the present, a visible past, as Nora puts it, today the past is experienced as invisible. Instead of a relation of continuity, there is an emphasis on discontinuity (xxxi). We no longer define ourselves or our societies via identification with what we and they once were, but instead by the difference between what we are now and what "they" were then. As Nora suggests, the past has become the "other" par excellence, allowing us to inversely define ourselves by what we are not, or what we are no longer. Michel de Certeau frames this problem slightly differently, in a way which points to the implications of this shift for historiography:

> In other words, the conclusion of history is what used to take the form of the incipit in formal historical narrative: "In times past, life was not the way it is today." Cultivated methodically, this distance ("life was not...") has become the result of research, instead of being its postulate and question. (83-4)

De Certeau goes on to elaborate on the effects of this reversal:

> More important than reference to the past is the introduction of the past by way of an assumed distance. A gap is folded into the scientific coherence of a present time, and how could this be, effectively, unless through something that can be objectified, the past, whose function is to indicate alterity? Even if ethnology has partly relieved history in this task of establishing a staging of the other in present time - the reason why these two disciplines have been in intimate rapport - the past is first of all the means of representing a difference. (85)

The task of the historiographer, as exemplified in the various contributions to the *Lieux de mémoire*, is the examination of the production and characteristics of this distance or gap. Certain "lieux" or "sites" such as monuments, commorations, texts, institutions and cultural concepts, which function as repositories of national memory, are examined through, and this is the crucial point, the lens of the present as they function in different ways at different times. As for Benjamin, the past, for these historians, is coherent only inasmuch as it is examined from a vantage point firmly anchored in the observor's present. But whereas Benjamin focuses on the constellation formed by the fragments of the explosion of the historical continuum, Nora and others are interested by the explosions themselves. This particular way of regarding and writing history, in many respects a revival and reworking of the notion of "histoire événementielle," constitutes an effort not to reestablish the former link between history and memory, but to forge a new relationship, highly political in its implications, between the two. The result, as Nora asserts for better or for worse, is nothing less that the creation of a new national identity based upon and surpassing difference (Comment écrire, 30-32).

Without ignoring the many criticisms which may be made of Nora's overall project: the absence of female and colonial "memory," the lack of theorization of the idea of collective memory, the predominance of republican memory, and the highly nationalistic tone of Nora's prefaces, the underlying theory of rupture and difference resembles the view of the past that emerges from Morand's *Venises*. Indeed, the past, and Morand as figure of that past, survives only as difference, as the "other" that serves to inversely identify the present. Perhaps the most striking example of this function of the past is one concerning the hippies on Crete in whom Morand, as we saw, discerned both resemblance and its radical denial. When Morand encounters the group for the second time, he notices the absence of one of its members: the girl, baptized "la Walkyrie," who so violently rejected Morand's city the previous year: "I shit on Venice" (196). One of the group explains that she died of a drug overdose and goes on to comment:

> "Au fond, elle souffrait de ne pas être fille de lord héréditaire" fit le chauffeur du mini-bus (accent Magdalen et B.B.C) en grattant une chevelure graisseuse comme du poil de caniche; "On dira ce qu'on voudra, mais le *Burke's Peerage*, ce fut toujours son petit livre rouge...". (207)

This book, *Burke's Peerage*, represents more than aristocracy, it is the record of the past as continuity, and as such earns the scorn apparent in the hippie's comment. The Walkyrie's obsession translates as desire not only of a certain identity but of the continuity with the past represented by that identity. Such a desire, which Nora cites as evidence that the past no longer "exists" in the present except as a measure of alterity (Entre, xxxii-iii), is all the more tragic because futile and, Morand seems to suggest, fatal.

This second "hippie" episode is, perhaps not fortuitously, situated just before the final two fragments of the book and constitutes what one might call the last "living memory" in the text. The penultimate and final fragments or, if you will, the last "post cards" are situated not in Venice but in Trieste, the site of Stendhal's "exile" from Venice, as Morand remarks. In the course of his description of his visit to his wife's family and to the cemetery where he will be interred in Hélène's mausoleum, Morand symbolically effectuates his own death. Standing before the family tomb, he remarks, in the last words of *Venises*:

> Là, j'irai gésir, après ce long accident que fut ma vie. Ma cendre, sous ce sol; une inscription en grec en témoignera; je serais veillé par cette foi orthodoxe vers quoi Venise m'a conduit, une religion par bonheur immobile, qui parle encore le premier langage des Evangiles. (215)

Morand's death is to be a return or rather an arrival at the endpoint of a journey punctuated and determined by Venice. For not only has the trajectory of *Venises*, the book, culminated here, but Venice as *Venises* has led him on a reverse journey, one which becomes a reintegration into the continuity of the past. Venice, as interlocutor, surrogate and now guide, has led him ultimately backward in time: to the Greek language and to the Orthodox faith, a religion "par bonheur immobile" and which restores, through its language, the linguistic harmony whose disturbance, as noted earlier, functioned as a metaphor of Morand's alienation from the postwar world. The curative role of language (and literature) is, for Morand, one of a redemptive return to the past.

V

MORAND RETRO

On July 2, 1968, Paul Morand was elected to the Académie française. Charles de Gaulle had withdrawn his threat of veto issued in 1959 and Morand received 21 of 28 votes. Whereas his doomed attempt to gain entry in 1959 had provoked a storm of media coverage and political outcry, his success in 1968 was duly if unsensationally noted, with little or no mention of his war-time activities that had prompted de Gaulle's opposition to his candidature in 1959. Morand had obviously been implicitly pardoned, "redeemed" of his collaboration to the point where he could take his place among the most "French of the French" in the Académie. What had happened? Most obviously, the recent events of May, 1968, no doubt deflected attention from the election. But one might also venture that de Gaulle's policy of the propagation of the myth of *resistencialisme* had worked. This myth, it will be recalled, reinforced the view that the vast majority of the French had resisted Nazi Occupation during the Second World War, with collaborators representing only a small fraction of the population. At work for almost 25 years, perhaps this myth had succeeded by marginalizing and thus blunting the crimes of the collaborators. Collaboration may have come to be seen as a relatively "harmless" anomaly, to be detested, naturally, but only as the abstract, inconceivable opposite of the Resistance, deified by its majuscule.

One finds, perhaps not surprisingly, this marginalization throughout Morand's postwar historical works. While opposing the deGaullian vision on a first level by examining the phenomenon of collaboration and thus bringing it to the center, at a deeper level, Morand seems to echo the mechanisms of *resistencialisme* in its marginalization of the collaborative position. By far the most persistent pattern found in these works is the recurrence of the figure of the pariah. All Morand's protagonists eventually find themselves in the position of pariah: historical losers in the complex and often arbitrary circumstances in which they are engulfed. And all suffer a similar fate: death, whether literal, as in the case of Loup de Tincé, Parfaite and Lassalle; or symbolic, as with don Luis in his self-condemnation to perpetual wandering, Escolastica in her madness, Fouquet in his cell at Pignerol, or Morand himself, in the living death described in *Venises*. This common fate, however, is just as persistently accompanied if not by redemption, then by its possibility, created by Morand's highly literary renditions of the very history which served to condemn. Don Luis is transformed into the sacred and penitential figure of don Pablo; dona Escolastica is "saved" by chess in the memory of her historical counterpart whose experience is in turn redeemed by her twentieth-century progeny; and Fouquet emerges restored, for if Colbert won the battle it is Fouquet who, in Morand's biography, wins the war with posterity. Even Morand himself, at the end of *Venises*, is cloaked in the Orthodox faith which restores him to a certain fantasy of the past and to a linguistic harmony with history. As I have argued, Morand achieves this salvatory effect by playing upon literary disruptions of historical continuity: the lifting-out of characters from their historical situations via reference to myth and to other texts; the stylistic and structural compression of temporal duration and spatial differences effectuated by both suspension and acceleration; the use of figures of speech, in particular, anachronistic metaphor; a calculated manipulation of historical fact; and a repeated structural and thematic insistence on the phenomenon of historical rupture.

Just as Morand's literary use of history functions to redeem the personal experiences of his protagonists, on another level, working both within the confines of the texts and projecting outside of them into the larger realm of history, these books point to another redemptive project. I have argued that Morand's practice of exploding history as a means of imparting meaning to individual historical experience reflects a broader intent: the redemption of the experience of the Occupation of France and its immediate aftermath, in particular, Morand's own experience. Without reiterating the many parallels emphasized in the texts themselves between the historical situations chosen as contexts and the experience of France during and immediately after the war, I would restate an observation made earlier a propos of *Fouquet ou le soleil offusqué*. The comparison, in that work, of Colbert's preparation of Fouquet's downfall to a "film de l'événement avant l'événement" suggests, in the context of Morand's highly anachronistic biography, that the work itself, along with his other postwar texts, themselves function as a series of "films of the event *before* the event (1940-44)," written, however, from the retrospective position of the "after" with all its attendant corrective advantages. The structure of this play of the "before" and the "after" reflects the way in which Morand exploits the often chiasmic parallels between the past event and the contemporary event, as relations of both similarity and difference. There is simultaneously similarity between the "fictive" events and the event of 1940-44: a country occupied (*Le Flagellant de Séville*), a victim of an purge (*Fouquet*), an experience of a Franco-French war ("Parfaite de Saligny"), and a love story with its own counterpart in the same text ("La Folle amoureuse"); and difference: France is the occupier, the literary establishment defended Fouquet, Loup de Tincé acts not out of political conviction but passion, and, in contrast to her ancestor, dona Escolastica does not wait for her Russian lover. And yet Morand's manipulations ultimately present a picture of eradicated difference: don Luis collaborates out of love for France, Fouquet is unjustly condemned for his oedipal-like blindness to the advent of Louis XIV (de Gaulle); Loup de Tincé is persecuted for having pursued his object of desire, Parfaite/France; both Escholaticas undergo a process of normalization, of "coming-to-reason."

What might at first appear to be the insertion of a particular experience (collaboration) into historical tradition is subverted by a vision of historical relativism made possible by the juxtaposition of events in a perversely Benjaminian constellation. The historical continuum that Morand explodes is the locus of true difference, while the difference perceptible in Morand's relativistic constellation is predicated on a perceived sameness. That this indeed is his intent is signaled, as we earlier saw, in a letter written during the writing of *Le Flagellant de Séville*:

> Et quand ils (les Français) disent qu'une armée régulière (l'armée allemande) n'avait pas le droit de fusiller une population civile qui tirait sur les soldats, ils seront obligés d'admettre que Napoléon a toujours donné des ordres contraires, exécutant des villages entiers qui n'avaient prise aucune part active à la lutte; en peu de mots, que les représailles sont aussi vieilles que les guerres. (Louvrier, 309)

Morand's intent is thus doubled: he writes and rewrites the story of the redemption of his historical protagonists, all the while repeating his own redemption. The stories act as a sort of lure, inviting, in their obsessive repetition, the reader to reach outside the texts for a hidden and yet visible meaning, a reading which Morand explicitly signals by continually rewriting, in historical guise, the experience of the Occupation.

This obsessive rewriting, even as it differs from the rewriting effectuated by the myth of *resistencialisme*, is nonetheless quite similar in its mechanisms. Quite simply put, these mechanisms resemble a continual constatation of difference, a marginalization of collaboration as an isolated event and of the collaborator as the Other, thus permitting a reestablishment of "sameness," a reintegration of the community along the lines of Girard's sacrificial structure, into a seamless, continuous identity only briefly and harmlessly "interrupted" by the Occupation. Morand's historical texts, while ideologically opposing the myth of *resistencialisme*, enact its process by continually bringing the reader into a particular position, inuring him or her with a vision of the

Occupation which while different in its terms, repeats the structure of the deGaullian myth.

But then again, Morand's redemption in 1968 may have only been due to the fact that it was, quite simply, 1968. The de Gaulle regime was waning, de Gaulle himself would be dead a little over a year later, an era was ending and perhaps its ghosts seemed less malevolent and certainly more senile. But the fact that it was perhaps merely 1968 is at the same time highly relevant as concerns Morand. For the new era subsequently ushered in was to have a profoundly different reaction to the ghosts of the Occupation, one which while not directly impacting Morand who died in 1976, does impact a reading of his postwar works as they uncannily also comment on the archaeology of the Occupation undertaken during what is known as the *"mode rétro"* in France.

1968 marked, according to some, the beginning of a period turned toward the future in France, but an uncertain future as that year also marked a turn towards new interrogations of the nature of French identity and of the nation itself. Looking forward, France was also forced to look back, to the Algerian War, to Indochina and to the Second World War, events crucial to the formation of contemporary France but which had been largely glossed over, successfully for a time, by de Gaulle's powerful unifying vision. In some ways, the uprisings of 1968 constituted more of a fundamental rupture than the period of the Occupation, at least vis-à-vis the exploding of the myth that had kept modern French identity intact in a historical continuum of a tradition of patriotic resistance to the Other (whether aristocrat, Jew, German or Algerian) stretching back to the French Revolution. This rupture amounted to an opening of the floodgates, at least in terms of inquiry, if not in immediate wide-spread attention. As earlier noted, Marcel Ophuls controversial 1971 film *Le Chagrin et la pitié* (*The Sorrow and the Pity*), debunking the belief that few French collaborated either actively or passively with the German occupiers, was not aired in France until 1981. But the *mode rétro* had nonetheless begun, marked progressively by the now famous trials of Klaus Barbie, Paul Touvier, and most recently René Bousquet, the publication of numerous books and articles on French collaboration and increasing media coverage. The extent of this swing in the object of interest has been such that one hears little if anything about the Resistance today, except as a sort of hallowed, dim memory. It is the collaborators, rather, who make the news, are known by name and deed. Indeed, so far-reaching is this phenomenon that collaboration now seems to be the "norm." Richard Golsan succinctly explores Stanley Hoffman's positing of "what he [Hoffman] labels the 'Lacombe Lucien' myth, which paints a portrait of 'a weak and complicituous France, where there would only have been a handful of resistance fighters, there the regime could not only further the desires and pressures of the occupier, but could count n the support of a debased people.'" (Golsan, 149).[1] More pertinent to my argument and perhaps more reflective of current attitudes in France is Alan Morris's assertion that certain pre-*mode rétro* works of fiction had already proposed yet another, if no less disquieting scenario according to which the distinctions between collaboration and resistance are weakened and transformed into mere incidents of chance or instances of opportunism. Certainly one must count Morand's texts, unmentioned by Morris, as contributing to such a scenario as his protagonists and secondary characters find themselves accidentally thrust into larger political situations and as they become involved for reasons far removed from those in question in the larger context.

If in this same vein Morand's postwar works appear to prefigure one result of the *mode rétro*, namely a balancing or putting into question of the *resistencialiste* myth via the erection of a counter myth that might be termed that of the "collaborationiste malgré lui," these works also enact and comment upon the a priori conditions and mechanisms of this new myth, not unlike the way in which they functioned vis-à-vis the deGaullian vision. For again, even as they ideologically oppose the terms of the collaborationist myth (redemption rather than condemnation), the other dominant pattern observed in these works, that of the thematic and structural role of the notion of "rupture," can be seen as having a similar function vis-à-vis the *mode rétro*. Just as the *mode rétro* was made possible by the rupture of 1968 and de Gaulle's death, and in many ways founds its underlying discourse upon a certain epistemology of rupture, a point I shall later expound upon, Morand's texts likewise take as their grounding points moments of rupture.

I would like to first look at the nature of the image of rupture in these texts. From the most detached perspective, each of the various historical contexts chosen by Morand as settings for his postwar works displays a rupture as one of its defining traits: the radical upheaval in Spain signalled by the dissolution of the Spanish monarchy and the rise of the cortès, the watershed of the French Revolution, the abrupt transformation of the French monarchy after the death of Mazarin, the weakening of the Spanish Empire in North America, the Spanish Civil War, and the wrenching experience of the Second World War. Within the stories themselves, historical rupture is narrated in a way which both reflects the

---

[1] See Golsan's study of the reception of Louis Malle's film *Lacombe Lucien* and how its critics embody the various positions taken on the *mode rétro*.

historical situation and effectuates redemption. In *Le Flagellant de Séville*, there are several points at which rupture occurs. The first is the radical change following the restoration of Ferdinand VII that permits don Luis' return to Seville not as an enemy of the monarchy but rather as its erstwhile defender against constitutional rebellion. The second is don Luis' discovery that he himself was responsible for his wife's murder. The third, in many ways a reintegration of the first two, is that which transforms don Luis into don Pablo, the Flagellant of Seville. The latter, it is recalled, describes this transformation as follows: "Quelque chose était brisé entre le présent et le passé; c'était une rupture sans brusquerie, un vide à l'intérieur de quoi il repensait ses aventures sans plus les sentir" (25). This void, created by the breaking down of something between the past and the present, provides don Pablo with a null space in which he can contemplate the past without pain and which renders the present tolerable. The break, the crumbling of the homogeneous time in the interval, permits a link between the past and the present. This rupture-that-resutures-itself receives its physical image in the act of flagellation itself. The lashes of the whip, I argued, ulcerate time as they signal a conformity with the historical figure of Christ, even as they quite literally ulcerate or rupture the flesh. But the act also implies a simultaneous healing, as an act of penance. The linking of the past and the present, a painful process of rupture, is itself a form of redemption

The movement of rupture and ensuing reassemblage in a significant form also comes to the fore in *Venises*. I argued that the twelve-year gap in the record emerges, in a manner reminiscent of Henry Adams, as not only the erasure of the personal and the historical, but also as the symbol of their relation, a relation which, in the context of *Venises*, is broken within that very void. However, unlike other instances of rupture in Morand's postwar work, that of *Venises* appears irreparable. Morand is fundamentally cut off from both what he was in the past and the present world in which he exists. But he does find redemption, as we noted, this time not in the structure of a constellation but in the very language of the constellation itself, a crucial point to which I shall return.

In addition to the thematic structures, literal and figurative, of rupture, these works demonstrate a persistence, bordering on obsession, of narrative and stylistic figures of rupture as well. The myriad references to myth and to other texts periodically sever the "present" of the narration and reach backward and forward in time as they work to keep differing temporal points in simultaneous play. In *Fouquet ou le soleil offusqué*, we saw a similar effect achieved by the use of both diachronic and synchronic narration. *Fouquet* also displays perhaps the clearest examples of temporal and spatial compression as suspensions and accelerations continually disrupt the flow of its narrative time. This technique is also strongly present in *Venises*, in its fragmentary structure and in its use of physical space as a means of telescoping and expanding duration. Stylistic rupture comes through in Morand's extensive use of metaphor, a trope which may be seen as a rupture of the signifier/signified relationship which then refashions an association between signifiers, especially in his use of anachronistic metaphor which stretches the established associations to the limit and even, as we saw in *Fouquet*, to the breaking point. The point of rupture in the latter text, between Mazarin/Fouquet's "reign" and Louis XIV, is also figured by a change in verbal tense from the imperfect to the simple past. Fouquet is ultimately condemned, according to Morand's biography, for his failure to perform this grammatical leap and to properly "read" Louis XIV. Shifts in tense also punctuate the scattered references in *Venises* to the rupture in that text, projecting forward in the conditional and then swinging back in the perfect tense. Narrative and syntactic rupture plays an important role in the creation of the redemptive constellation of the past and present.

Nowhere is this more evident than in "La Folle amoureuse," a constellatory story in and of itself, and an exemplary model of Morandian rupture. It is the story of the relationship of two stories, of two Escolasticas and of two encounters of Spain and Russia, one hundred years and thousands of miles apart. But it is exactly this distance, this rupture, which ultimately links the two and enables them to be read. Only when read together is each completed and endowed with meaning: the second Escolastica reveals the end of the story of the first, a story which in turn explains her own. This process, as I argued, is made possible by the recurrence of the chess motif. Dona Escolastica's comment at the beginning of the second story, "les échecs m'ont sauvé la vie" eradicates the rupture of the two stories in its confusion of identities, since the mad Escolastica too was "*saved by chess,*" and invites the simultaneous reading or superimposition of each woman's encounter with a chess-playing Russian.

At the same time that chess integrates time and space, it must also be seen as the figure for the creation of the rupture itself, as a game which is played simultaneously within the confines of history and traditional historical chronology and without. Chess permits the playing out of historical context (feudal society) outside of the original context, and thus is ahistorical. But even as the players are removed from the continuum of history, chess cannot be considered to be achronological but rather as belonging to a particular chronological order, both spatial and temporal, created as the players move the pieces in a particular sequence over a period of time. In addition, each time the game is played, this action of rupture and reordering is repeated, differently. Within the novella, it is the tension between the two "games" of chess, separated by a century, which cuts the two stories loose from their fixed historical position. Chess is the lever with which Morand pries each story out of its position in the historical continuum and thus constitutes the figure, the key, which makes the story readable by making the past legible in the present.

Such is the key employed by Ferdinand Le Galeux in *Montociel, rajah aux Grandes Indes* to "faire sauter les serrures d'un texte" (19). The work of the cryptanalyst Le Galeux is not only the deciphering of a text but the decoding of the past as well. The ultimate import of the coded document he deciphers proves to be that it furnishes a link to the past, his past, a link which gives meaning to the present in the discovery that he is the son of Montociel and half-brother of the current Rajah. But this discovery, the connection of the past and the present, is only possible because of a prior process of rupture. The act of deciphering occurs at the moment when two texts, two languages coincide, creating a rupture or breaking of the code. At that moment, the cryptanalyst is himself redeemed: "Arrivé au mot, le décrypteur est sur terre ferme: le voilà sauvé"(31). As we saw, Le Galeux's tool, his means of breaking the code, is a word: ESARINTULO. It is a word which, through its capacity to rupture, enables him to arrive at *the* word.

I would now draw a deceptively simple conclusion: in Morand's postwar historical works, historical rupture is created by linguistic rupture. This appears, on the one hand, overly obvious since it is language which creates and constitutes the text, including its ruptures. On the other hand, it may not be quite so simple. In these works, Morand persistently demonstrates how language works on history, indeed that it is language which writes and ultimately *makes* history, as de Certeau argues. But it must be recalled that for Morand, historical rupture also creates linguistic rupture. From the depths of Loup de Tincé's prison, the new France in its birth "parlait une langue neuve" (199); Louis XIV's language is incomprehensible to Fouquet; and the present, in *Venises*, "[...] se parle une langue étrangère que je n'entends plus; d'ailleurs il n'existe pas de dictionnaire"(172). There is no "word" to express the past in this new lexicon, until another rupture, the rupture of the historical continuum, provides a new word, indeed a new language itself, in the form of Morand's own constellation.

Morand seems to suggest that the method of looking at history as and in a constellation is a sort of language. By learning to "read" this language, being presented with it in text after text, the reader is able to decode Morand's message. This language is peculiar in that it comprehends the idea of a void or a silence, that of the rupture, in its semiotics and syntax. Viewed in this way,

Venises comes to be seen in a different light. For it is written, as we saw, in a language of rupture and silence, not only the silence of Morand but the deeper silence of the past as well. *Venises* recreates identity and the past in a discourse of fragmentation whose condition is rupture, the condition in which Morand and we live. Leo Bersani notes:

> The modern is understood not merely as a break with the past but as an inability to understand the past. The modernity of the twentieth century includes the loss of what other modernities did not necessarily give up when they defined their own distinctiveness: an understanding of the tradition to which that modernity added something new. The break with the past now is marked by a mournful sense of the break itself as unique. (48)

When viewed as a literature not only of redemption but of rupture, as the context and agent of the former, Morand's postwar work seems to insert itself into a certain vision of contemporary historiography in France. Pierre Nora, it is recalled, argues for a new history of France, written with the consciousness of a fundamental rupture. But while Nora and Morand both concur on the need for a rewriting of history in what amounts to a new syntax of the past and the present, both err insofar as the "new" revised history carries all the germs, latent or full blown, of relativism and revisionism. The constellation that would redeem Morand's identity and, in Nora's case the identity of France, resides on a refashioning of a ruptured identity which ultimately rests on a notion of recuperated sameness.

In many ways, the basic premises of the *mode rétro*, itself affecting and affected by the work of historians such as Nora, follow a similar if not identical logic. As I suggested above, one might view the *mode rétro* as predicated upon a "rupture," as is of course all historical inquiry, between the present moment and the past. However, rarely if ever has it been so self-consciously posited as significant as in recent years. Thus a difference is inscribed, between the moment of the *mode rétro* inquiry and, in this case, not one but two pasts: the Occupation (what might be termed its primary object) and the "de Gaulle era," as the myth that must be dismantled in order to attain or access the primary moment of the Occupation. A distancing from or rupture with the "middle" period emerges as the necessary condition for the *mode rétro* to be possible at all. The success of Morand's historical structures is likewise dependant, as we have seen, on the removal or "blasting out" of the time period separating the two moments in questions in his texts, removing the veil that obscures their mutual relevance. This crucial relationship between the past and present moments is central to much recent historiographical theory and certainly informs the *mode rétro* in ways that were impossible because both ideologically and perhaps epistemologically unthinkable for earlier investigators. Certainly, as many have suggested, the *mode rétro* is as revelatory of the past thirty years in France as it is of the extent of collaboration between 1940 and 1944, just as the resistencialiste myth is of the deGaullian era.[2]

In conclusion, I would like to stress that it has never been my intent nor, I believe, the result of this study to somehow mar the important contributions of the work of those thinkers, researchers, writers and filmmakers of the *mode rétro* to our continued understanding of the complex history of the Occupation. Nor has it been my design to repeat Morand's own gesture by seeking to redeem his collaborationist activities. Rather, I hope to have suggested how the study of Morand's postwar historical works may aid in understanding the myriad struggles of our time to come to terms with the past.

---

[2] See Morris, Golsan and Bonitzer.

BIBLIOGRAPHY

WORKS BY PAUL MORAND

Lampes à arc. 1920. Paris: Au Sans Pareil; Paris: Gallimard, 1992. (poems)

Feuilles de température. 1920. Paris: Au Sans Pareil; Paris: Gallimard, 1973. (poems)

Tendres Stocks. 1921. Paris: Nouvelle Revue française; Paris: Gallimard, 1996. (novel)

Ouvert la nuit. 1922. Paris: Nouvelle Revue française; Paris: Gallimard, 1987. (short stories)

Fermé la nuit. 1923. Paris: Nouvelle Revue française; Paris: Gallimard, 1993. (short stories)

Poèmes (1914-1924). 1924. Au Sans Pareil; Paris: Gallimard, 1973.

Lewis et Irène. 1924. Paris: Grasset; Paris: Grasset, 1987. (novel)

L'Europe galante. 1925. Paris: Grasset, 2000. (short stories)

Rien que la terre. Paris: Grasset, 1926. (travel journal)

Bouddha vivant. 1927. Paris: Grasset, 1988. (novel)

East India and Company. 1927. New York: Boni; trans. B. Vierne. Paris: Arléa, 1987. (travel journal)

Le Voyage. Paris: Hachette, 1927. (essay)

Magie Noire. 1928. Paris: Grasset, 1987. (short stories)

Paris-Tombouctou. Paris: Flammarion, 1928. (travel journal)

Hiver caraïbe. 1929. Paris: Flammarion, 1991. (travel journal)

Champions du monde. 1930. Paris: Grasset, 1990. (novel)

New York. 1930. Paris: Flammarion, 1988. (city-portrait)

Route de Paris à la Méditerranée. Paris: Firmin-Didot et Cie, 1931. (travel journal)

Papiers d'identité. Paris: Grasset, 1931. (essays)

1900. 1931. Paris: Les Editions de France; Paris: Flammarion, 1942. (essay)

Flèche d'Orient. 1932. Paris: Gallimard, 1999. (travel journal)

Air indien. 1932. Paris: Grasset, 1988. (travel journal)

L'Art de mourir. 1932. Paris: Ed. des Cahiers libres; Paris: PUF, 1992. (essay)

Londres. 1933. Paris: Plon, 1990. (city-portrait)

Rococo. Paris: Grasset, 1933. (short stories)

France-la-Doulce. Paris: Grasset, 1934. (novel)

Rond-Point des Champs-Elysées. Paris: Grasset, 1934. (chronicles)

Bucarest. 1935. Paris: Plon, 1990. (city-portrait)

Bug O'Shea. 1936. Les Laboratoires Deglaude; Paris: Editions du Rocher, 1994. (short stories)

Les Extravagants. 1936. Paris: Gallimard, 1986. (short stories)

La Route des Indes. 1936. Paris: Plon; Paris: Arléa, 1990; Paris: Livre de poche, 1992. (travel journal)

Apprendre à se reposer. Paris: Flammarion, 1937; republished as *Eloge du repos.* Paris: Arléa, 1992. (essays)

Le Réveille-matin. Paris: Grasset, 1937. (chronicles)

L'Heure qu'il est. Paris: Grasset, 1938. (chronicles)

Méditerranée, mer des surprises. 1938. Tours: Mame; Paris: Ed. du Rocher, 1991. (travel journal)

Réflexes et Réflexions. Paris: Grasset, 1939. (chronicles)

Chroniques de l'homme maigre. Paris: Grasset, 1941. (chronicles)

L'Homme pressé. 1941. Paris: Gallimard, 1990. (novel)

Feu M. le duc. Genève: Ed. du Milieu du Monde, 1942. (short stories)

Vie de Guy de Maupassant. 1942. Paris: Flammarion. Paris: Pygmalion, 1998. (biography)

Petit Théâtre. Paris: Grasset, 1942. (theater)

Propos de 52 semaines. 1942. Genève: Ed. du Milieu du Monde; Paris: Arléa, 1992. (chronicles)

Excursions immobiles. Paris: Flammarion, 1944. (chronicles)

Montociel, rajah aux Grandes Indes. 1947. Genève: Editions du Cheval Ailé; Paris: Gallimard, 1960; Paris: Livre de Poche, 1970. novel)

Le Dernier Jour de l'Inquisition. followed by *Parfaite de Saligny.* 1947. Paris: La Table Ronde. Paris: Stock, 1985. (novellas)

Journal d'un attaché d'ambassade, 1916/1917. 1948. La Table Ronde; Paris: Gallimard, 1996. (memoir)

Giraudoux, souvenirs de notre jeunesse. Genève: La Palatine, 1948. (essay)

L'Europe russe annoncée par Dostoïevsky. Paris: Pressédition, 1948. (essay)

Le Visiteur du soir. Genève: La Palatine, 1949. (essay)

Le Flagellant de Séville. 1951. Paris: Librairie Arthème Fayard; Paris: Gallimard, 1982. (novel)

Hécate et ses chiens. 1954. Paris: Flammarion, 1984. (novel)

L'Eau sous les ponts. Paris: Grasset, 1954. (essays)

La Folle amoureuse. 1956. Paris: Librairie Stock, 1986. (novella)

Fin de siècle. 1957. Paris: Librairie Stock; Paris: Gallimard, 1986. (short stories)

Le Prisonnier de Cintra. 1958. Paris: Fayard; Paris: Livre de Poche, 1989. (short stories)

Le Lion écarlate. Paris: Gallimard, 1959. (theater)

Bains de mer, bains de rêve. 1969. Lausanne: Guide du livre et Clairefontaine; Paris: Arléa, 1990. (travel essay)

Fouquet ou le Soleil offusqueé. 1961. Paris: Gallimard, 1985. (biography)

La Dame blanche des Habsbourg. 1963. Paris: Robert Laffont. Paris: Perrin, 2000. (biography)

Tais-toi. 1965. Paris: Gallimard, 1998. (novel)

Nouvelles du coeur (Nouvelles d'une vie, I). Paris: Gallimard, 1965.

Nouvelles des yeux (Nouvelles d'une vie, II). Paris: Gallimard, 1965.

Anthologie de la littérature équestre. Paris: Perrin, 1966.

Monplaisir ... en littérature. Paris: Gallimard, 1967. (essays)

Monplaisir ... en histoire. Paris: Gallimard, 1969. (essays)

Ci-gît Sophie-Dorothée de Celle. Paris: Flammarion, 1968. (biography)

Discours prononcé dans la séance publique tenue par l'Académie française pour la réception de M. Paul Morand, le 20 mars 1969. Paris: Gallimard, 1969.

Venises. 1971. Paris: Gallimard, 1990. (memoir)

Les Ecarts amoureux. Paris: Gallimard, 1974. (short stories)

L'Allure de Chanel. 1976. Paris: Hermann, 1996. (biographical essay)

Morand, Paul, Jean des Cars, and Roger Commault. *Sleeping story, l'épopée des wagons-lits*. 1976. Paris: Julliard, 1978.

Monsieur Dumoulin à l'Isle de la Grenade. Paudex: Fontainemore, 1976. (essay)

Lettres à des amis et à quelques autres. Paris: La Table Ronde, 1978.

Lettres du voyageur. Paris: Editions du Rocher, 1988.

Lettres à Lisette Haas. Paris: Editions des Cendres, 1988.

Un lésineur bienfaisant (M. de Montyon). Paris: Gallimard, 1989. (essay)

Entretiens avec Paul Morand. Paris: Editions de la Table ronde, 1990.

Escales. La Table Ronde, 1993. (unedited texts)

Nouvelles complètes. 2 vols. Paris: Gallimard, 1992.

East India and Company. Paris: Arléa, 1993.

Les Ecarts amoureux. Paris: Gallimard, 1994.

Mes débuts. Paris: Arléa, 1994.

Le Voyage. Paris: Pocket, 1996.

Des artistes sans mensonge. Lausanne: Bibliothèque des arts, 1996.

Eloge du repos. Paris: Arléa, 1996.

Lettres de Paris. Trans. Bernard Delvaille. Paris: Salvy, 1996.

Paris. Lausanne: Bibliothèque des arts, 1997.

Chroniques: 1931-1954. Paris: Grasset, 2001.

Journal inutile. Paris: Gallimard, 2001.

ANNOTATED BIBIOGRAPHY OF WORKS DEVOTED TO PAUL MORAND

Books

Bory, Jean-Louis. *Tout feu tout flamme: musique II*. Paris: Julliard, 1986. 114-120.

Bory's essay, "Paul Morand ou le mélancolique survolté," discusses Morand's style in the context of the early short stories. One interesting aspect is his explanation of how he, a liberal, came to read and love Morand's work.

Burrus, Manuel. *Paul Morand, voyageur du XXème siècle*. Paris: Librairie Séguier, 1986.

An extended biographical essay, evoking Morand's many world travels. Burrus includes many photographs and anecdotal information about diplomatic posts and trips to the Far East in particular.

Delvaille, Bernard. *Paul Morand*. 1966. Paris: Pierre Seghers, 1984.

Part of the "Poètes d'aujourd'hui series," Delvaille's study of Morand's early poetry bases itself for a large part on biographical information. Specific poems are singled out as expressions of the era following the First World War and of Morand's involvement in the avant-garde.

Fogel, Jean-François. *Morand-Express*. Paris: Grasset, 1980.

The best of the full-length biographical works, *Morand-Express* is the account of Fogel's journey, around Europe, in quest of Morand. It is particularly interesting for the information provided on the time spent by Morand in Tanger, before and after the war, and in Switzerland. Fogel's style is reminiscent of Morand's own, though not so much as to overpower his work.

Guitard-Auviste, Ginette. *Paul Morand.* Paris: Editions Universitaires, 1956.

A brief biographical sketch with commentary on his early works.

---, *Paul Morand.* Paris: Hachette, 1981.

The first extensive biography of Morand. Guitard-Auviste was a long-time friend of both Paul and Hélène Morand, and her work reflects this intimacy. Her commentary on his literary works is limited to the context of Morand's life. Guitard-Auviste's documentation is extensive; however, many bibliographical references are to personal, undocumented conversations or anecdotes.

Hebey, Pierre. *La Nouvelle Revue française des années sombres (1940-1941).* Paris: Gallimard, 1992. 391-397.

Brief, but insightful discussion of the anti-semitic nature of Morand's novel *France-la-doulce* (1934) and the article "De l'air...de l'air" (1933).

Louvrier, Parcal, and Eric Canal-Forgues. *Paul Morand: Le sourire du hara-kiri.* Paris: Perrin, 1994.

This new biography contains much of the information provided by Guitard-Auviste with several additions, including many previously uncited letters and official documents, and much new information on Morand's diplomatic service during the twenties and thirties. The book is lengthy and very prosaic; its style resembles that of Fogel's book, except that the authors are not content only to borrow Morand's style but often his words as well - without attribution.

Place, Georges. *Paul Morand.* Paris: Editions de la chronique des lettres françaises, 1975.

An exhaustive bibliography of Morand works, including articles, prefaces and illustrations. Also includes a brief biographical sketch.

Rousso, Henry. *The Vichy Syndrome.* trans. Arthur Goldhammer. Cambridge: Harvard University Press, 1992. 64-68.

Very good explanation and contextualization of Morand's ill-fated bid for the Académie française in 1958.

Sarkany, Stéphane. *Morand et le cosmopolitisme littéraire.* Vevey: La Table Ronde, 1968.

Interesting study of the theme of cosmopolitanism. Sarkany analyzes Morand's works as they pertain to his legend of globe-trotter. His study of the later works is ketchy, with more emphasis on the psychological aspects than the historical. The book also contains the transcripts of three interviews Sarkany conducted with Morand.

Schneider, Marcel. *Paul Morand.* Paris: Gallimard, 1971.

Written with Ginette Guitard-Auviste, who provided a short biographical sketch, this is more an essay on Morand in general than a critical study. It is noteworthy in that the section entitled "Documents" contains several short commentaries on Morand, including Proust's preface to *Tendre Stocks*, Bory's essay, and essays by Valéry Larbaud, Léon Daudet, Roger Nimier, and others.

Thibault, Bruno. *L'Allure de Morand: du modernisme au pétainisme.* Birmingham: Summa Publications, 1992.

Excellent analysis of Morand's early style. Thibault moves from the stylistic to the political without, however, much theoretical foresight. He makes the argument that Morand's style is "fitted" to his political motives, without explicitly stating what those motives were. The book also relies heavily on quotes from *Venises* as authoritative and factual statements without situating them in the context of that far-from-objective work.

Articles and Prefaces

Bienvenu, Reine. "Autour et au-dela du récit de voyage: Mediterranée, mer de surprises de Paul Morand." *Les Récits de voyage.* Ed. Alain Niderst. Paris: Nizet, 1986. 162-189.

Charrière, Christine. "Le Prince du modern style." *Le Figaro littéraire.* 27 January, 1992.

Collomb, Michel. "Paul Morand: *Fin de siècle* et péril jaune." *Fin de siècle: Terme – évolution – révolution?* Ed. Gwenhael Ponnau. Toulouse: PU du Mirail, 1989. 597-602.

Dambre, Marc. "Paul Morand à l'heure allemande." *Paris sous l'occupation.* Eds. Wolfgang Drost, Geraldi Leroy, et al. Heidelberg: Carl Winter University, 1995. 84-93.

Delvaille, Bernard. "Morand et son double." *Magazine littéraire.* 305 (December, 1992): 49-52.

Dion, Robert. "La Machine humaine à l'épreuve de la vitesse: *L'Homme pressé,* de Paul Morand." *Tangence.* 55 (Sept. 1997): 95-107.

Hechter, Michèle. "Premier Morand." *Libération.* 25 December, 1986.

de Lacretelle, Jacques de. "Proust et Paul Morand." *Bulletin de la Société des Amis de Marcel Proust et de Combray.* 27 (1977): 387-91.

Loselle, Andrea. "The Historical Nullification of Paul Morand's Gendered Eugenics." *Gender and Fascism in Modern France.* Eds. Richard J. Golsan and Melanie Hawthorne. Hanover: University Press of New England. 1997. 101-118.

---. *History's Double: Cultural Tourism in Twentieth-Century French Writing.* New York: St. Martin's Press, 1997.

Naud, François. "Paul Morand, portraits de villes." *Littératures.* 24 (1991): 155-63.

Osburn, Charles B. "Literary Sidelights: Bernard Grasset and Paul Morand." *Revue des Langues Vivantes.* 42 (1976): 155-64.

Proust, Marcel. Preface. *Tendre Stocks.* By Paul Morand. 1921. Paris: NRF; Paris: Gallimard, 1981.

Schneider, Marcel. "L'écrivain de la fin d'un monde." *Le Figaro littéraire*. 14 March, 1988.
Sollers, Philippe. Preface. *New York*. By Paul Morand. Paris: Flammarion, 1981.
---. "Le Swing de Morand." *Le Monde*. 31 January, 1992.
Struve-Debeaux, Anne. "L'Espace de Paul Morand." *Etudes de Langue et Littérature française*. 60 (1992): 124-32.
Tallett, Nicholas. "Paul Morand on America: Geopolitics in Fictional Representation." *Claudel Studies*. 23.1 (1996): 31-36.
Thibault, Bruno. "Erotisme et exotisme: L'art du portrait moderniste dans les premières nouvelles de Paul Morand." *Romance Languages Annual*. 1(1989): 332-336.
van Noort, Kimberly. "Sleeping with Europe: Paul Morand's Body Politic and the Twenties in *L'Europe galante*." *Romance Notes*. 40 .2 (1999): 213-221.
---. "Postcards from Venice: Life and the City in Paul Morand's *Venises*." *Studies in Twentieth-Century Literature*. Forthcoming.

Journal numbers devoted to Morand

Magazine littéraire. October, 1977.

Nouvelle Revue de Paris. 8 (1988).

Roman 20-50. 8 (1989).

WORKS CONSULTED

Adams, Henry. *The Education of Henry Adams*. 1907. Boston: Houghton, 1973.

Avni, Ora. "Narrative Subject, Historic Subject: Shoah and *La Place de l'Etoile*." *Poetics Today*. 12.3 (1991): 495-516.

Assouline, Pierre. *L'Epuration des Intellectuels en France*. Bruxelles: Ed. Complexe, 1990.

Azéma, Jean-Pierre and Olivier Wieviorka. *Vichy: 1940-1944*. Paris: Perrin, 2000

Badr, Ibrahim. *Giono et la guerre: idéologie et imaginaire*. New York, Peter Lang, 1999.

Bahti, Timothy. *Allegories of History: Literary Historiography after Hegel*. Baltimore: Johns Hopkins University Press, 1992.

Bartov, Omer. *Mirrors of Destruction: War, Genocide, and Modern Identity*. Oxford: Oxford University Press, 2000.

Beaujour, Michel. *Miroirs d'encre*. Paris: Seuil, 1980.

Berkvan, Michael. *Writing the Story of France in World War II: Literature and Memory, 1942-1958*. New Orleans: University Press of the South, 2000.

Benjamin, Walter. "Theses on the Philosophy of History." *Illuminations*. Trans. Harry Zohn. New York: Harcourt, Brace and World, 1968.

Bersani, Leo. *The Culture of Redemption*. Cambridge: Harvard University Press, 1990.

Bontizer, Pascal and Serge Toubiana. "Anti-Rétro: Entretien avec Michel Foucault." *Cahiers du cinéma*. July-August 1974. 251-251

Bourget, Marie-Noëlle, Lucette Valensi, and Nathan Wachtel. *Between Memory and History*. Chur, Switzerland: Harwood Academic Publishers, 1990.

Brée, Germaine. *Narcissus Absconditus: The Problematic Art of Autobiography in Contemporary France*. Oxford: Clarendon, 1978.

Brenner, Jacques. *Histoire de la littérature française de 1940 à nos jours*. Paris: Fayard, 1978.

Bulthaup, Peter. *Materialien zu Benjamins Thesen "Uber den Begriff der Geschichte"*: *Beiträge und Interpretationen*. Frankfurt am Main: Suhrkamp, 1975.

Burke, Peter. "History as Social Memory." Butler 97-114.

---. *The French Historical Tradition: The Annales School*. Stanford: Stanford University Press, 1990.

Butler, Thomas, ed. *Memory: History, Culture, and the Mind*. Oxford: Basil Blackwell, 1989.

Carrard, Philippe. *Poetics of the New History: French Historical Discourse from Braudel to Chartier*. Baltimore: Johns Hopkins University Press, 1992.

Céline, Louis-Ferdinand. *D'un château l'autre*. Paris: Editions de la Pléiade. 1962.

Chevigny, Hector. *Russian America: The Great Alaskan Venture 1741-1867*. New York: Viking, 1965.

Churchill, Kenneth. *Italy and English Literature 1764-1930*. Totowa, NJ: Barnes and Noble, 1980.

Collier, Peter. *Proust and Venice*. Cambridge: Cambridge University Press, 1989.

Conan, Eric and Henry Rousso. *Vichy, un passé qui ne passe pas*. Paris: Fayard. 1994.

Connerton, Paul. *How Societies Remember*. Cambridge: Cambridge University Press, 1989.

Cowart, David. *History and the Contemporary Novel*. Carbondale: Southern Illinois University Press, 1989.

Clarke, H. Butler. *Modern Spain 1815-1898*. New York: AMS Press, 1969.

Curtius, Ernst Robert. *Essays on European Literature*. Trans. Michael Kowal. Princeton: Princeton University Press, 1973.

de Certeau, Michel. *The Writing of History*. Trans. Tom Conley. New York: Columbia University Press, 1988.

Davies, Peter Jonathan. *France and the Second World War: Occupation, Collaboration and Resistance*. London: Routledge, 2001.

Derrida, Jacques. *La Carte postale: de Socrate à Freud et au-delà*. Paris: Flammarion, 1980.

Dessert, Daniel. *Fouquet*. Paris: Fayard, 1987.

Eakin, Paul John. *Touching the World: Reference in Autobiography.* Princeton: Princeton University Press, 1992.

---. *Fictions in Autobiography: Studies in the Art of Self-Invention.* Princeton: Princeton University Press, 1985.

Epton, Nina. *The Spanish Mousetrap: Napoleon and the Court of Spain.* London: MacDonald, 1973.

Felman, Shoshana, ed. *Testimony: Crises of Witnessing in Literature, Psychoanalysis, and History.* New York: Routledge, 1991.

Finkenzeller, R., W. Ziehr, and E. Bührer. *Chess: A Celebration of 2000 Years.* Trans. C. Badger and L. Crossley. New York: Little, Brown and Co., 1989.

Foley, Barbara. *Telling the Truth: The Theory and Practice of Documentary Fiction.* Ithaca: Cornell University Press, 1986.

Footman, David. *Ferdinand Lassalle: Romantic Revolutionary.* New Haven: Yale University Press, 1947.

Fort, Bernadette. ed. *Fictions of the French Revolution.* Evanston: Northwestern University, 1991.

Freud, Sigmund. *Leonardo da Vinci and a Memory of His Childhood.* Trans. Alan Tyson. New York: Norton, 1964.

Friedlander, Saul, ed. *Probing the Limits of Representation: Nazism and the "Final Solution."* Cambridge: Harvard University Press, 1992.

Fussell, Paul. *Abroad: British Literary Traveling Between the Wars.* New York: Oxford University Press, 1980.

Golsan, Richard J. "Collaboration and Context: *Lacombe Lucien*, the *Mode Rétro*, and the Vichy Syndrome." Ungar and Conley 139-55.

---. *Vichy's Afterlife: History and Counterhistory in Postwar France.* Lincoln: University of Nebraska Press, 2000.

Golsan, Richard and Melanie Hawthorne, eds. *Gender and Fascism in Modern France.* Hanover: University Press of New England, 1997.

Golsan, Richard and Christopher Flood, eds. *The Invasion and Occupation of France, 1940-44; Intellectual and Cultural Responses.* Spec. issue of *Journal of European Studies.* 23.1-2 (1993).

Gossman, Lionel. *Between History and Literature.* Cambridge: Harvard University Press, 1990.

Greenlee, James W. *Malraux's Heroes and History.* Dekalb: Northern Illinois University Press, 1975.

Griedson, Anthony, ed. *New Directions in Biography.* Honolulu: University Press of Honolulu, 1981.
Hartman, Geoffrey, ed. *Holocaust Remembrance: The Shapes of Memory.* Oxford: Blackwell, 1994.
Hibbert, Christopher. *Venice: The Biography of a City.* New York: Norton, 1980.
Higgins, Lynn. *New Novel, New Wave, New Politics: Fiction and the Representation of History in Postwar France.* Lincoln: University of Nebraska Press. 1996.
Hirschfeld, Gerhard and Patrick Marsh, eds. *Collaboration in France: Politics and Culture during the Nazi Occupation 1940-1944.* Oxford: Berg, 1989.
Honan, Park. "The Theory of Biography." *Novel.* 13.1 (Fall 1979): 109-120.
Hull, Anthony. *Goya: Man among Kings.* New York: Hamilton Press, 1987.
Judt, Tony. *Past Imperfect: French Intellectuals 1944-1956.* Berkeley: University of California Press, 1994.
Kaes, Anton. *From Hitler to Heimat.* Cambridge: Harvard University Press, 1989.
Kaplan, Alice Yaeger. *The Collaborator: The Trial and Execution of Robert Brasillach.* Chicago: University of Chicago Press, 2000.
Kitchen, Martin. *Europe between the Wars.* London: Longman, 1988.
Kline, T. Jefferson. *André Malraux and the Metamorphosis of Death.* New York: Columbia University Press, 1973.
Krieger, Leonard. *Time's Reasons.* Chicago: Chicago University Press, 1989.
Kritzman, Lawrence D., ed. *Auschwitz and After: Race, Culture, and "The Jewish Question" in France.* New York: Routledge, 1994.
LaCapra, Dominick. *History and Criticism.* Ithaca: Cornell University Press, 1985.
---. *History, Politics and the Novel.* Ithaca: Cornell University Press, 1985.
---. "Representing the Holocaust: Reflections on the Historian's Debate." Friedlander 108-127.
Lejeune, Philippe. *Le Pacte autobiographique.* Paris: Seuil, 1975.
Licht, Fred, ed. *Goya in Perspective.* New Jersey: Prentice Hall, 1973.

Littlejohn, David. *The Patriotic Traitors: The History of Collaboration in German Occupied Europe, 1940-45*. Garden City: Doubleday, 1972.

Loiseaux, Gérard. *La Littérature de la défaite et de la collaboration*. Paris: Fayard, 1984.

Loselle, Andrea. *History's Double: Cultural Tourism in Twentieth-Century French Writing*. New York: St. Martin's Press, 1997.

Lovett, Gabriel H. *Napoleon and the Birth of Modern Spain*. 2 vols. New York: New York University Press, 1965.

Lukács, Georg. *The Historical Novel*. Trans. Hannah and Stanley Mitchell. London: Merlin Press, 1962.

Maurois, André. *Aspects of Biography*. Trans. Sydney C. Roberts. New York: D. Appleton, 1929.

Mehlman, Jeffrey. "Writing and Deference: The Politics of Literary Adulation." *Representations*. 15 (1986): 1-14.

---. *Genealogies of the text: Literature, Psychoanalysis and Politics in Modern France*. Cambridge: Cambridge University Press, 1995.

---. *Legacies of Anti-Semitism in France*. Minneapolis: University of Minnesota Press, 1983.

Middleton, David and Derek Edwards, eds. *Collective Remembering*. London: Sage, 1990.

Morris, Alan. *Collaboration and Resistance Reviewed: Writers and the "Mode Retro" in Post-Gaullist France*. New York: Berg, 1992.

---. "Attacks on the Gaullist 'Myth' in French Literature." *Forum for Modern Language Studies*. 21.1 (1985): 71-83.

Nadel, Ira Bruce. *Biography: Fiction, Fact and Form*. New York: St. Martin's Press, 1984.

Nettlebeck, Colin. "Getting the Story Right: Narratives of the Second World War in Post-1968 France." *Journal of European Studies*. 15.2 (1985): 77-116.

Nora, Pierre. *Les Lieux de mémoire*. 3 vols. Paris: Gallimard, 1984-86.

---. "Entre mémoire et histoire." *Lieux*: I.

---. "Comment écrire l'histoire de France?" *Lieux*: III.

Oncken, Hermann. 1924. *Lassalle: Zwischen Marx und Bismark*. Stuttgart: W. Kohlhammer, 1966.

Ory, Pascal. *Les Collaborateurs 1940-1945*. Paris: Seuil, 1976.

Peters, Margot. "Group Biography: Challenges in Methods." Griedson 35-52.

Poe, Edgar Allen. "Maelzel's Chess-Player." Salzmann 128-147.
Ricoeur, Paul. *The Rule of Metaphor.* Trans. Robert Czerny. Toronto: University of Toronto Press, 1977.
---. *Time and Narrative.* Trans. K. McLaughlin and D. Pellauer. Chicago: University of Chicago Press, 1985.
Riffaterre, Michael. *Text Production.* Trans. Terese Lyons. New York: Columbia University Press, 1983.
Roberts, James. *The Counter-Revolution in France 1787-1830.* New York: St. Martin's Press, 1990.
Rosand, David. *Painting in Cinquecento Venice: Titian, Veronese, Tintoretto.* New Haven: Yale University Press, 1982.
Rousso, Henry. *La Collaboration.* Paris: M.A. Editions, 1987.
---. *The Vichy Syndrome.* Trans. A. Goldhammer. Cambridge: Harvard University Press, 1991.
Salzmann, Jerome, ed. *The Chess Reader: The Royal Game in World Literature.* New York: Greenburg, 1949.
Santner, Eric. "History Beyond the Pleasure Principle: Some Thoughts on the Representation of Trauma." Friedlander 143-154.
---. *Stranded Objects: Mourning, Memory and Film in Postwar Germany.* Ithaca: Cornell University Press, 1990.
Sartre, Jean-Paul. *Qu'est-ce que la literature?* Paris: Gallimard, 1997.
---. "Qu'est-ce qu'un collaborateur?" *Situations III.* Paris: Gallimard, 1949.
Schneidau, Herbert N. *Waking Giants: The Presence of the Past in Modernism.* Oxford: Oxford University Press, 1991.
Scullion, Rosemarie. "Unforgettable: History, Memory and the Vichy Syndrome." *Studies in Twentieth-Century Literature.* 23.1 (1999):11-26.
Seward, Desmond. *Napoleon and Hitler: A Comparative Biography.* New York: Viking, 1988.
Shaw, Harry E. *The Forms of Historical Fiction: Sir Walter Scott and His Successors.* Ithaca: Cornell University Press, 1983.
Shotter, John. "The Social Construction of Remembering and Forgetting." Middleton 120-138.
Smith, Rhea Marsh. *Spain: A Modern History.* Ann Arbor: University of Michigan Press, 1965.
Sternhell, Zeev. *Ni droite ni gauche: L'Idéologie fasciste en France.* Paris: Seuil, 1983.

Suleiman, Susan Rubin. *Authoritarian Fictions, The Ideological Novel as a Literary Genre*. New York: Columbia University Press, 1983.
Taguieff, Pierr-Andre, Grégoire Kauffmann and Michael Lenoire. *L'Antisémitisme de plume, 1940-1944: Etudes et documents*. Paris: Berg, 1999.
Tanner, Tony. *Venice Desired*. Cambridge: Harvard University Press, 1992.
Thomas, Hugh. *The Spanish Civil War*. New York: Harper Row, 1961.
Todorov, Tzvetan. *The Poetics of Prose*. Trans. Richard Howard. Ithaca: Cornell University Press, 1977.
Ulmer, Gregory. "The Post-Age." *Diacritics* 11 (1981): 39-56.
Ungar, Steven and Tom Conley, eds. *Identity Papers: Contested Nationhood in Twentieth-Century France*. Minneapolis: University of Minnesota Press, 1996.
VanderWolk, William. *Rewriting the Past: Memory, History and Narration in the Novels of Patrick Modiano*. Amsterdam: Rodopi, 1997.
Venner, Dominique. *Histoire de la Collaboration*. Paris: Pygmalion, 2000.
Watts, Philip. *Allegories of the purge: How Literature Responded to the Postwar Trials of Writers and Intellectuals in France*. Stanford: Stanford University Press, 1998.
Webster, Paul. *Petain's crime: The Full Story of French Collaboration in the Holocaust*. London: Pan, 2001.
Weiner, Margery. *The French Exiles 1789-1815*. Westport, CT: Greenwood Press, 1960.
White, Hayden. *The Content of the Form: Narrative Discourse and Historical Representation*. Baltimore: Johns Hopkins University Press, 1987.
---. *Metahistory: The Historical Imagination in Nineteenth-Century Europe*. Baltimore: Johns Hopkins University, 1974.
----. *Tropics of Discourse*. Baltimore: Johns Hopkins University Press, 1978.
Williams, Gwyn A. *Goya and the Impossible Revolution*. New York: Pantheon, 1976.

Wolfarth, Irving. "On the Messianic Structure of Walter Benjamin's Last Reflections." *Glyph 3*. Eds. S. Weber and H. Sussmann. Baltimore: Johns Hopkins University Press, 1978.

Wood, Nancy. *Vectors of memory: Legacies of Trauma in Postwar Europe*. Oxford: Berg, 1999.

INDEX

Académie francaise, 9, 14, 90, 114-15, 161
Adams, Henry, *The Education of Henry Adams*, 155-56; gap in, 155, 166; theory of history, 156
afrancesado, 29
Annales, (Les), 92, 156
Anne of Austria, 101
Aragon, Louis, 115
Argüello, Concepcíon, 64
Auric, Georges, 15
autobiography, 11, 121, 124-129; anonymity and, 121-24, 127; autobiographical pact, 127; distancing in, 124; intertextuality and, 130-32; origins, 140-41; travel writing and, 122-24, 129
Automaton Chess Player, 75-77, 87
Bahti, Timothy, 47
Balzac, Honoré de, 97, 111
Barrès, Maurice, 22
Beaujour, Michel, 128
Benda, Julien, 115
Benjamin, Walter, 21, 46-49, 76-77, 79; 163; Automaton Chess Player, 76-77, 87
Benöist-Méchin, Jacques, 13
biography, 11, 92-93; segment biography, 93; group biography, 99-100; use of tropes, 93-96, 105; temporal compression, 108-111; and naming, 110; diachronic and synchronic narratives, 110; historical present-ness, 110-11; anachronism, 111-113
Bismarck, Otto von, 81
Blanchot, Maurice, 150-52
Bonaparte, Joseph, 19, 26
Bonnard, Abel, 13
Bory, Jean-Louis, 16
Bracke-Desrousseaux, 85
Browning, 130
Brünhilde, 83
Burke, Kenneth, 93
Byron, Lord George, 22, 130
Casanova, 132
Céline, Louis Ferdinand, 12-13, 15; *D'un château l'autre*, 35
CENE (Comité national des écrivains), 33-34, 113, 115
Chanel, Coco, 14-15
Chateaubriand, François René de, 22, 130-31, 141
chess, 72-76, 87, 167-68
chiasmus, 10, 29-30, 44, 52-53, 61-62, 63-64, 67, 162-64
city portrait, 122
Cocteau, Jean, 12, 15
collaboration, 9, 15, 32, 35-37, 67, 85-86. 114-117, 162-65
Combats, 13
Connerton, John, 40
Corneille, Pierre, 107

Corvo, Baron (Frederick Rolfe), 2, 130
Counter-Revolution, 53, 63
da Vinci, Leonardo, 89
Daudet, Léon, 12
de Bestegui, Don Carlos, 149
de Celle, Sophie Dorothée, 19
de Certeau, Michel, 22, 154, 157
de Gaulle, Charles, 9, 10, 13-14, 161, 164
Derrida, Jacques, *La Carte postale*, 122
Don Juan legend, 84
Drieu la Rochelle, Pierre, 13, 15
Eakin, John Paul, 155-56,
Edda Saga, 83,
Eluard, Paul, 115,
Engels, Friedrich, 81
Fabre-Luce, Alfred, 13, 25
flagellation, 32, 48, 166; as commemoration, 41
Flaubert, Gustave, 19, 44, 62
Fogel, Jean-François, 16
Foley, Barbara, 34-35
Footman, David, 81
Fort Ross, California, 64
Fouquet ou le soleil offusqué,21, 148, 162, 166; artists and writers, 102; biography and, 108, 111; contem-porary literature and, 107; intertextuality and, 106-107, 111; metaphors,95-99, 106; metonymy, 93-94, 103-105; Oedipal myth, 101-103, role of Louis XIV in, 97-105; temporal com-pression, 105-110, 130-32; 134-36, 167;
Fouquet, François, 94-95
Freud, Sigmund, 89
Giono, Jean, 118
Girard, René, 163
Giraudoux, Jean, 12; *LaGuerre de Troie n'aura pas lieu*, 58, 83, 84
Goethe, Johann Wolfgang von, 22, 131, 132
Golsan, Richard, 10, 164
Gossman, Lionel, 92
Goya, 18-19, 25-28; *Five Paintings on Panel*, 25; *Disasters of War*, 25
Grasset, Bernard, 9, 12
Guitard-Auviste, Ginette, 16
Habsburg Empire, 14, 116
historical fiction, 11, 34-35, 80
historical materialism, 47
historicization, 11, 154
history, 18, 20, 154; language and, 168; historical rupture, 150, 60-61, 113-114, 148, 150, 162, 165-166; historiography, 34, 156-59, 69; Benjamin's theory of, 46-49; 76-77; Morand's use of, 38, 43, 52-53, 63-64, 79-81, 44-49, 118, 162-63, 168; Morand's theory of, 70, 72, 77-79, 156; memory and, 156-59
Hitler, Adolf, 84
Honan, Park, 110
identity, 33; as absence, 126-27
intertextuality, 18-19, 107' *Le Flagellant de Séville* and,

Index 193

27-28, 38-40; *Le Lion écarlate* and, 83-84; *Fouquet ou le soleil offusqué* and, 102-03, 106-107, 111-166; *Venises* and, 128-32, 135-37
Jouhandeau, Marcel, 13
Kline, T. Jefferson, 108 (n.)
Kornprobst, Louis, 26
La Gerbe, 13,
LaCapra, Dominick, 92
"La Folle amoureuse," chess and, 72-76, 87; madness, 68-70; narrative structure of, 63-64, 65-67, 167-68; redemption and, 78-79; use of history, 52, 63-64, 70-72, 77-79; vampirism, 69-70
LaFontaine, 106, 107
Lalique, Suzanne, 15
Language, and rupture, 60, 114 150, 156, 159, 168-169; history and, 168-69
Larbaud, Valéry, 12
Lassalle, Ferdinand, 19,
Laval, Pierre, 1,
Lawrence, D.H., 22
Le Flagellant de Séville, 11, 16, 20, 53, 91; collaboration and, 29-30, 32, 35-37, 62, 63, 130; Don Juan legend, 38, 84; flagellation, 32, 41, 48. 166; intertextuality, 27-28, 38-40; myth, 38, 40-41; ritual, 40; rupture and, 166; use of history, 42-44
Lister, Enrique, 65
literature and politics, 116

Malraux, André, 65 (n.), 108 (n.)
Marx, Karl, 81, 84,
Maupassant, Guy de, 90
Mauriac, Francois, 9, 90
Maurois, André, 8,
Maurois, André, 9
McCarthy, Mary, 141
memory, affective, 131; collective, 11; monumental,131; individual, 157, 164-165
Milhaud, Darius, 15
Mlle de la Vallière, 101
mode rétro, 10-11, 23, 164-65,169-70
Montherlant, Henry de, 9, 15
Morand, Hélène, 13, 85
Morand, Paul, early career, 12-16; shift to historical works, 16-17; *Bouddha vivant*, 51; *Chroniques d'un homme maigre*, 13; *Ci-gît Sophie Dorothée de Celle*, 90, 99; "Les Clés du souterrain," 91; Morand, "La Dame blanche des Hapsbourg," 90, 99; "Le Dernier jour de l'Inquisition,16, 37, 91; *Fermé la nuit*, 15; "Le Festin de pierre," 38, 84; "Fleur du ciel," 91; "La Folle amoureuse," 16, 19, 21, 52, 53-54, 63-79, 80, 87, 91, 167-68; *Fouquet ou le soleil offusqué*, 21, 148, 162, 166; *France-la doulce*, 13 (note); *Hiver- Caraïbe*, 15; *Isabeau de Bavière*, 16; *L'Allure de Chanel*, 90;

L'Homme pressé, 14, 125; *La Route des Indes*, 15; *Le Flagellant de Séville*, 11-16, 20, 53, 91; *Le Lion écarlate*, 21, 79-87, 91; *Montociel: le rajah aux grandes indes*, 51-52, 77-78, 168; *New York*, 12-13, 90; *Ouvert la nuit*, 15; "Parfaite de Saligny," 16, 21, 52, 54-63, 114, 150; *Paris-Tombouctou*, 15, 90; "Le Ravissement de l'Europe," 84; "Rien que la terre," 90; *Tais-toi*, 33, 147; *Venises*, 19, 21-22, 85, 169. See also *Le Flagellant de Séville, Fouquet ou le soleil offusqué,* "Parfaite de Saligny," "La Folle amoureuse," and *Venises*.
Morris, Alan, 10-11, 23, 165
Murube, Joaquin Romero, 32
myth, 38, 40-41
Napoleon, occupation of Spain, 11, 28-29
Nora, Pierre, *Les Lieux de mémoire*, 156-59, 169
Oedipal complex, 101, 102-103, 139
Oncken, Hermann, 81
Ophuls, Marcel, *Le Chagrin et la pitié*, 164
"Parfaite de Saligny," arbitrary alliances in, 57-59; Counter-Revolution and, 53, 63; decadance of Europe and, 60-61; chiasmus in, 52-53, 61-64; Giroudux and, 57-58

pariah, 19, 82, 91, 161
Paulhan, Jean, 33, 92, 113; "De la paille et du grain," 113, 115-117,
Pétain, Philippe, 13
Poe, Edgar Allan, 75
post-card theory, 122
postmark, 112
Pound, Ezra, 9, 12
Proust, Marcel, 9, 12, 14, 22, 141, 144
Rakowitza, Yanko, 86
Ravel, Maurice, 15
redemption, 39, 48, 78-77, 87, 161-162
Renan, Ernst, 12
résistantialisme, 10-11, 34, 161, 163-165, 170
Rezanov, Nikolai Petrovich, 64
Ricoeur, Paul, 92
Riffaterre, Michael, 13,
ritual, 40
Rolland, Romain, 117
Romains, Jules, 90
Rosand, David, 136-37
Rousso, Henry, 10, 90
rupture, historical, 21, 59-60, 60-61, 113-114, 147-48, 150, 155-56, 162, 165-166; linguistic, 60, 114 150, 156, 159, 168-169; stylistic, 166-168
Ruskin, John, 22
Russian-American Fur Company, 64
Saint-Simon, 136
Sarkany, Stéphane, 91
Sartre, Jean-Paul, 36-37
Satie, Erik, 15

Index 195

Scudéry, Mme de, 107
Sévigné, Mme de, 106
Siegfried, André, 90
Sollers, Phillippe, 12-13, 16
Spanish Civil War, 54, 65, 67
Stendhal, Henri Beyle, 12, 19, 22, 97, 107, 140; *Le Rouge et le noir*, 117, 140; *La Chartreuse de Parme*, 97, 140
Sternhell, Zeev, 53
Strachey, Lionel, *Washington and Jefferson*, 99
Taine, 131
temporal compression, 43-46, 105-110, 130-32, 134-36, 167
temporal superimposition, 131
Thibault, Bruno, 150
Todorov, Tzvetan, 109
Traité de Fontainebleau, 28
Ulmer, Gregory, 123
Valéry, Paul, 97, 107
vampire, 69-70
Vaux-le-Vicomte, 90, 103
Venice, physical structures, 132-38, 139; plurality, 127-28; literary representations of 127-32
Venises, 19, 21-22, 85, 169; alienation, 124-27; autobiography and city portrait, 121-24, 127-28, 133; autobiographical pact in, 128, 146; destiny and, 125-26, 146; dialogue with city, 127, 152; eroticisation, 128-29; fragmentation in, 122, 127, 146-48; historical representations of, 130; intertextuality and, 127-32, 136-37; father in, 139; mother in, 139; WWI, 142; interwar period, 144; 12-year gap in text, 123, 146-48, 154, 166; use of physical structures, 126, 132-38, 139
Veronese, Pablo, 133; *Feast in the House of Levi*, 136-37
Verseilles, 104 ,
Vie de Guy de Maupassant, 16,
Villedieu, Mme de, 107
Voix francaises, 13
von Kempelen, Baron Wolfgang, 75
von Langsdorff, Georg, 64
von Stülpnagel, General, 114
Vuillemin, Jules, Le Miroir de Venise, 128
White, Hayden, 92

OHIO UNIVERSITY LIBRARY

Please return this book as soon as you have finished with it. In order to avoid a fine it must be returned by the latest date stamped below. All books are subject to recall after two weeks or immediately if needed for reserve.

CF